Lighter
quicker
better

Lighter
quicker
better

Cooking for the Way We Eat Today

Richard Sax and Marie Simmons

William Morrow
An Imprint of HarperCollins*Publishers*

Many of the recipes in this book appeared, in different form, in our column, "Cooking for Health," in *Bon Appétit*. We gratefully acknowledge *Bon Appétit*'s generous permission to use this material.

A hardcover edition of this book was published in 1995 by William Morrow.

First paperback edition published 2000

Designed by Don Morris Design

Library of Congress Cataloging-in-Publication Data
Sax, Richard.
    Lighter, quicker, better : cooking for the way we eat today / Richard Sax and Marie Simmons.—1st paperback ed.
        p.   cm.
    ISBN 0-688-17761-1
    1. Cookery. 2. Low-fat diet—Recipes. I. Simmons, Marie. II. Title.
TX714.S29 2000
    641.5'638—dc21   99-053287
Paperback ISBN 0-688-17761-1

00 01 02 03 04 QW 10 9 8 7 6 5 4 3 2 1

Contents

Pasta   110

Sandwiches, Pizza, and Eggs   136

Vegetables   162

Bean & Grain Side Dishes   202

Meatless Main Dishes   220

Fish and Shellfish   252

Cakes and Other Baked Goods **382**

Acknowledgments **406**

Index **407**

Introd

OUR FRIENDS OFTEN SAY, "I know I should eat less fat, but I don't have any good recipes." Everyone wants to eat lighter, but the question is, how to go about it?

Over the years, almost instinctively and without conscious effort, we've both watched our cooking styles change. As professional cooks (and passionate eaters), we both like foods with full flavor—and aren't about to give up their pleasures. Although our experience includes all kinds of food, from spa cuisine to chocolate extravaganzas, we always come back to the simple foods in which our tastes are grounded, and these are thick soups, luscious pastas, mashed potatoes, hearty stews, and comforting desserts.

We still want those full flavors, but with less fat, fewer calories, less cholesterol. We've both found that

uction

we feel better when we don't eat a steady diet of rich foods, as tantalizing as they might once have seemed. And while we're both food writers who love to cook, we don't want to spend all of our time in the kitchen.

Why this evolution to lighter more healthful eating? Is it because we're getting older, and our bodies are responding to time's relentless march? Or have our eating habits changed because eating healthfully is now headline news?

Well, it's definitely not because healthy eating is trendy—we eat for taste, not to keep up with fads. What's happened is that we've gradually redefined our cooking style, trimming the richness without losing the flavor. In short, we've developed a repertoire of delicious food that satisfies. And happens to be healthier, too. We eat lots of vegetables, grains, and fruits—foods that are inherently healthful, and we have learned to eat less (smaller portions) of dairy products and meats.

Our answer to our friends' question is moderation, not deprivation.

Eating more healthfully is largely a matter of common sense. When we spoke with Dr. Marion Nestle, chairman of New York University's nutrition department and editor of the Surgeon General's Report on Nutrition and Health, about the conflicts in official advice on the ideal amounts of fat in our diet, and asked her what the ideal percentage of fat should be, she had only one thing to say: "Eat more fruits and vegetables, and you'll be doing fine."

About eight years ago, *Bon Appétit* magazine approached us to write a monthly column, "Cooking for Health." It was a serendipitous match, because this is what each of us had already been doing in our own home kitchens. When we stop to think about it, our cooking has changed in three ways: *ingredients*, *equipment*, and *cooking techniques*.

For instance, a decade ago, when cooking onions, we would have automatically started by throwing a chunk of butter into a heavy skillet over high heat. Now we coat a nonstick pan, which has become the rule rather than the exception, with a thin film of olive oil, and slowly coax the flavor from the onions.

These days, we're more likely to roast vegetables than to steam them; roasting caramelizes their natural sugars, adding depth and a dimension of flavor (without that dab of butter) that are missing when vegetables are simply steamed or blanched. Carbohydrate-rich pasta, which we could both happily eat every day, is a healthy dish when you sauce it with a trace of olive oil, fresh vegetables, and herbs, all moistened with a ladle of the pasta cooking liquid instead of butter and cream. This kitchen trick is actually nothing new; Marie's Italian grandmother did this all the time.

We've moved meat from the center of the plate to the perimeter. Instead of eating meat every day, our meals are now as likely to be centered around fish or poultry, grains, and vegetables. Where we'd once devour an eight- or twelve-ounce steak, we now use small quantities of meat to augment the flavor of generous amounts of grains and vegetables. And there's virtually never a container of sour cream or heavy cream in our refrigerators, though there is a container of yogurt.

Cooking lighter and more healthfully sometimes calls for adjustments in our cooking habits, as well. A skinless chicken breast quickly becomes dry and leathery under the broiler. But when seared in a nonstick skillet, it turns out tender and juicy. In your favorite meat loaf, substituting ground turkey for ground beef cuts way back on fat. But because the turkey is leaner, the meat loaf will be dry without the compensating addition of moist vegetables and extra liquid.

And because we're cooking with less fat, which does add appealing moisture and flavor, it's crucial to be generous with naturally flavorful ingredients: orange and lemon zest, fresh herbs, spices, roasted garlic and peppers, various vinegars, and mustards.

We also dip into the palette of flavors from around the world, not just the "holy trinity" of French, Italian, and Tex-Mex. In this book, you'll find adaptations of dishes from India, North Africa, the Middle East, and Asia, all streamlined so they don't take a long time in the kitchen. When Richard's sister Diana, a vegetarian for over twenty years, heard we were working on a healthy cookbook, she answered immediately: "Go spicier and more ethnic. Ethnic foods from all over the world are so interesting, especially the carbohydrate and grain-based foods. Spread the word that eating healthy doesn't have to be eating boring." And so we have.

One of the challenges in devising healthy versions of traditional peasant dishes is that it's all too easy to cut out the fat—and wind up losing all the depth of flavor. It's the slow intermingling of ingredients, their gradual melding of flavors, that leads to that homey extra something that makes this sort of dish—whether it's chicken paprikás, coq au vin, osso buco, a meat loaf, or a well-simmered stew—so soul-satisfying. And so you'll find several of these dishes here, in versions that cut back on fat but not on old-fashioned flavor.

And so, our own home cooking fertilized our *Bon Appétit* column, and vice versa. When you cook for a living, your professional and personal lives often influence each other to the point where they're almost one. We both feel there is no celebration in life greater than eating wonderful food—a perfect ripe tomato or ear of corn, a bowl of homemade soup, the best bread. We never forget how fortunate we both are to make our livings from food, which provides both sustenance and pleasure.

The food in this book, then, is a positive, upbeat approach to healthier eating, from soup to (dry-roasted) nuts, from appetizers to desserts. This is not a diet book; we don't like diets, and they don't work. Rather, it is a healthier approach to everyday eating. In short, lighter, quicker, better—cooking for the way we eat today.

just how healthy are these recipes?

We've decided specifically not to include nutrition analysis for each recipe in this book. Why? Because we find numbers can be confusing and misleading (if not downright frightening). Rather than slavishly following numbers for each dish, we embrace the commonsense approach, pacing our protein, calorie, and fat intake over one or more days' eating.

When we cook, we know instinctively when the fat level is within reason, for both taste and health. For instance, we try to keep added fat in any recipe to 1 tablespoon (or less) per serving. And we aim to eat a large proportion of carbohydrates, fruits, and vegetables, which are the cornerstone of a healthy diet. And remember that this is not food for weight loss but for generally healthier eating.

Lighter
quicker
better

Appe

snacks

&

tizers

WHEN WE STARTED WORKING on this book, we
kicked off the project by throwing a party on
the backyard terrace; we featured many of
the recipes in this chapter. It was a perfect
night, summer just emerging in full
bloom, with long lingering light. Earlier
in the day we had gone to New York's Union
Square Greenmarket and come back laden
with a rainbow of colorful produce—peppers in
three colors, ripe tomatoes, pencil-thin green beans
and asparagus, baby eggplants, sugar snap peas, freshly made mozzarella, and bouquets of fresh herbs. We
spent a delightful afternoon cooking in high gear, then
set out platters of

- ◆ Tomato Bruschetta with Roasted Garlic
- ◆ Marinated Mozzarella Nuggets with roasted
  peppers and fresh basil
- ◆ Roasted Red and Yellow Pepper Dips,
  Romesco Style

◆ Ginger and Garlic Eggplant Dip
◆ Pickled Shrimp
◆ Crunchy Pita Chips
◆ assorted vegetable crudités

Served with plenty of Champagne, our guests gave us the best compliment we could have received: Digging into the brilliantly colored, vibrant-tasting platters of food, they asked, "*This* is healthy?!"

Few foods are as irresistible as the tidbits that kick off a meal. When appetite is honed to a sharp edge, the first juicy morsels always seem to be the most delicious, the most packed with flavor. Unfortunately, when appetites are at their keenest, it's easy to throw caution to the wind. The result: loading up on saturated fat and excess alcohol. A few nachos here, some crackers and cheese there, chips and dip everywhere, and those fat grams add up quickly.

Appetizers should do what they say—perk up the appetite. A plateful of cheese and crackers is likely to fill you up prematurely, dulling the senses for the events to come.

But even when the goal is to trim the fat, appetizers should also feel like a celebration; this is no time for spartan fare. Smoked salmon, wild mushrooms, luxurious shellfish; dips and spreads made with vegetables, yogurt, and herbs and scooped with crisp vegetables, tortilla wedges, and pita triangles instead of deep-fried chips—these are the way to go.

A good strategy is to bring out the flavor of the food itself. By using plenty of fresh vegetables, even traditionally fat-rich guacamole, for example, is within reach. And dips can be made without the usual culprits (full-fat mayonnaise, sour cream, cream cheese) by building them on a base of such healthier alternatives as yogurt or Yogurt Cheese, part-skim (1%) cottage cheese, or pureed cooked beans.

Salsas—chunky mixtures of citrus-accented vegetables and sometimes fruits—are naturally low in fat, packed with lively flavor and nutrient-rich vegetables, and can be used not only as colorful dips but also as sauces for all sorts of grilled dishes.

Seafood is always a festive starter, extravagant yet naturally low in fat. Our colorful Pickled Shrimp can be made ahead, actually improving in flavor as the shrimp marinate. Steamed mussels or clams are a no-fat indulgence.

When trying to come up with tempting appetizer foods, think vegetables. You may think stuffed mushrooms are so old they're retro, but when filled with chopped wild mushrooms, onion, and fresh herbs, they take on a whole new life.

Foods served before a meal should lend themselves to advance preparation. With no fussing at the last minute, you can enjoy your friends and family at your own parties.

avoid snack fat attacks

Here's the lowdown on some favorite snack foods:

	Calories	Fat g	Cholesterol mg	Sodium mg
1-inch cube cheddar	110	9	30	180
¼ cup salsa	12	0	0	340
1 shrimp	28	.3	54	64
2 thin Crisp bread crackers	30	.5	0	20
15 potato chips	150	10	0	170
6 thin pretzels	110	1	0	290
8 Ritz crackers	140	8	0	240
1 cup tortilla chips	280	12	0	460

Guilt-free Guacamole

Guacamole—delicious as it is—is usually disastrously high in fat. It is sometimes made with sour cream and/or mayonnaise, which drive calories, fat, and cholesterol through the roof. Besides, the avocado itself is a concentrated source of fat—one of the highest in the vegetable kingdom, with over 300 calories in each one, and 80 percent fat by calories. But that fat is mostly monounsaturated, so it may help reduce blood cholesterol.

We've cut back on fat by adding diced tomatoes, cucumbers, and red onion to the basic mixture, while keeping all the luscious flavor in.

Makes about 3 cups

1 ripe avocado, halved, peeled, and pit removed
1 cup diced (¼ inch) ripe plum tomatoes
½ cup diced (¼ inch) seeded hothouse or Kirby cucumber
½ cup diced (¼ inch) red onion
2 tablespoons fresh lime juice
2 tablespoons chopped cilantro or parsley
1 tablespoon minced seeded jalapeño or other chili pepper (see Note)
½ teaspoon salt, or more to taste

1. Dice the avocado into small pieces, about ¼ inch. Place in a mixing bowl and add the tomatoes, cucumber, onion, lime juice, cilantro, jalapeño, and salt.

2. Stir with a spoon until the mixture is blended and the avocado is roughly mashed. Serve as a dip.

Note: Pickled jalapeños can be substituted. Adjust the amount to taste and heat of chili.

White Bean Dip with Roasted Garlic Gremolata

6   garlic cloves, loose skins removed, thin skin left on, drizzled
     or brushed very lightly with olive oil

⅓   cup (packed) flat-leaf parsley, roughly cut up

2   strips (2 × ¾ inch each) lemon zest, cut up

1   can (19 ounces) cannellini beans, rinsed and drained,
     or 2½ cups cooked dried beans (page 204)

3   tablespoons fresh lemon juice, or more to taste

1   tablespoon olive oil

¼   teaspoon salt
     Freshly ground black pepper

Vegetables for dipping
     Endive leaves
     Radicchio leaves
     Snow peas
     Fennel sticks
     Small carrots
     Cucumber slices

1. Heat the oven to 400°F. Place the garlic cloves in a pie plate and roast until garlic is soft when pierced with a knife, 12 to 15 minutes. Do not brown. Cool the garlic slightly. Slip off peels and trim hard ends. There should be about 2 tablespoons.
2. Meanwhile, finely chop the parsley and lemon zest in a food processor. Remove and reserve a spoonful of this mixture for garnish. Add the beans, lemon juice, olive oil, salt, pepper, and the roasted garlic. Process until blended and fairly smooth.
3. Place the bean dip in a bowl and serve surrounded with fresh vegetables. If not serving immediately, place a piece of plastic wrap directly on the surface of the dip and refrigerate. Just before serving, sprinkle the reserved parsley-lemon mixture on top.

Gremolata is a combination of minced garlic, parsley, and lemon zest traditionally used to garnish osso buco in Milan. We make it with garlic that's been roasted to tame and sweeten its flavor. Then we fold the gremolata into pureed white beans—a low-calorie way to pack a high-flavor punch. The vegetables we suggest below are only that—suggestions. Buy whatever you find in season and arrange a colorful presentation.

Makes about 1½ cups

Lighter Caponata

By roasting the eggplant, instead of dicing and frying it, it's possible to cut back on much of the olive oil traditionally used to prepare this sweet-and-sour Sicilian specialty. Serve it as a dip or on toasted Italian bread.

Makes about 2 cups

1	large or 2 small eggplants, halved lengthwise (about 1½ pounds)
2	tablespoons olive oil
1	cup diced (¼ inch) sweet onion
½	cup diced celery, with a few leaves
1	garlic clove, minced
1	can (14½ ounces) Italian-style plum tomatoes, drained, seeded, and chopped; juice reserved (about ⅔ cup)
2	tablespoons finely chopped flat-leaf parsley
1	tablespoon red wine vinegar, or more to taste
1	tablespoon chopped pitted brine-cured black olives
2	tablespoons capers, rinsed and drained
1	teaspoon sugar, or more to taste
½	teaspoon salt, or more to taste
	Freshly ground black pepper
1	tablespoon extra virgin olive oil, for serving (optional)

1. Heat the oven to 350°F. Line a large baking pan with foil.
2. Place the eggplant, cut side down, on the baking pan. Add about ¹/₄ cup water to moisten the bottom of the pan. Roast until the eggplant is tender when pierced with a skewer, about 45 minutes, adding small amounts of water as needed to prevent burning during roasting. Cool to room temperature. Peel the eggplant and cut the flesh into ¹/₄-inch dice. You should have about 2 cups.
3. Meanwhile, heat the oil in a large skillet, preferably nonstick, over medium-low heat. Add the onion, celery, and garlic and sauté over medium-low heat, stirring occasionally, until the onion is golden and the vegetables are tender, about 10 minutes. Add the diced eggplant and sauté, stirring occasionally, until the eggplant browns slightly, 10 to 15 minutes.

4. Add the tomatoes and 3 or 4 tablespoons of the reserved tomato juice, or as needed to keep the mixture moist. Stir in the parsley, vinegar, olives, capers, sugar, salt, and black pepper to taste. Cover and cook over low heat for 5 minutes. Cool completely before serving.

5. Just before serving, correct the seasonings with small amounts of vinegar, sugar, and salt to taste. Spoon into a small bowl and drizzle with olive oil, if desired.

Roasted Red and Yellow Pepper Dips, Romesco Style

Based on Romesco, the traditional Catalan sauce of hot nyora peppers and ground almonds, this simple dip, when made with two colors of peppers, is truly beguiling. We've cut the olive oil and nuts, which are also high in fat, back to a fraction of the original. You can also make this with half almonds, half hazelnuts.

Makes about 1 ¹/₂ cups

2   red bell peppers
2   yellow bell peppers
8   garlic cloves, thin skins left on
12 whole unblanched almonds, toasted
1   teaspoon sherry or red wine vinegar, or more to taste
2   tablespoons olive oil
    Salt and freshly ground black pepper
    Cayenne

1. Place the broiler rack about 2 inches from the flame and heat the broiler.

2. Place a large sheet of foil on a baking sheet. Arrange the peppers in the center and surround with the garlic cloves. Broil the peppers, turning frequently, until the peppers and garlic are evenly charred, about 15 minutes. Remove from the broiler and wrap up the peppers and garlic in the foil; let stand until cool enough to handle.

3. Keeping the red and yellow peppers separated and working over the foil to catch the juices, remove the charred skins, seeds, and stems from the peppers. Cut the flesh into 1-inch pieces and reserve the 2 colors of peppers separately. Strain the pepper juices and reserve. Peel the skins from the garlic and trim off the hard stem ends. Coarsely chop the garlic and add half to the red peppers and half to the yellow.

4. Chop six of the toasted almonds in the food processor. Add the reserved yellow peppers and garlic, 1 tablespoon of the reserved pepper juices, and ¹/₂ teaspoon of the vinegar. Process until pureed. With the motor running, add 1 tablespoon of the olive oil in a slow stream until puree is smooth. Add salt, pepper, and cayenne to taste. Transfer to a small bowl.

5. Rinse out and dry the food processor. Repeat with the red peppers and garlic, the remaining almonds, 1 tablespoon of the reserved pepper juices, the remaining vinegar, and the remaining olive oil. Add salt, pepper, and cayenne to taste. Transfer to another small bowl.

6. To serve, select a shallow serving bowl and scrape the red pepper puree into half of the bowl. Scrape the yellow pepper puree into the other half. Shake the bowl gently so that the purees meet in the center.

Hummus-style Chick Pea Dip

Think of this as a streamlined hummus, the Middle Eastern blend of chick peas and tahini (toasted sesame) paste. Chick peas are a nutrient-rich legume, dense with carbohydrates and protein. Tahini, on the other hand, is primarily fat. We've kept the characteristic flavorings in hummus—lemon juice, garlic, olive oil, mint, and dill—and left the tahini behind.

Makes about 1 ¹/₂ cups

1 can (19 ounces) chick peas, rinsed and drained
3 tablespoons fresh lemon juice, or more to taste
2 tablespoons extra virgin olive oil
2 tablespoons cold water
1 garlic clove, finely chopped
Cayenne
1 tablespoon chopped mint
1 tablespoon chopped parsley
1 tablespoon chopped dill

Puree the chick peas, lemon juice, olive oil, water, and garlic until smooth and fluffy. Transfer the mixture to a shallow soup bowl or other deep plate. Smooth the top with a spatula. Sprinkle lightly with cayenne and top with the combined chopped herbs.

lighter dippers

Instead of deep-fried chips or fat-laden crackers, try some of these healthier alternatives:

◆ **Carrot slices, cut in long, thin diagonals**

◆ **Cucumber slices**

◆ **Endive leaves**

◆ **Bell pepper wedges**

◆ **Crunchy Pita Chips (page 20)**

◆ **Spicy Tortilla Chips (page 21)**

Ginger and Garlic Eggplant Dip

2   medium eggplants, halved lengthwise
    (about 1 pound each)
2   tablespoons extra virgin olive oil
1   tablespoon minced garlic
1   teaspoon ground cumin (see Note)
1   tablespoon grated fresh ginger
¼   cup minced red bell pepper
¼   cup finely chopped parsley
    Salt and freshly ground black pepper

1. Heat the oven to 400°F. Line a heavy baking sheet with foil.

2. Brush the cut sides of the eggplant with 1 tablespoon of the olive oil and arrange, cut side down, on the baking sheet. Bake until the cut sides are well browned and the eggplant is very soft, about 25 minutes. Cool slightly.

3. Combine the remaining olive oil and garlic in a large skillet and heat, stirring, over low heat until the garlic begins to sizzle. Stir in the cumin and remove from heat.

4. Scoop the softened eggplant from the eggplant shells, chop fine, and add to the skillet. Add the ginger, bell pepper, and parsley. Heat, stirring, over medium-low heat until blended. Add salt and pepper to taste. Serve warm or at room temperature.

Note: For maximum flavor, toast 1½ teaspoons cumin seeds in a small, dry nonstick skillet over medium-low heat until fragrant, about 5 minutes, and grind them in a spice mill; measure after grinding.

To bring out the flavor of cumin in this Middle Eastern-flavored dip, toast whole cumin seeds and grind them. You'll be surprised at how much flavor is released this way.

Makes about 2 cups

Smoked Salmon Mousse

This easy mousse, made with light cream cheese and lowfat yogurt, can be served as a dip with cucumber rounds or chilled and piped onto the rounds and served as canapés. If you can, prepare this a day or two in advance so the flavors have a chance to develop. Many delis sell inexpensive smoked salmon trimmings, which work fine for this mousse.

M a k e s   1 1/3

c u p s

2   ounces sliced smoked salmon, cut into
     1/2-inch pieces, or trimmings
8   ounces light cream cheese
1/3 cup lowfat or nonfat yogurt
1   tablespoon minced scallion, white part only,
     or more to taste
1   tablespoon fresh lemon juice, or more to taste
2   tablespoons chopped dill, or more to taste
     Freshly ground white pepper
     Tiny dill sprigs, for garnish
1   seedless cucumber, scrubbed and cut into
     1/4-inch slices

1. Combine the smoked salmon, cream cheese, yogurt, scallion, lemon juice, dill, and pepper in a food processor and process until smooth. Correct seasonings, adding more scallions, lemon juice, dill, and/or pepper to taste.

2. Transfer to a bowl and serve as a dip, garnished with dill sprigs and with the cucumber slices arranged around the bowl. Or chill the salmon mixture until stiff enough to pipe through a fluted pastry tube onto the cucumber slices. Garnish each with a small dill sprig.

Yogurt Cheese

1   pint nonfat or lowfat yogurt

Line a strainer with cheesecloth or a coffee filter and place it over a bowl. Put the yogurt in the strainer and refrigerate for at least 4 hours or overnight. The longer the yogurt drains, the thicker the cheese.

Garlic and Herb Yogurt Dip: Stir $^1/_4$ cup chopped dill, 2 tablespoons chopped parsley, and 1 tablespoon chopped roasted garlic (page 28) into 1 cup yogurt cheese. Spoon into a bowl, cover with plastic wrap, and refrigerate at least 1 hour before serving.

Mustard-Dill Yogurt Dip: Stir $1^1/_2$ tablespoons smooth Dijon mustard, $1^1/_2$ tablespoons grainy Dijon mustard, and 3 tablespoons chopped dill into 1 cup yogurt cheese.

When you drain the excess whey (the liquid part) from yogurt, you wind up with a thick, rich mixture that's about the texture of sour cream. (You can use the whey to bake biscuits or bread.) Let the yogurt drain further, and it's concentrated almost to the texture of cream cheese. Either makes a versatile base for a dip or spread, which can be flavored in several different ways.

Makes about 1 cup

Fresh and Easy Salsa

Salting tomatoes, then letting them drain in a colander for about twenty minutes, draws out excess moisture and concentrates the flavor.

Makes about 3 cups

3 ripe tomatoes, cored, seeded, and diced
1 yellow tomato, cored, seeded, and diced
½ yellow bell pepper, stemmed, seeded, and cut into ¼-inch dice
¼ cup finely chopped red onion or scallion
2 tablespoons minced cilantro or parsley
2 jalapeños, seeded and minced
   Juice of 1 lime, or more to taste
   Salt

Combine the tomatoes, pepper, onion, cilantro, jalapeños, lime juice, and salt to taste in a small bowl. Let stand at room temperature for about 1 hour before serving.

lighter, quicker, better salsas

Salsas have sneaked up on the American table, overtaking even ketchup, the great American staple, in sales. While storebought salsas can be perfectly good, homemade ones are much fresher in taste. They are very easy to throw together. Tomato-based salsas are the most common, but you can also base salsas on other vegetables and fruit. Salsas make great appetizer dips, but you can also spoon them over grilled fish, chicken, or meat.

Wear rubber gloves when handling fresh chilies; capsaicin, the compound that gives them their heat, is a powerful skin irritant. If handling chilies without gloves, wash your hands thoroughly with soap and water immediately afterward.

Roasted Three-Pepper Salsa

1	red bell pepper
1	green bell pepper
1	yellow bell pepper
1	rib celery, with a few leaves, halved lengthwise if large, sliced thin
2	tablespoons finely chopped flat-leaf parsley
2	tablespoons finely chopped pitted brine-cured black olives
1	tablespoon olive oil
1	teaspoon small capers, rinsed and drained
1	teaspoon finely shredded orange zest
1	teaspoon minced fresh rosemary leaves or a pinch of dried rosemary
½	garlic clove, crushed
	Salt and freshly ground pepper
1	to 2 teaspoons fresh lemon or lime juice

The peppers, olives, capers, orange zest, and rosemary in this salsa are faintly reminiscent of the flavors of Provence. We love it as a dip or served on salmon steaks, grilled hamburgers, or a baked potato.

Makes about 1 ¾ cups

1. Roast the peppers as described on page 10. Coarsely chop the peppers. Measure ¼ cup of the roasted pepper juices and add to the chopped pepper.

2. Add the celery, parsley, olives, olive oil, capers, orange zest, rosemary, and garlic and stir to blend. Season to taste with salt and pepper. Cover and set aside at room temperature for about 1 hour, or until the flavors blend. Stir in lemon or lime juice to taste and correct seasonings. This salsa is best served at room temperature.

Grilled Tomato and Vegetable Salsa

This mixture of vegetables was inspired by a Spanish-style cooked sauce usually served with fresh cod. The ingredients can be varied as availability and taste dictate, but the tomatoes and onions are essential. The vegetables can be grilled over a hot fire or cooked under the broiler. If grilling outdoors, arrange the tomatoes in a wire basket so they hold their shape; skewer the onions crosswise so they don't fall apart during cooking. Serve as a side dish with grilled chicken or steak. Great served as a topping for grilled fish or boneless chicken breasts.

Makes about 2 cups

2 medium-size, firm ripe tomatoes, cored and halved crosswise

1 medium-size sweet onion, peeled and halved crosswise

2 scallions, trimmed

1 large or 2 small frying peppers, halved lengthwise, seeds and stems removed (see Note)

1 carrot, halved lengthwise

1 small zucchini, halved lengthwise

3 tablespoons olive oil, preferably extra virgin

2 teaspoons minced fresh oregano or pinch of dried oregano

2 teaspoons fresh thyme leaves, stripped from stems, or pinch of dried thyme

1 garlic clove, crushed

¼ cup chopped basil

1 tablespoon balsamic or red wine vinegar

Salt and freshly ground pepper

1. Heat a grill or broiler. Prepare all the vegetables and arrange on a large tray. Combine 1½ tablespoons of the olive oil, the oregano, thyme, and garlic and stir to blend. Brush over all the surfaces of the vegetables.

2. Grill or broil the vegetables, turning as needed. Transfer them to the tray as they become charred and tender. Cool slightly.

3. Carefully peel the skin from the pepper. Scrape the centers of the tomatoes into a bowl. If any of the tomato flesh remains quite firm, chop it up. Cut the onion, scallions, pepper, carrot, and zucchini into ¼-inch dice and add.

4. Combine the vegetables with the remaining 1½ tablespoons olive oil, the basil, vinegar, and salt and pepper to taste.

Note: These thin-walled peppers are sometimes called Italian or Hungarian peppers or Cubanelles.

Papaya and Vegetable Salsa

1   large ripe papaya, halved, seeded, peeled, and finely
    chopped
1   cup finely chopped juicy ripe tomatoes, with juice,
    with or without seeds
½   cup finely chopped seeded and peeled cucumber
¼   cup finely chopped scallion
3   tablespoons fresh lime juice
1   tablespoon finely chopped cilantro or parsley
2   teaspoons finely chopped jalapeño or other chili
    pepper, or to taste
    Salt

In a medium bowl, combine the papaya, tomato, cucumber, scallion, lime juice, cilantro, jalapeño, and a pinch of salt. Stir to blend. Let stand at room temperature until the mixture becomes juicy, about 20 minutes. Taste and correct seasonings.

In a recent study of more than three dozen fruits, papaya had the highest amounts of vitamins, minerals, and fiber. This pretty, fresh-tasting salsa goes well with lowfat white or blue corn chips.

**Makes about
2 cups**

Crunchy Pita Chips

This lowfat chip, perfect with dips, can replace potato, corn, or any other fried chips. Store dry pita in the freezer until you're ready to make the chips.

Makes 16 chips

2 pita breads, whole wheat or white
2 teaspoons olive oil
½ garlic clove, crushed

1. Heat the oven to 350°F.

2. Using a small knife or kitchen scissors, cut along the circumference of each pita bread, cutting it into 2 circles. Combine the olive oil and garlic in a small bowl. Lightly brush on the surface of the bread. Stack the circles and cut into 8 wedges. Arrange in a single layer on a baking sheet. Bake until golden, 8 to 10 minutes.

all dips are not created equal

	Calories	Fat g	Cholesterol mg
1 cup mayonnaise	1600	176	80
1 cup reduced-calorie mayonnaise	800	80	80
1 cup cholesterol-free mayonnaise (without egg yolk)	640	48	0
8 ounces cream cheese	792	80	248
8 ounces lowfat cream cheese	490	35	105
8 ounces sour cream	416	40	92
8 ounces lowfat yogurt	140	3.4	14
8 ounces nonfat yogurt	110	0	5
1 cup Yogurt Cheese from lowfat	220	6.8	28
1 cup Yogurt Cheese from nonfat	288	0	10
8 ounces part-skim ricotta cheese	342	19.6	68

Spicy Tortilla Chips

8 thin flour or corn tortillas (about 6 inches in diameter)

1 tablespoon vegetable oil

1½ teaspoons cumin seeds, crushed with a mortar and pestle, or chopped with a knife, or 1 teaspoon chili powder

1. Heat the oven to 400°F.

2. Brush both sides of each tortilla with oil. Sprinkle with cumin. Stack and cut into 6 triangular wedges.

3. Arrange the wedges in a single layer on a nonstick baking sheet and bake, stirring once or twice, until golden and crisp, about 10 minutes. Serve warm. *(The chips can be made ahead and rewarmed.)*

While there are several lowfat tortilla chips now on the market, they'll never be as tasty as the ones you can make yourself in minutes. We have to laugh at the tortilla and potato chips that conspicuously announce that they have no cholesterol. What they don't say is that those cholesterol-free chips are fried in vegetable oil and have plenty of fat.

Fresh flour and corn tortillas are available in the dairy sections of most supermarkets. The thinner the tortilla, the better the chips.

Makes 48 chips

Salsa and Cheese Nachos

For these and the following nachos—and for other dishes involving melted cheese—we suggest using a small amount of full-fat cheese, rather than low-fat cheese. Not only does it have better flavor, it melts better, too. If you like, you can spread a dab of bean dip (page 7) on each chip before adding the other toppings.

Makes 24 chips

½ recipe tortilla chips (24 wedges) (page 21)
½ cup salsa, homemade (page 16) or storebought, as needed
½ cup grated jack and/or cheddar cheese

1. Heat the oven to 400°F.
2. Scatter the chips on a baking sheet in a single layer. Spoon about 1 teaspoon salsa on each chip. Sprinkle a teaspoon of cheese over and bake until the cheese is melted and bubbly, about 4 minutes. Serve hot.

Jalapeño and Cheese Nachos

Makes 24 chips

½ recipe tortilla chips (24 wedges) (page 21)
4 or 5 pickled jalapeños, stem ends cut off, seeds pulled out, and sliced, or use sliced pickled jalapeños
½ cup grated jack and/or cheddar cheese

1. Heat the oven to 400°F.
2. Scatter the chips on a baking sheet in a single layer. Place 2 jalapeño slices on each chip. Scatter the cheese over and bake until the cheese is melted and bubbly, about 4 minutes. Serve hot.

Crostini

12 slices (½ inch) Italian bread, preferably
whole wheat

1 tablespoon extra virgin olive oil

1 garlic clove, halved (optional)

1. Heat the oven to 350°F.

2. Using a pastry brush, lightly brush one side of the bread with a little olive oil. Arrange on a baking sheet. Bake until the edges are golden, about 25 minutes. Cool slightly.

3. Rub each slice of bread lightly with the cut side of the garlic, if desired.

Crostini are simply thick slices of toasted bread, usually topped with something savory. In Tuscany, crostini are frequently spread with a chicken liver mixture and served with drinks before dinner. Whole wheat Italian bread makes especially delicious crostini. The bread can be toasted on a grill, under a broiler, or in a toaster oven as well as in the oven. Crostini are usually served with the topping already spread on the toasts, but don't assemble them more than half an hour in advance.

Makes 12

White Bean Crostini Topping

Makes enough

for 12

crostini

1	can (19 ounces) cannellini beans, drained and rinsed, or 2½ cups cooked dried beans (page 204)
3	tablespoons fresh lemon juice
3	teaspoons extra virgin olive oil
1	teaspoon finely chopped garlic
1	teaspoon chopped fresh oregano leaves or ¼ teaspoon dried oregano

Combine the beans, lemon juice, 2 teaspoons of the olive oil, garlic, and half of the oregano in a food processor. Process until nearly smooth. Spread the mixture in a shallow bowl and drizzle the remaining oil on top. Sprinkle with the remaining oregano.

Roasted Eggplant Crostini Topping

Makes enough

for 12

crostini

4	thick (½ inch) slices peeled eggplant
2	teaspoons extra virgin olive oil
½	garlic clove, crushed
¼	cup chopped fresh roasted peppers (page 10) or rinsed and drained jarred roasted peppers
½	teaspoon small capers, rinsed and drained
	Freshly ground black pepper

1. Heat the oven to 425°F.

2. Arrange the eggplant slices in a single layer on a nonstick baking sheet. Stir the oil and garlic together in a small bowl and lightly brush the mixture on both sides of the eggplant.

3. Roast the eggplant slices until lightly browned, turning once, about 20 minutes per side. Cool slightly. Coarsely chop the eggplant and combine with the red peppers and capers. Season with black pepper to taste. Serve warm or cold.

Escarole Crostini Topping

1½   to 2 pounds escarole, trimmed, cut, or torn
      into 1-inch pieces
      Salt
1   tablespoon extra virgin olive oil
1   garlic clove, crushed
      Pinch of crushed red pepper, or more to taste
      Freshly ground black pepper

Makes enough for 12 crostini

1. Prepare the escarole and set aside. Half-fill a large saucepan with water and bring to a boil. Add salt and stir in the escarole. Cook, stirring, until just tender, 3 to 5 minutes. Drain the escarole well, pressing on the escarole with the back of a spoon to remove excess moisture.

2. Combine the olive oil, garlic, and red pepper in a large skillet. Heat over low heat just until the garlic begins to sizzle. Add the escarole all at once and stir to coat with the oil.

3. Cook briefly over high heat to cook off some of the juices. Season with salt and black pepper to taste. Serve spooned onto crostini.

pretzels vs. chips

Next time you have a snack attack, reach for a handful of pretzels instead of potato chips.

Fifteen chips (1 ounce) have 10 grams of fat, while 6 pretzels (1 ounce) have only 1 gram.

Savory Mushroom Crostini Topping

Makes enough for 12 crostini

2	cups chopped white button mushrooms
2	tablespoons finely chopped onion
1	teaspoon finely chopped garlic
1	tablespoon extra virgin olive oil
1	tablespoon finely chopped flat-leaf parsley
1	tablespoon finely chopped plain sundried tomatoes
	Salt and freshly ground black pepper

Combine the mushrooms, onion, garlic, and olive oil in a large skillet. Cook, stirring, over medium-high heat, until the mushrooms are tender and liquid has evaporated, about 5 minutes. Add the parsley, sundried tomatoes, and salt and pepper to taste. Cook stirring, until blended, about 1 minute. Transfer to a food processor and puree. Serve warm or at room temperature.

Frank Stitt's Sweet Potato Crostini

4 slices (½ inch) sourdough bread

3 teaspoons extra virgin olive oil

1 garlic clove, halved

2 ounces fresh goat cheese, crumbled

4 round slices (½ inch) baked and peeled sweet potato

1 fresh roasted pepper (page 10) or jarred roasted pepper, drained and patted dry, cut into thin strips

1 teaspoon thyme leaves
   Freshly ground black pepper

1. Drizzle each piece of bread with ½ teaspoon olive oil and rub with the cut side of the garlic. Broil or toast until lightly browned. Arrange the slices on a platter.

2. Distribute the goat cheese evenly on the crostini. Top each with a potato slice. Using a small knife, spread the cooked potato evenly.

3. Combine the red pepper, remaining 1 teaspoon olive oil, and thyme in a small bowl. Arrange on the crostini, dividing evenly. Grind black pepper over all and serve.

This unusual variation on crostini comes from Frank Stitt, chef-owner, with his wife, Frances, of Highlands Bar & Grill and Bottega in Birmingham, Alabama. Born and raised in Cullman County, Alabama, Frank has been a pioneer at devising new, but always sensible, ways with traditional southern ingredients.

S e r v e s   4

Tomato Bruschetta with Roasted Garlic

Bruschetta is a southern Italian specialty. Slices of toast, usually in thicker slabs than crostini, are spread with various toppings. This one is based on the recipe for bruschetta rossa *from* chef Michael Romano at Union Square Café.

When you salt tomatoes this way, they turn almost into a marmalade, which soaks into the grilled bread. Put the tomato mixture together in the afternoon, then serve the bruschetta as the late summer sun begins to set. You'll need knives and forks.

S e r v e s   6

2½ to 3 pounds ripe tomatoes, peeled, seeded, and cut into ½-inch dice
   Kosher salt
½ cup shredded basil leaves
4 to 6 large garlic cloves
3 tablespoons olive oil
¾ teaspoon chopped fresh not dried oregano (optional)
¾ teaspoon chopped fresh not dried thyme leaves (optional)
   Freshly ground black pepper
6 large slices sourdough or coarse country bread
6 small basil sprigs, for garnish (optional)

1. Place the tomatoes in a nonaluminum colander in a bowl or over a large plate with a rim. Sprinkle the tomatoes lightly with salt (usually about 1½ teaspoons) and ¼ cup of the basil. Toss to combine. Let the tomatoes stand for 45 minutes to 1 hour, tossing once or twice.

2. Heat the oven to 375°F.

3. Peel the garlic cloves, leaving a thin layer of skin on each one. Place in a pie plate or other shallow baking dish and drizzle with a little olive oil. Roast the garlic until soft when pierced with a small knife but not yet browned, usually 12 to 15 minutes. Set aside to cool.

4. Peel the garlic, cut each clove lengthwise into 4 or 6 sections, and slice thin crosswise. Place garlic in a mixing bowl with the remaining olive oil, remaining basil, and oregano and thyme, if using. Drain the tomatoes well, discarding the juices. Add the tomatoes to the mixing bowl and sprinkle generously with pepper. Taste and add a little more salt if needed to bring out the tomato flavor. *(The tomato mixture can be prepared up to 2 or 3 hours in advance and kept at room temperature.)*

5. At serving time, toast the bread on a grill, in a toaster, or under the broiler until lightly golden on both sides. Place a slice of toast on each serving plate. Spoon the tomato mixture over each slice of bread, letting some of the oil and juices run over the edges. Garnish each serving with a small basil sprig and serve with a knife and fork.

Mushroom Caps Stuffed with Wild Mushrooms

Mushrooms upon mush-rooms upon mushrooms. These mushrooms are stuffed with a duxelles (a mixture of chopped wild mushrooms, onions, and herbs)—both fresh and dried.

Makes 20

½ cup dried porcini (about 1 ounce)

½ cup boiling water

20 medium white button mushrooms, wiped clean, stems removed and reserved

1 tablespoon olive oil
Salt and freshly ground black pepper

½ cup finely chopped onion

4 ounces fresh shiitake mushrooms, stems discarded, caps finely chopped (about 1 cup)

1 garlic clove, crushed

2 tablespoons finely chopped parsley

2 tablespoons chopped chives or finely chopped scallion

1 teaspoon fresh lemon juice
Freshly grated nutmeg

1. Combine the dried porcini and boiling water in a small bowl, cover, and let stand until the mushrooms have softened, about 15 minutes. Drain through a coffee filter, reserving the liquid. Rinse the mushrooms under cool water to remove any grit and pat dry with paper towels. Finely chop by hand or in a food processor. Set aside.

2. Brush the tops of the mushroom caps lightly with a little of the oil and arrange on an ovenproof platter or baking dish, bottoms up. Sprinkle lightly with salt and pepper. Set aside.

3. Heat the remaining oil in a heavy skillet, preferably non-stick. Add the onion and sauté over low heat, stirring, until golden, about 5 minutes.

4. Finely chop the reserved white mushroom stems. You should have about 1 cup. Add the stems, the chopped shii-takes, the porcini, and the garlic to the skillet and stir to blend.

Cover and cook over very low heat until the mushrooms begin to release some of their liquid. Uncover, raise the heat, and stir in the reserved porcini liquid. Cook over high heat, stirring constantly, until all the liquid has reduced and the mushroom mixture is dry when pressed with the back of a spoon, about 4 minutes.

5. Heat the oven to 375°F.

6. Stir the parsley, chives, lemon juice, ¼ teaspoon salt, a grinding of pepper, and a grating of nutmeg into the mushroom mixture. Carefully spoon the mixture into the mushroom caps, dividing the mixture evenly. *(The mushrooms can be filled several hours in advance and refrigerated, then baked just before serving.)* Bake until the caps are tender, 15 to 20 minutes. Serve hot.

Potato Tortilla with Chives

This isn't the flat, pan-cakelike Mexican bread, but the potato omelet that is virtually the national dish of Spain. Cut into bite-size squares; it's a great party nibble.

Our version contains just enough egg to bind the potato and onion mixture. Wiping the potatoes dry and layering them as we do keeps the starch in the potatoes. The finished omelet then holds together neatly.

Makes about 28 squares

2   tablespoons olive oil
2   pounds russet (baking) potatoes, peeled, wiped clean with a damp towel (do not rinse), and sliced thin (about 4 cups)
¼   cup minced onion
    Salt and freshly ground black pepper
2   large eggs, beaten
½   cup lowfat or nonfat yogurt
½   bunch chives, cut into 2-inch lengths, or 2 scallion tops, thinly sliced

1. Heat a 10- to 12-inch nonstick skillet over medium heat until hot enough to evaporate a drop of water upon contact. Add 1 tablespoon of the olive oil and tilt the pan to coat evenly.

2. Spread about a third of the potato slices on the bottom of the pan; sprinkle half of the onion and salt and pepper to taste over the potatoes. Top with another layer of potato slices and sprinkle with the remaining onion and salt and pepper to taste. Spread with the remaining potato slices. Drizzle with the remaining tablespoon of olive oil. Press down firmly on the potatoes with the back of a large spatula.

3. Cover the pan and cook over medium-low heat until the potatoes are tender when pierced with the tip of a knife, 20 to 25 minutes. As the potatoes cook, press down firmly on the potato slices every 5 minutes or so.

4. Whisk the eggs until blended. Drizzle over the top of the potatoes, avoiding the outside edges as much as possible. Cover and cook until the eggs have set, 5 to 8 minutes. Remove from the heat and let the tortilla stand, covered, for 5 minutes.

5. Loosen the edges of the tortilla from the skillet with a spatula. Place a round platter on top of the skillet and carefully invert the tortilla. The bottom should be crisp and browned. Cool at least 10 minutes.

6. Cut the tortilla into strips about 1½ inches wide. Then cut across, forming 1½-inch squares. Serve warm or at room temperature, topping each square with about ½ teaspoon of yogurt and 2 pieces of chive.

Wine-steamed Mussels with Oregano and Orange

Steaming shellfish is a perfect way to get full flavor with almost no fat. This technique for steaming mussels also works well with clams, particularly small ones. When steaming mussels or clams, cook them, tightly covered, just until the shells open, no longer.

**M a k e s
4   a p p e t i z e r
s e r v i n g s**

1   tablespoon olive oil
2   cups diced (¼ inch) sweet onion
2   tablespoons fresh oregano leaves, chopped, stems removed, or 1 teaspoon dried oregano
1   garlic clove, crushed
3   strips (3 × ½ inch) orange zest
1   cup white wine
2   pounds fresh mussels, scrubbed, debearded, and rinsed

Orange Gremolata
½   cup (packed) flat-leaf parsley leaves and thin stems, chopped
2   whole garlic cloves
3   ripe plum tomatoes, cored, halved, seeded, and chopped (optional)
    Diced pulp of 1 orange, peel, pith, and seeds removed (½ to ¾ cup)
    Fresh oregano sprigs, for garnish (optional)

1. Heat the olive oil and onion in a wide saucepan or deep skillet, preferably nonstick, over low heat. Cook, stirring, until the onion is crisp-tender but not browned, about 3 minutes. Stir in the oregano, crushed garlic, and 1 strip of the orange zest and sauté 30 seconds. Add the wine, raise the heat to high, and bring to a boil.

2. Add the mussels, cover the pan tightly, and cook over medium heat, shaking the pan once or twice, until the mussels have opened, about 5 minutes. Remove any opened mussels into a large serving bowl or deep platter and cover with foil.

Continue cooking the others until they open, about 5 minutes longer. Discard any unopened mussels.

3. Meanwhile, combine the parsley, the remaining 2 strips orange zest, and the whole garlic and chop fine with a chef's knife or small food processor. Set aside.

4. Stir the parsley mixture and tomatoes, if using, into the broth in the pan and bring to a boil. Stir in the orange pulp and turn off the heat. Ladle the broth over the mussels and serve immediately, garnished with sprigs of oregano.

Pickled Shrimp

Based on a Carolina Low Country classic, this dish has lots of shrimp and plenty of colorful vegetables. The dish can be made one or two days ahead; the flavor improves as the shrimp marinate.

Serves 10

1	small onion, halved
1	bay leaf
3	allspice berries, crushed
1	teaspoon salt
1½	pounds medium shrimp (26 to 30 per pound), peeled with tails left on and deveined
½	cup olive oil
½	cup white wine vinegar
½	red bell pepper, stemmed and seeded, cut into thin strips
½	yellow bell pepper, stemmed and seeded, cut into thin strips
½	cup coarsely chopped dill, including thin stems
½	cup thinly sliced scallion, cut into diagonals
1	lemon, cut into paper-thin slices, seeds removed
1	garlic clove, bruised
1	strip orange zest (3 × ½ inch), cut into thin julienne strips
	Freshly ground black pepper
	Hot pepper sauce

1. Fill a large saucepan three-quarters full with water. Add the onion, bay leaf, allspice, and salt. Heat to a full rolling boil. Stir in the shrimp and cook, uncovered, stirring occasionally, just until cooked through, about 3 minutes. Drain immediately and rinse with cold tap water.

2. In a large nonaluminum container with a tight-fitting lid, combine the oil, vinegar, pepper strips, dill, scallion, lemon slices, garlic, orange zest, and a generous grinding of pepper. Add the shrimp and toss to blend.

3. Cover and refrigerate at least 8 hours or up to 2 days before serving, stirring occasionally. Correct seasonings, if necessary, and add hot sauce to taste. To serve, spoon the mixture into a shallow serving bowl, preferably glass, and serve with picks or small forks.

Marinated Mozzarella Nuggets

2 tablespoons olive oil

2 teaspoons red wine vinegar

½ garlic clove, crushed

½ teaspoon crushed red pepper

16 squares (1 inch) roasted red pepper, fresh (page 10) or jarred

½ pound fresh mozzarella, either small balls or cut into 16 cubes (½ to ¾ inch) or use part-skim mozzarella

16 small fresh basil leaves or 1-inch torn pieces

1. Whisk the oil, vinegar, garlic, and red pepper until blended. Add the roasted peppers and marinate 15 minutes. Add the mozzarella and toss gently, just to coat.

2. Use small party picks and skewer a piece of mozzarella, a piece of red pepper, and a basil leaf together. Arrange on a platter and drizzle with any marinade left in the bowl. Serve at room temperature.

As with all cheese appetizers, the secret here is to indulge in small portions. To make that easier, many cheese stores and Italian markets sell small balls of mozzarella called bocconcini *(little mouthfuls). If these are not available, cut larger mozzarella cheese into* ¹/₂- to ³/₄-inch cubes.

Makes 16 pieces

all mozzarella is not created equal

	Calories	Fat, gm per ounce
Whole-milk mozzarella	80	6
Part-skim mozzarella	80	5
Reduced-fat mozzarella	60	3

We don't recommend no-fat mozzarella; this is a case where no fat means loss of flavor and texture.

u p s

WE ARE BOTH ENTHUSIASTIC, dedicated soup makers and eaters. Saturday mornings, especially in winter, or on a cool, rainy morning of any season, Richard can be found in his Manhattan kitchen happily chopping vegetables and contemplating the soup of the day. Meanwhile, across the Brooklyn Bridge, Marie, very likely, is doing the same thing. When you have prepared a good homemade soup for dinner, you don't need much else on the menu, except perhaps a salad and a loaf of bread.

Soup moves effortlessly through the seasons. Fall and winter find our soup pots brimming with hearty bean and root vegetable soups. Although soups made with dried beans are not quick, you can substitute canned beans in many of our recipes. Of course, if time allows, a slow simmering soup requires little attention, leaving the cook free to do other things. When we make a batch of bean soup, we often double the recipe and freeze some for later. In spring and summer, we gravitate toward fresh vegetable soups, either pureed or chunky, served chilled or hot.

Soups, especially when they are broth based, are one of the most nutrient-dense dishes in a meal. Nutritional density refers to the food value—or protein, vitamins, and minerals—a food delivers for the calories. For instance, a cup of chicken broth has fewer than 35 calories and beef broth fewer than 20 calories, but the broths are a good source of nutrients and, when properly prepared, little fat.

We use very simple techniques for trimming the fat profile of our favorite soups. We spoon the fat from the surface of canned broth. When we make our own broth, we chill it and lift off the solidified fat. To keep the fat used in preparing the vegetables for soup to a minimum, we use one tablespoon (or less) of olive oil, a small amount of water, a nonstick pan and very low heat to cook the vegetables slowly and to coax out their natural juices.

Many soups, especially hearty broth-based vegetable soups, are inherently healthful, but rich creamy soups and chowders can be lethal, especially when they are thickened with heavy cream, egg yolks, roux, or *beurre manié* (kneaded butter and flour). To pare the fat and cholesterol in these soups without sacrificing their flavor and texture, we use lowfat substitutions for dairy products—lowfat milk for whole milk or yogurt for sour cream. We add texture and body to soups that are traditionally thickened with flour and butter by using pureed potatoes, carrots, or other vegetables. This adds not only flavor but nutrients, too. The Three-Mushroom Bisque and the Two-Potato Chowder make good use of these two fat-saving techniques.

We've learned the hard way that if we simply omit the fat from a soup recipe, we remove much of the flavor as well. Fat not only tastes good, it carries and brings alive other flavors. And taste is, after all, what eating well is all about. We often add a special topping or seasoning to soups. That might be finely chopped fresh herbs or gremolata (a mixture of finely chopped parsley, garlic, and lemon zest) or pureed basil and yogurt, a dusting of grated cheese, intense spices such as curry and ginger, and, of course, garlic.

soup is good food

Studies indicate that by starting a meal with soup—which has a lower caloric density than most solid foods and takes longer to sip than solid food takes to chew—you are less likely to overload on the main course and dessert. One study at the Institute for Behavioral Education in King of Prussia, Pennsylvania, involving a group of people in a weight-loss program, showed a 5 percent greater weight reduction in participants who ate soup four or more times a week compared to those who ate soup less than four times a week. Additional studies have shown that people who had a cup of soup before a meal consumed up to 25 percent fewer calories than people who ate a more caloric appetizer. One study of participants on a weight-loss maintenance program showed that soup eaters were better able to maintain their weight loss than non–soup eaters.

Chicken Broth

Although there are many good quality reduced-sodium canned chicken broths on the market, there really is nothing like homemade broth. It is lighter in flavor and less obtrusive in soups and sauces. Make the broth in small batches and freeze it in one- or two-cup plastic containers. Chill the broth overnight first; all the fat will rise to the top of the broth and solidify. The next day, the solid layer of fat can be easily lifted off.

If you prefer, you can make broth entirely without salt and add salt as needed when you prepare the soup, sauce, or whatever.

Makes about 8 cups

2 to 3 pounds chicken wings, backs, and/or necks
3 quarts water
1 onion, halved
1 leafy rib celery
1 carrot
1 garlic clove, halved
1 bay leaf
1 flat-leaf parsley sprig
1 teaspoon salt, or to taste

1. Rinse the chicken thoroughly in 2 changes of water. Drain and pat dry. Place in a large stockpot. Add the water, onion, celery, carrot, garlic, bay leaf, parsley, and salt. Heat over medium-high heat until mixture begins to boil. Reduce the heat and skim any foam from the surface. Simmer the broth, uncovered, over medium-low heat until reduced by one-third, about 3 hours. Cool slightly.

2. Set a large fine-mesh strainer over a large bowl and strain the broth. Discard the solids. Chill the broth overnight.

3. Next day, lift the solid fat from the surface. Ladle the broth into 1- and 2-cup freezer containers, leaving behind the layer of cloudy broth on the bottom of the bowl. This should be discarded. Broth will keep 4 months in the freezer.

Beef Broth

2   slices (1 inch) beef shank with meat attached
    (2 to 3 pounds)
    Olive oil
1   large onion, halved
1   carrot, halved lengthwise
1   garlic clove, halved
3   quarts water
1   leafy rib celery
1   flat-leaf parsley sprig
1   bay leaf
1   teaspoon salt, or to taste

For rich, amber beef broth, brown the beef and the vegetables first in a nonstick pan that has been coated with a thin film of olive oil.

Makes about 8 cups

1. Wipe the surfaces of the meat with a dampened paper towel. Brush the bottom of a very large wide saucepan, preferably nonstick, with a thin film of olive oil. Heat pan over medium-high heat until hot enough to sizzle the meat.

2. Add the meat, onion, carrot, and garlic to the pan. Cook over medium to medium-high heat until the meat is well browned on both sides. Add the water, celery, parsley, bay leaf, and salt. Heat to boiling and skim any foam from the surface. Reduce the heat and simmer, uncovered, over medium-low heat, until the broth is reduced by one-third, about 3 hours. Cool slightly.

3. Set a large fine-mesh strainer over a large bowl and strain the broth. Transfer the pieces of meat to a side dish. Discard the remaining solids. Pick over the meat, discarding any fat and gristle. Shred the meat and reserve for soup. Refrigerate the broth overnight.

4. Next day, lift the solid fat from the surface. Ladle the broth into 1- and 2-cup freezer containers, leaving behind the layer of cloudy broth on the bottom of the bowl. This should be discarded. Broth will keep 4 months in the freezer.

Vegetable Broth

2 cups chopped onions
2 cups sliced carrots
1 cup diced (¼ inch) parsnips
1 leek, washed, trimmed, and sliced
½ head garlic
2 teaspoons olive oil
2 cups chopped savoy cabbage
1 pound untrimmed spinach, rinsed
1 cup sliced mushrooms
1 cup sliced celery, with a few celery leaves
1 small zucchini, trimmed and diced (¼ inch)
1 small yellow squash, trimmed and diced (¼ inch)
1 can (14½ ounces) whole tomatoes, with juice
½ cup (packed) parsley leaves
1 bay leaf
1 fresh thyme sprig or ½ teaspoon dried
3 quarts water
1 teaspoon salt, or to taste

1. Combine the onions, carrots, parsnips, leek, and garlic in a stockpot. Add the olive oil and stir to blend. Cook, uncovered, over medium heat, stirring often, just until the vegetables are wilted, about 15 minutes.

2. Add the cabbage, spinach, mushrooms, celery, zucchini, yellow squash, tomatoes, parsley, bay leaf, and thyme; stir to blend. Add the water and salt. Heat to boiling.

3. Reduce the heat and simmer, uncovered, over medium-low heat, until reduced by one-third, about 2 hours. Strain through a sieve into a large bowl. Press down on solids to extract juices. Discard solids.

4. Ladle into 1- and 2-cup freezer containers and cover tightly. Broth will keep 4 months in the freezer.

While it is difficult to make a strong broth without the protein and richness that are extracted from meat or poultry bones, a good all-vegetable broth can be prepared by lightly browning the vegetables before simmering them. When onions, carrots, parsnips, and other aromatic vegetables are browned, their natural sugars caramelize from the heat of cooking to add a depth of flavor and color to the broth. While you can use virtually any combination of vegetables, don't add more than two cups of cabbage, or its flavor will overwhelm the other vegetables.

Makes about 8 cups

a quick blast of flavor

Top a bowl of soup with a spoonful of any of the following garnishes just before serving.

ROASTED RED PEPPER PUREE Rinse and drain 2 jarred red bell peppers. Coarsely chop the peppers. Heat 1 tablespoon olive oil in a skillet and add the peppers and 1 finely chopped garlic clove. Cook over low heat just until the garlic is tender, about 1 minute. Add 1 teaspoon fresh thyme leaves or a pinch of dried thyme, a pinch of salt, and freshly ground black pepper. Transfer to a food processor and puree. MUSHROOM SAUTÉ WITH HERBS AND GARLIC Combine 2 cups chopped mushrooms and 1 tablespoon olive oil and 1 tablespoon water or broth in a nonstick skillet. Cook, stirring, over medium heat until the mushrooms are tender. Increase heat and cook, stirring until they are lightly browned. Add 1 finely chopped garlic clove, 1 tablespoon chopped parsley, and a pinch of thyme. Cook, stirring, 1 minute. Season to taste with salt and pepper. PUREED ROASTED GARLIC Separate the cloves of garlic from the head. Discard the loose papery skins, but do not peel. Place in a small shallow baking dish and drizzle with 2 teaspoons oil. Toss to coat. Bake in a preheated 300°F oven until the garlic is softened, about 45 minutes. Cool. Cut the hard end off each clove of garlic and squeeze out the garlic into a small bowl. Mash the garlic, add any oil or juices left in the baking dish, and season with salt and pepper. Add a teaspoonful to each bowl of soup at serving time. SPICY TOMATO PUREE Cook 1 slice bacon in a small nonstick skillet. Drain bacon on paper towels, chop very fine, and set aside. Wipe skillet clean. Add ½ cup chopped seeded tomato, fresh or canned, 1 teaspoon chili powder, and a pinch of cayenne. Heat, stirring, until the tomato cooks to a thick puree. Set aside at room temperature. Add the bacon just before using.

Hearty Pasta Soup with Two Beans

Pasta e due fagioli *is a classic example of a nutrient-dense, lowfat, cholesterol-free, protein complementary dish. The joy of this type of hearty soup is the scope of improvisation it allows the cook. We've used limas and cannellini beans, but you can sub-stitute other dried beans, peas, or lentils, fresh green beans, or green peas. Use any small pasta shape you happen to have on hand—elbows, acini di pepe, or tubettini, plus chicken, beef, or vegetable broth. In place of spinach, use escarole, chicory, or chard.*

Makes 6 servings

2 cups small pasta, such as small elbows, tubetti, or farfalline
½ cup reserved pasta cooking liquid
½ cup chopped onion
2 tablespoons olive oil
¼ cup diced (¼ inch) red bell pepper
¼ cup diced (¼ inch) green bell pepper
2 garlic cloves, minced
2 cups Chicken Broth (page 42) or reduced-sodium canned broth, fat skimmed, or water, as needed
1 can (14½ ounces) whole tomatoes, with juice, pressed through a strainer or food mill
1 cup frozen baby lima beans
2 tablespoons chopped flat-leaf parsley
Salt
1 can (about 1 pound) cannellini beans, drained and rinsed
¼ pound fresh spinach, trimmed and torn (about 2 cups)
Generous grinding of black pepper
2 scallions, cut into 1-inch lengths
Freshly grated parmesan cheese

1. Cook the pasta in plenty of boiling salted water for 3 to 5 minutes; pasta should be undercooked. Ladle ½ cup pasta cooking liquid from the pot and set aside. Drain pasta and set aside.

2. Combine onion and olive oil in a large wide saucepan, preferably nonstick. Cook over low heat, stirring occasionally, until tender, about 10 minutes. Add red and green peppers and garlic. Cook 3 more minutes. Add the broth, tomatoes, lima beans, 1 tablespoon of the parsley, and salt to taste. Bring to a boil over medium heat. Reduce heat, cover, and simmer 5 minutes.

3. Add the cannellini beans, pasta, and reserved pasta cooking liquid. Simmer over low heat, covered, until pasta is tender and has absorbed enough liquid to make the mixture more stewlike than soupy in consistency, about 15 minutes. Add broth or water if mixture is too thick. Fold in the spinach; cover and simmer over very low heat 5 minutes longer.

4. Stir in the remaining tablespoon of parsley. Season with ground pepper. Serve in shallow soup bowls, scattering scallion greens and plenty of grated parmesan over each portion.

Green Minestrone with Farfalline

This is a light spring version of the traditional Italian vegetable and bean soup. You can make it with any small pasta shape. Farfalline (small butterflies) are pretty here.

Makes 8 servings

1   pound leeks, green tops trimmed, washed, and diced (¼ inch)
1   cup diced (¼ inch) carrot
1   tablespoon olive oil
1   tablespoon water
6   to 8 cups Chicken Broth (page 42) or reduced-sodium canned broth, fat skimmed
½   cup farfalline or other small pasta shape
1   can (19 ounces) cannellini beans, drained and rinsed
1   cup sliced (¼ inch) green beans
1   cup diced (¼ inch) zucchini
1   cup diced (¼ inch) yellow squash
1   cup fresh or frozen small green peas
1   cup diagonally sliced trimmed fresh asparagus
1   tablespoon (packed) flat-leaf parsley leaves
1   tablespoon (packed) cut-up fresh dill or basil sprigs
1   scallion, coarsely chopped
1   strip lemon zest
1   garlic clove
    Salt and freshly ground black pepper
    Grated Parmigiano-Reggiano (optional)

1. Combine the leeks, carrot, olive oil, and water in a large wide saucepan, preferably nonstick. Cook over low heat 30 seconds. Cover and cook until the leeks are very tender, about 15 minutes. Do not brown.

2. Add 6 cups of the broth to the leek mixture and bring to a boil. Add the farfalline and cook, stirring occasionally, until almost tender, about 10 minutes. Add the cannellini beans, green beans, zucchini, yellow squash, peas, and asparagus. Simmer, uncovered, over medium heat, until the vegetables are tender, about 8 minutes.

3. Finely chop the parsley, dill, scallion, lemon zest, and garlic all together into a fine mixture. Stir into the simmering soup.

4. Add additional broth to thin soup, if desired. Season to taste with salt and pepper. Ladle into bowls and serve with a light sprinkling of grated parmesan, if desired.

a little cheese goes a long way

Flavor-packed hard cheeses, especially the Italian parmesan and romano, are full-fat cheeses, but since they are served grated, a little goes a very long way. One tablespoon grated parmesan or romano has only 25 calories and 1.5 grams fat.

White Bean Soup with Parmesan Rinds and Gremolata

Leave a pot of this hearty soup simmering on the back of the stove on a Saturday morning as you go about other chores. Although some beans can be soaked for as little as three or four hours, the dryness of beans is unpredictable, so it's always a good idea to soak them overnight. The parmesan rinds are not essential, but they make a delicious addition to this soup. As you use up your wedge of Parmigiano-Reggiano, cut the hard rinds into ¼-inch strips and freeze them in a plastic container. Then when you make a pot of white bean soup, simmer the rinds along with the beans.

1   pound dried cannellini beans, rinsed

2   cups chopped onion

2   garlic cloves, finely chopped

2   tablespoons olive oil, preferably extra virgin

2   tablespoons water

8   to 10 cups unsalted Chicken or Vegetable Broth, fat skimmed (pages 42, 44)

2   or 3 whole carrots

1   bay leaf

1   fresh or dried sage leaf (optional)

8   pieces (¼ × 2 inches) Parmigiano-Reggiano rind
    Salt and freshly ground black pepper
    Gremolata (page 7)

1. Soak the beans overnight or give them a short soak as on page 204. Drain beans.

2. Combine the onion, garlic, olive oil, and water in a large wide saucepan, preferably nonstick. Cook, stirring frequently, over low heat until golden, about 15 minutes. Do not brown.

3. Add 8 cups of the broth, carrots, bay leaf, and sage, if using. Add the beans. Heat to boiling. Cook, uncovered, over medium-low heat, stirring occasionally, until beans are tender and liquid is reduced to an almost creamy consistency, about 1½ to 2 hours. Add more broth as needed throughout the cooking time. Add the parmesan rinds during the last hour of cooking.

4. Remove the carrots to a side dish. Discard the bay leaf. Using a slotted spoon, transfer 2 cups of the beans to a food processor and puree them. Return to the saucepan. Cut the carrot into ¹/₂-inch slices and return to the saucepan. Season to taste with salt and pepper.

5. Ladle the soup into bowls and sprinkle lightly with Gremolata.

They impart a nice salty edge to the soup. Depending on how hard and dry they are, the rinds will turn to soft, or just chewy, morsels. Bits of ham or prosciutto also make a nice addition.

Makes 8 servings

Ribollita

This baked bread and vegetable soup is the ultimate comfort food. Ribollita, which means reboiled, was devised by Tuscan cooks as a way to serve minestrone soup left from the previous day. The soup is layered with peasant bread and baked—it can also be simmered—until hot and bubbly. This recipe is our lower-fat adaptation of Tuscan Ribollita. The recipe may look long and involved, but it can be prepared in advance and in stages.

Makes 6 servings

Crostini

6 slices (¼ inch thick) day-old white or whole wheat Italian bread

Soup

1 large onion, halved and thickly sliced (about 1½ cups)

2 tablespoons olive oil

1 tablespoon water

2 carrots, cut into ¼-inch slices (about 1 cup)

2 leafy ribs celery, cut into ¼-inch slices

1 garlic clove

1 small zucchini, thinly sliced (about 1 cup)

½ cup diced (¼ inch) red bell pepper

   Pinch of dried or fresh rosemary leaves

   Salt and freshly ground black pepper

1 pound escarole (4 cups), trimmed and coarsely cut up

1 can (19 ounces) cannellini beans, rinsed and drained

1 can (14½ ounces) Italian plum tomatoes, drained and coarsely cut up, with juice reserved

1 to 1½ cups Beef Broth or Chicken Broth (pages 43, 42) or reduced-sodium canned broth, fat skimmed, or more if desired to thin soup

2 tablespoons grated parmesan cheese

   Extra virgin olive oil, for drizzling (optional)

1. Heat the oven to 350°F.

2. Place the bread on a baking sheet and bake, turning once, until golden, about 15 minutes. Cool slightly. Set crostini aside.

3. Combine the onion, 1 tablespoon of the olive oil, and the water in a large Dutch oven or other large stovetop-to-oven pan. Heat over medium heat, stirring, until the oil is hot, about 1 minute. Reduce heat to low, cover, and cook, stirring occasionally, until the onion is tender and golden, about 10 minutes.

4. Stir in the carrot and celery. Crush the garlic through a press and stir into the onion mixture. Cover and cook over medium-low heat for 10 minutes, stirring occasionally. Do not brown. Add the zucchini, red pepper, and rosemary and cook over medium heat, stirring, just until the zucchini is crisp-tender, about 5 minutes. Sprinkle with salt and pepper.

5. Fill a large saucepan three quarters full of water and bring to a boil. Add salt to taste. Stir in the escarole and cook over high heat, stirring occasionally, until tender, about 10 minutes. Drain well, cool slightly, and squeeze out excess moisture.

6. Combine the escarole, cannellini beans, tomatoes, remaining olive oil, a pinch of salt, and grinding of black pepper in a large bowl. Stir to blend.

7. Heat the oven to 400°F.

8. Using a spatula, spread the onion mixture evenly in the Dutch oven. Top with the bean and escarole mixture and spread in an even layer. Arrange the crostini on top. Add the juice from the tomatoes and just enough of the broth to come almost to the top of the vegetables. Press down on the crostini so that the underside is slightly moistened. Sprinkle with the cheese.

9. Bake, uncovered, until surface is golden, about 25 minutes. Let stand 5 minutes before serving. Spoon into shallow soup bowls, dividing the crostini, vegetables, and juices evenly. You can add additional broth, if desired, but soup is supposed to be very thick. Drizzle each serving with olive oil, if desired.

Nine-Bean Soup

Now that both health and good taste dictate contemporary eating styles, bean dishes are back. Dried beans are high in complex carbohy-drates and fiber, low in fat, and contain no cho-lesterol. Use one of the bean mixes sold in super-markets and gourmet shops or make your own from what you have in the cupboard.

Makes 6 to 8 servings

½   pound mixed dried beans
2   medium-large red or yellow onions, chopped
1   tablespoon olive oil
1   tablespoon water
4   carrots, sliced
2   garlic cloves, sliced thin
4   teaspoons paprika, preferably Hungarian
1   teaspoon dried marjoram
1   small dried hot chili or a pinch of crushed red pepper
1½   tablespoons tomato paste
3   cups reduced-sodium canned chicken broth, fat skimmed, or Vegetable Broth (page 44)
6   cups water
    Salt and freshly ground black pepper
2   tablespoons chopped parsley
1   tablespoon balsamic or wine vinegar, or to taste
4   scallions, sliced thin on a sharp diagonal

1. Soak beans overnight or give them a short soak as described on page 204. Drain and rinse.

2. Combine onions, oil, and water in a large wide saucepan, preferably nonstick. Cook over low heat for 5 minutes. Add carrots and garlic and cook, stirring, for 5 minutes. Add pa-prika, marjoram, and chili and cook, stirring, 1 minute longer. Add tomato paste, beans, broth, and water. Bring to a boil. Skim foam, reduce heat, and partially cover. Simmer the soup until the beans are tender, about 1½ hours.

3. Season to taste with salt and pepper, add parsley and vine-gar, and serve, sprinkling scallions on top.

Papazoi

1	cup dried white navy beans or other small white beans
1	tablespoon olive oil
1	cup slivered lean baked ham (about 4 ounces)
1	cup chopped onion
1	garlic clove, minced
1	cup barley
1	cup fresh, canned, or frozen corn kernels
10	cups unsalted Chicken or Vegetable Broth, fat skimmed (pages 42, 44)
1½	cups diced peeled potato
	Salt and freshly ground black pepper
¼	cup finely chopped flat-leaf parsley
	Extra virgin olive oil

1. Soak the beans overnight or give them a quick soak as described on page 204. Drain and set aside.

2. Heat the oil in a large heavy saucepan. Add the ham, onion, and garlic and sauté until onion is soft, about 5 minutes. Add the drained beans, barley, and corn and stir to coat with oil. Add the broth.

3. Bring to a boil, reduce the heat, and cook over medium-low heat, stirring occasionally, 1½ hours. Stir in the potatoes and continue to cook until the soup has thickened and the vegetables are very tender, about 45 minutes longer.

4. Season to taste with salt and pepper. If possible, cool the soup and refrigerate overnight. Reheat at serving time, correcting seasonings and adding water or broth to thin consistency, if necessary.

5. Just before serving, stir in chopped parsley. Drizzle each serving with olive oil.

Marie first sampled this creamy barley, bean, and corn soup at Piccolo, a charming Italian-style restaurant in Ketchum, Idaho. Further research revealed that it is popular in the region of Friuli in the northeastern part of Italy. It's delicious the day it's made, but the flavors mellow and improve on standing, so don't hesitate to make it a day or more ahead. It also freezes well.

**M a k e s   8
s e r v i n g s**

Lentil Soup with Curried Vegetables and Rice

Lentils require no soaking and cook quickly. For this soup, spice up the lentils with cinnamon, cloves, and bay leaf. Brown rice adds a nutty flavor. Serve the soup as a main course, topped with yogurt and cilantro leaves.

M a k e s 8
s e r v i n g s

1	pound brown lentils, rinsed and sorted
6	cups water
1	cinnamon stick (2 inches)
1	small onion pierced with 2 whole cloves
1	bay leaf
1	garlic clove, bruised
1	leafy rib celery
1½	to 2 cups lowfat milk
1	cup chopped sweet onion
1	red bell pepper, stemmed, seeded, and cut into ¼-inch dice
1	large carrot, diced (¼ inch)
1	tablespoon chopped garlic
1	tablespoon olive oil
1	teaspoon curry powder, or more to taste
	Salt and freshly ground black pepper
1	cup cooked long- or short-grain brown rice (optional)
½	cup lowfat yogurt
¼	cup chopped cilantro

1. Combine the lentils, water, cinnamon stick, onion stuck with cloves, bay leaf, bruised garlic, and celery in a large heavy saucepan. Cook, stirring, until mixture boils. Cook, covered, over low heat until lentils are soft, about 25 minutes. Remove the cinnamon, onion, bay leaf, and celery and discard. Working in batches, puree the lentils. Transfer to a large wide saucepan. Add enough milk to get the desired consistency.

2. In a large skillet, preferably nonstick, combine the chopped onion, red pepper, carrot, chopped garlic, and olive oil. Cook over low heat, stirring, until mixture is coated with oil, about 30 seconds. Cover and cook the vegetables over low heat until tender, about 10 minutes. Uncover and turn heat to medium. Cook, stirring, until vegetables begin to turn golden. Add the curry powder and cook, stirring, 1 minute. Add salt and pepper to taste.

3. Stir the vegetables and rice, if using, into the lentil soup. Taste for salt and pepper. Ladle into bowls and garnish each with a spoonful of yogurt and a sprinkling of cilantro.

thicken soup with vegetable purees

Pureed cooked starchy vegetables, like dried beans and potatoes, add the most body to soups. For a more lightly thickened soup, puree cooked carrots, onions, mushrooms, broccoli, or peas, and add them. About 1 cup pureed cooked vegetables will add body to 3 to 4 cups of broth or other liquid.

Winter Squash and Apple Soup

A simple, brightly colored soup, made spicy with curry and ginger. Add finely chopped fresh mint and/or cilantro, if you like.

Makes 4 servings

2   medium acorn squash, halved, and seeded

2   tart green apples, such as Granny Smith or Greening, cored, peeled, and chopped (about 2 cups)

½   cup chopped onion

2   teaspoons curry powder

3   cups Chicken Broth (page 42) or reduced-sodium canned broth, fat skimmed

1   cup unsweetened apple juice

2   teaspoons grated fresh ginger
    Salt

1   tablespoon fresh lemon juice
    Freshly ground white pepper

1   cup lowfat or nonfat Yogurt Cheese (page 15)

1   tablespoon finely chopped mint (optional)

1   tablespoon finely chopped cilantro (optional)

1. Partially steam the squash halves, cut sides down, on a rack over gently boiling water until tender, about 10 minutes. Cool briefly. Scrape squash pulp from the shells with a spoon and set aside.

2. Combine the apples, onion, curry powder, and ¼ cup of the broth in a medium saucepan. Cook the mixture over low heat, covered, for 10 minutes. Add the squash pulp, the remaining broth, apple juice, ginger, and ½ teaspoon salt. Simmer over low heat, covered, for 20 minutes.

3. Working in batches, puree the soup in a food processor or blender until smooth. Rinse the saucepan and set a sieve over the pan. Press the puree through the sieve. Reheat the soup, add the lemon juice and additional salt and pepper to taste.

4. Discard the yogurt water and transfer the yogurt from the strainer to a small bowl. Stir in the mint and cilantro, if using. Garnish each serving with a spoonful of yogurt.

Mess o' Greens Soup

1	pound escarole, collards, chicory, swiss chard, or any combination, torn into 1-inch pieces (about 8 cups)
2	garlic cloves, finely chopped
1	tablespoon vegetable oil
8	cups Chicken Broth (page 42) or reduced-sodium canned broth, fat skimmed
1	carrot, sliced into thin rounds
½	teaspoon salt, or to taste
1	cup cooked pasta, such as tubetti, acini di pepe, semi de melone, or quadrettini
2	strips lemon zest, chopped
2	medium garlic cloves, chopped
6	large basil leaves, chopped
1	tablespoon thin-sliced scallion greens
	Freshly ground black pepper

Greens are good for you. They're rich in vitamins, minerals, and fiber, easy to prepare and cook, fresh and good tasting, too.

Makes 5 servings

1. Combine the escarole, garlic, and oil in a large heavy saucepan. Cook over low heat, covered, stirring occasionally, until escarole is tender, about 15 minutes.

2. Add the broth, carrot, and salt. Heat to a simmer, cover, and cook until carrots are just tender, about 5 minutes. Add pasta to soup.

3. Just before serving, heat soup to a simmer. Place lemon zest, garlic, and basil on a cutting board and finely chop the mixture together. Stir it into the soup and simmer for 3 minutes. Sprinkle soup with scallions and pepper. Serve hot.

Thai-style Salmon Soup

The popularity of Asian food has presented a whole new palette of ingredients for the home cook. Here we use fresh ginger, fermented fish sauce, and bok choy. Cilantro, familiar to many through Southwest cooking, is also popular in Thai cuisine.

Makes 4 servings

2 teaspoons curry powder, preferably Madras

2 cups Chicken Broth (page 42) or reduced-sodium canned broth, fat skimmed

2 cups water

½ cup thinly sliced onion

1 tablespoon finely chopped fresh ginger

1 garlic clove, coarsely chopped

1 sprig basil

1 sprig cilantro

1 sprig thyme

Pinch of crushed red pepper, or more to taste

¼ cup thin carrot slices

8 snow peas, trimmed and cut into ½-inch-diagonal strips

2 large inside leaves bok choy, cut into thin crosswise slices (1 cup)

12 ounces skinless salmon fillet or boned salmon steak, cut into 1-inch chunks

1 tablespoon oriental fish sauce

½ cup (lightly packed) watercress leaves

4 thin slices cucumbers

2 tablespoons torn cilantro leaves

Salt

1 lime, quartered

1. Sprinkle curry in a large wide saucepan. Place over low heat and heat, stirring, just until the curry is fragrant, about 30 seconds. Add the broth, water, onion, ginger, garlic, basil, cilantro, thyme, and red pepper. Heat to a boil, reduce heat, cover, and simmer over low heat 30 minutes. Drain the broth through a sieve and discard solids. Return broth to saucepan and keep warm over low heat.

2. Meanwhile, place a vegetable steamer in a saucepan over 1 inch of boiling water. Add the carrot slices, snow peas, and bok choy. Cover and steam 2 minutes. Remove from steamer and rinse with cold water.

3. Add the salmon to the broth. Cover and cook over low heat until opaque, about 2 minutes. Add the steamed vegetables, fish sauce, watercress, cucumber slices, and cilantro leaves. Add salt to taste. Stir carefully so fish does not break up. Ladle into bowls distributing ingredients evenly and serve with a wedge of lime.

lighter soup recipes

◆ Use a nonstick pan and cook or sauté vegetables in half the usual amount of oil or in a mixture of oil and water or broth.

◆ Cook the vegetables in oil and/or water, covered, over low heat; this is sometimes called sweating.

◆ Substitute oil for butter—same calories and fat, but no cholesterol.

Onion Soup with White Wine and Parmesan Toasts

French onion soup with gobs of gooey cheese used to be the height of sophistication. Not anymore. Our version is lighter yet even more flavorful. Naturally sweet onions, which are slowly cooked until caramelized, produce a mahogany-brown soup when simmered in beef broth. For a golden hue, use a combination of beef and chicken broth.

Makes 4 servings

4 cups chopped sweet onions (about 1¾ pounds)
1 tablespoon olive oil
1 to 2 tablespoons water, or as needed
1 teaspoon minced garlic
1 cup dry white wine
4 cups Beef Broth (page 43), or 2 cups each Beef Broth and Chicken Broth (page 42), or reduced-sodium canned broth, fat skimmed
¼ cup minced carrot

Parmesan Toasts

8 slices (½ inch thick) day-old French bread or whole wheat Italian bread
1 tablespoon olive oil
Parmesan cheese, preferably in a solid piece

Freshly ground black pepper
1 tablespoon minced fresh parsley

1. Combine the onions, oil, and water in a large wide saucepan, preferably nonstick, and cook over medium-high heat until onions are coated with oil, about 1 minute. Cover and cook over low heat until onions are very tender, about 10 minutes. Uncover and continue cooking until onions turn a rich golden brown, about 10 minutes. Stir in garlic and cook, stirring occasionally, for 5 minutes longer.

2. Turn heat to high. Add the wine and cook, stirring, until wine reduces by half, about 3 minutes. Add the broth and carrot. Cover the pan and simmer over low heat until the carrot is very tender, about 20 minutes. Set aside.

3. Heat the oven to 350°F.

4. Lightly brush bread with olive oil and place in a single layer on a baking sheet. Bake until lightly toasted, about 10 minutes.

5. Using a cheese slicer or vegetable peeler, cut thin wide curls of parmesan cheese. Cover the surface of each piece of toast with 1 or 2 curls of cheese. If only grated cheese is available, sprinkle each slice of toast with about 1 teaspoon.

6. Toast the cheese-topped bread in the oven until cheese has melted slightly, about 6 minutes.

7. At serving time, add pepper to soup and ladle into bowls. Float 1 or 2 pieces of parmesan toast on each portion of soup. Sprinkle with parsley and serve piping hot.

Three-Mushroom Bisque

This light soup gets its smoothness from finely pureed fresh mushrooms and its intense flavor from the dried porcini and their soaking liquid.

Makes 4 servings

6 cups Beef or Chicken Broth (pages 43, 42) or reduced-sodium canned broth, fat skimmed

½ cup dried porcini (1 ounce)

2 tablespoons extra virgin olive oil

4 cups cut-up white button or cremini mushrooms

2 tablespoons finely chopped shallots

1 garlic clove, finely chopped

½ teaspoon fresh chopped rosemary or a pinch of dried rosemary

½ teaspoon fresh thyme leaves or a pinch of dried thyme
Salt and freshly ground black pepper

1 teaspoon fresh lemon juice

½ cup lowfat milk, or as needed, at room temperature

Garnish

1 cup thinly sliced shiitake mushroom caps

1 teaspoon olive oil

1 tablespoon finely chopped parsley

¼ cup Yogurt Cheese (page 15)
Fresh thyme leaves, for garnish

1. Combine the broth and dried porcini in a large wide saucepan and bring to a boil. Reduce heat, cover, and simmer over low heat 15 minutes. Line a large fine-mesh strainer with a dampened paper towel and set over a bowl. Strain broth, reserving the porcini and the broth separately. Rinse saucepan of any grit left behind from the reconstituted porcini and wipe dry. Mince the porcini, discarding any hard or gritty pieces. Set aside minced porcini.

2. Heat the oil in the saucepan and add the cut-up mushrooms. Cook, stirring, over medium to medium-low heat until the mushrooms have given up some of their moisture and begin to brown, about 10 minutes. Stir in the shallots, garlic, rosemary, and thyme. Cook, stirring, 5 minutes. Season with a little salt and pepper. Add the reserved porcini broth, bring to a boil, reduce heat, and simmer, uncovered, over medium-low heat until broth is full flavored, about 15 minutes. Cool slightly.

3. Using a slotted spoon, transfer the mushrooms from the broth to a food processor. Puree the mushrooms. With the motor running, gradually add about $1/2$ cup of the broth. Puree until mixture is very smooth. Transfer mixture back to the saucepan. Add lemon juice and salt and freshly ground black pepper to taste. Spoon some of the hot soup into the milk, then stir the milk into the soup. Add the reserved minced porcini. Warm soup over low heat. Do not boil.

4. Meanwhile, combine the shiitake and 1 teaspoon oil in a nonstick skillet and cook, stirring, over medium heat until golden and tender. Add the parsley and a pinch of salt and a little pepper. Stir to blend.

5. Taste the soup and correct the seasonings. Add the shiitake mixture and ladle into bowls. Serve with a swirl of yogurt cheese. Garnish with fresh thyme leaves.

Curried Cream of Carrot Soup

Despite the title, you won't find any cream in this recipe. Pureed cooked potato is used to thicken the soup and make it creamy. Try it with other traditionally creamed soups. In summer we serve the soup chilled, seasoned with fresh lime and/or cilantro. In winter, we season it with fresh lemon juice and serve it piping hot, garnished with yogurt and thinly sliced scallion tops.

Makes 4 servings

1	pound carrots, cut into ½-inch lengths
2	medium potatoes, peeled and cut into ½-inch dice (about 8 ounces)
1	medium onion, chopped
3	cups Chicken Broth (page 42) or reduced-sodium canned broth, fat skimmed
1	tablespoon curry powder
2	teaspoons grated fresh ginger
1	teaspoon ground coriander
	Salt
1	teaspoon fresh lemon juice
4	teaspoons lowfat or nonfat yogurt
4	paper-thin slices lemon, seeds removed
1	tablespoon very thinly sliced scallion tops

1. Combine the carrots, potatoes, onion, broth, curry powder, ginger, and coriander in a large saucepan. Bring to a simmer over medium heat. Cover and cook until the carrots and potatoes are very tender, about 20 minutes. Set aside, covered, for about 10 minutes to cool slightly.

2. With a slotted spoon, transfer all the solids to a food processor. Puree until as smooth as possible. With the machine running, gradually add the hot broth. Return the soup to the saucepan, bring to a simmer, and season with salt to taste. Stir in the lemon juice. Ladle the soup into bowls and garnish each with yogurt, lemon slices, and scallion tops.

Note: To serve this soup cold, season with 1 teaspoon lime juice instead of the lemon juice. Garnish with paper-thin slices of lime and cilantro leaves.

Two-Potato Chowder

1   cup vertically slivered onion

1   tablespoon thinly sliced garlic

2   tablespoons water

1   tablespoon olive oil

1   cup sliced (¼ inch) celery

¾   teaspoon dried thyme

3   cups Chicken Broth (page 42) or reduced-sodium canned
    broth, fat skimmed

2½ cups thinly sliced peeled sweet potatoes (about 3 potatoes)

2½ cups thinly sliced peeled russet (baking) potatoes
    (about 3 potatoes)

1   teaspoon salt, or to taste

1   cup milk, or as needed
    Freshly ground black pepper

2   tablespoons thin diagonal slices scallion tops, for garnish

Traditionally made with butter, flour, and cream, this version of chowder can be made instead with milk and thickened with pureed potatoes. Sweet potatoes give the soup a lovely pale orange color. You can reduce the fat content even further by using lowfat or skim milk instead of whole milk.

Makes 6 servings

1. Combine the onion, garlic, water, and oil in a large wide saucepan. Cook, stirring, over low heat until the onion is tender and golden, about 10 minutes. Stir in the celery and thyme.

2. Add the broth, sweet potatoes and russet potatoes, and salt and bring to a boil. Cover and simmer until the potatoes are very tender and break apart when stirred, about 25 minutes. Remove from heat and cool slightly.

3. With a slotted spoon, transfer about 2 cups of the cooked potatoes and some broth to a food processor. Puree the potatoes, working in batches, if necessary. With the machine running, gradually add the milk. Pour the pureed mixture back into the saucepan and reheat over low heat. Do not boil. Taste and add salt, if needed, and freshly ground black pepper.

4. Ladle the chowder into bowls and garnish with scallion.

Corn and Shrimp Chowder with Tomatoes

A thick chowder made without flour or cream. Packed with vegetables, this soup is full-bodied enough for a main course. It's not quick, but it's worth the time and trouble. Make it when corn is fresh, sweet, and crisp. You can also make this without the shrimp.

Makes 8 servings

2 slices bacon, cut into ½-inch lengths

2 medium-large onions, coarsely chopped

2 carrots, sliced ¼ inch thick on a sharp diagonal

2 ribs celery, trimmed, strings peeled, and sliced on a diagonal

½ pound new or boiling potatoes, peeled, quartered lengthwise, and cut crosswise into ½-inch slices (4 or 5 small to medium potatoes)

3 fresh thyme sprigs or ½ teaspoon dried thyme

4 cups Chicken Broth (page 42) or reduced-sodium canned broth, fat skimmed

1½ cups water, or as needed

7 cups corn kernels with milky pulp, cut and scraped from 11 to 15 ears, 4 or 5 cobs reserved

2½ cups lowfat (1%) milk, or more as needed
Salt and freshly ground black pepper

¾ pound small to medium shrimp, peeled and deveined

3 large ripe tomatoes, peeled, cored, seeded, and cut into large dice (see Note)

3 tablespoons fresh chives, cut into ½-inch lengths
Pilot, oyster, or other plain crackers

1. Place the bacon in a large heavy saucepan or casserole over medium heat. Cook fairly slowly, stirring frequently and pouring off any excess fat once or twice, until bacon is lightly golden and nearly crisp, 10 to 15 minutes. With a skimmer or slotted spoon, transfer the bacon to paper towels to drain. Set aside. Pour off all but 2 teaspoons bacon fat from the pan.
2. Add the onions, carrots, and celery to the pan, tossing to coat. Sauté over medium heat, tossing frequently, until the vegetables have softened slightly but are not brown, about 5 minutes. Add the potatoes, thyme, broth, and enough water to

partially cover the vegetables. Break or cut the reserved corn cobs in half; tuck into the mixture. Cover and simmer until the potatoes are tender but not mushy, about 15 minutes.

3. Uncover the soup and set it aside to cool at room temperature for about 1 hour, if you have time. Remove and discard the thyme sprigs. Using a small knife, scrape all possible pulp and liquid from each cob back into soup, then discard. Skim fat and froth from surface.

4. Stir in corn kernels with their liquid and simmer 3 minutes. With a skimmer, transfer about 3½ cups of the solids to a food processor or blender. Process until coarsely pureed. Stir the puree back into soup, add the milk, and return to a simmer. Do not boil. Adjust consistency so soup is lightly thickened. If it is too thin, puree more solids and return puree to soup. If it is too thick, thin as needed with a little more milk. Season to taste with salt and a generous grinding of pepper. *(The chowder can be made in advance to this point; it improves with standing.)*

5. Return the chowder to a simmer, if necessary. Stir in the reserved bacon and scatter the shrimp over the surface. Cover tightly and simmer just until the shrimp turn pink, about 3 minutes. Do not boil. Correct seasonings again and add a little more milk, if needed. Stir in the tomatoes and half of the chives and cook for a few moments to heat the tomatoes through. Serve hot in wide soup bowls, sprinkling each portion with the remaining chives. Serve with pilot, oyster, or other plain crackers.

Note: If time allows, place diced tomatoes in a colander, sprinkle with kosher salt, and let drain for a few minutes.

New England-style Clam Chowder

Unlike an old-fashioned New England clam chowder, which is thickened with flour and enriched with heavy cream, ours is thickened with a puree of vegetables, and enriched with lowfat milk. In a pinch, canned or frozen chopped clams can be used in this recipe, but fresh ones are best. You can make the soup ahead, but it may need to be thinned slightly with a little more milk before serving.

Makes 4 servings

2 dozen small cherrystone clams, shucked, liquid reserved (see Note) or about 12 ounces shucked clams

2 teaspoons vegetable oil

2 tablespoons minced lean cooked ham

2 medium onions, chopped

2 ribs celery, trimmed, strings peeled, halved lengthwise, and chopped

1 carrot, halved lengthwise and sliced ¼ inch thick

1 garlic clove, minced

2 fresh thyme sprigs or ¼ teaspoon dried thyme

4 parsley sprigs, with stems

1 bay leaf

¾ teaspoon salt, or as needed

1 pound all-purpose or boiling potatoes, peeled, quartered lengthwise, and sliced

1 cup bottled clam juice

1 cup lowfat (1%) milk, or as needed

Freshly ground white pepper

Hot pepper sauce

2 tablespoons chopped flat-leaf parsley

Paprika, for garnish

1. Combine clam liquid with water to make 1½ cups and set aside. Heat oil and ham in a large saucepan and cook over low heat, stirring, for 3 minutes. Stir in onions, celery, carrot, garlic, thyme, parsley, bay leaf, and salt. Cover and cook vegetables over low heat, stirring from time to time, 5 to 7 minutes.

2. Stir in potatoes, reserved liquid, and clam juice. Cover and boil until potatoes are tender, about 15 minutes. Remove and discard thyme, parsley, and bay leaf. With slotted spoon, transfer slightly less than half of vegetables to a food processor or blender. Add a little liquid and puree. Return puree to soup. Add clams; simmer for 3 minutes. Add milk and bring soup almost to a simmer.

3. Season to taste with salt, pepper, and hot pepper sauce. *(Chowder can be prepared in advance to this point. Reheat without boiling.)* Just before serving, add parsley and correct seasonings. Ladle hot chowder into bowls and sprinkle each serving with paprika.

Note: Ask the fish store to shuck the clams and save the liquid for you or shuck them yourself. To make shucking easier, spread the clams on a baking sheet and place in the freezer. Freeze for about 1 hour. The clams will open slightly as they begin to freeze and will be much easier to pry open with a clam knife.

instant lower fat or nonfat substitutions for soups

If a recipe calls for

◆ **whole milk, use lowfat or skim milk**

◆ **whole milk, use half broth or tomato juice**

◆ **heavy cream or half-and-half, use whole milk**

◆ **sour cream or whole milk yogurt, use lowfat or nonfat yogurt**

Chilled Tomato and Yogurt Soup

This soup is so refreshing we have been known to pour it into a tall glass and drink it through a straw.

Makes 4 servings

1 pound ripe red tomatoes, peeled, cored, seeded, and cut into 1-inch cubes

2 cups plain lowfat or nonfat yogurt

¼ cup chopped sweet onion

1 tablespoon sugar

1 tablespoon chopped basil leaves

½ teaspoon salt, or to taste

Pinch of cayenne

2 large basil leaves, rolled tightly and cut crosswise into thin strips, for garnish

1. Combine the tomatoes, yogurt, onion, sugar, chopped basil, salt, and cayenne in a food processor or blender. Puree the mixture until smooth. Transfer to a bowl and refrigerate until well chilled.

2. Ladle the chilled soup into bowls and garnish with the thin strips of basil.

Tomato Soup with Basil Aïoli

1 cup vertically slivered onion
1 leafy inner rib celery, cut into thin diagonal slices
1 leafy basil sprig
1 tablespoon extra virgin olive oil
1 tablespoon water
3 pounds ripe tomatoes, peeled, cored, and quartered, or about 6 cups imported canned (two 28-ounce) Italian plum tomatoes, with juices
2 cups Chicken Broth (page 42) or reduced-sodium canned broth, fat skimmed
  Salt and freshly ground black pepper
  Basil Aïoli (recipe follows)

This soup can be served hot or cold, and it can be made with fresh or good quality canned tomatoes. Aïoli is garlic mayonnaise from the South of France. We've made a lowfat version, with basil to be added to the soup at the table.

Makes 4 servings

1. Combine the onion, celery, basil, olive oil, and water in a large heavy saucepan. Cover and cook over low heat until the vegetables are very tender, about 20 minutes.

2. Meanwhile, place a large strainer over a bowl. Working in the strainer, gently squeeze the seeds and juice from the tomatoes. Chop the tomato flesh and add to the saucepan. Rub the seeds and pulp in the sieve to extract as much juice as possible. Add the strained tomato juice to the saucepan. Discard the seeds. Add the broth to the tomato mixture and heat to a simmer over low heat.

3. Remove the basil sprig and season the soup with salt and pepper to taste. Serve hot, with aïoli. This soup can also be served cold.

Basil Aïoli

**Makes about
¹/₂ cup**

½   cup (packed) basil leaves
2   garlic cloves, minced
     Pinch of salt
1   teaspoon fresh lemon juice
½   cup reduced-fat mayonnaise

Very finely chop the basil with the garlic and a pinch of salt in
a food processor. Add the lemon juice. Gradually add the mayonnaise, 1 tablespoon at a time, until mixture is well blended.
Refrigerate until ready to serve.

Roasted Tomato Gazpacho

2½ pounds ripe tomatoes, cored and quartered

1 large red bell pepper, seeded and quartered

1 large sweet onion, peeled and cut into eighths

1 carrot, halved lengthwise

8 garlic cloves, peeled

2 tablespoons extra virgin olive oil

Salt and freshly ground black pepper

1 basil sprig

1 oregano sprig

1 thyme sprig

2 cups Chicken Broth (page 42) or reduced-sodium canned broth, fat skimmed

½ cup diced (⅛ inch) seedless or seeded cucumber

½ cup diced (⅛ inch) yellow bell pepper

½ cup thinly sliced scallion including green parts

½ cup diced yellow or red tomato

2 tablespoons thinly slivered basil leaves or Basil Puree (recipe follows)

The natural sugars in the tomatoes, red bell pepper, and onion caramelize and lend a smooth round flavor to this rich—in flavor, not in fat—soup. A puree of basil is swirled on the surface of the soup for a stunning and great-tasting garnish. You can also garnish each bowl of soup simply with slivered basil leaves.

Makes 4 servings

1. Heat oven to 450°F.

2. Arrange the tomatoes, red bell pepper, onion, carrot, and garlic in a large roasting pan. Drizzle with the olive oil and sprinkle with salt and pepper. Roast 30 minutes, stirring the vegetables and turning the pan so the vegetables brown evenly. Place the sprigs of basil, oregano, and thyme on top of the vegetables and roast for 20 minutes more, or until the vegetables are very tender. Remove from oven and cool slightly. Remove the carrot and set aside separately.

3. Place a food mill over a large bowl. Transfer the roasted vegetables and all the liquid in the roasting pan to the food mill. Add about ½ cup of the chicken broth to the pan and scrape up any browned bits. Add to the food mill. Press the vegetables through the food mill, using the remaining chicken broth to keep the vegetables moist and to extract as much from the vegetables as possible. Discard the solids in the food mill. There should be about 5 cups of pureed vegetables and broth combined.

4. Cut the carrot into small (⅛ inch) dice. Add the carrot, cucumber, yellow pepper, scallion, and diced tomato to the puree. Taste and correct seasonings. Refrigerate until very cold.

5. Serve chilled in large shallow bowls. Garnish each with a few slivers of basil or a swirl of Basil Puree.

Basil Puree

½ cup (packed) basil leaves
1 garlic clove
2 tablespoons extra virgin olive oil
   Pinch of salt

Makes about
¼ cup

Combine the ingredients in a food processor and process until smooth.

compare fat and calories

4 ounces (½ cup)	Fat g	Calories
Heavy cream	44	416
Sour cream	20	208
Half-and-half	13	120
Whole milk	4	72
Lowfat yogurt	4	72
Lowfat (1%) milk	1	48
Buttermilk (1%)	1	49
Nonfat yogurt	0	56
Skim milk	0	40
Chicken broth	1	18
Tomato juice	0	23

Salads
& *and*
dres

TO US A SALAD CAN BE ANYTHING from sliced ripe tomatoes with olive oil to a toss of baby greens with oil and vinegar, to a mélange of cooked lentils, green peas, celery, and scallions with vinaigrette. We like salads cool and crisp in the summer, but we also like salads served warm or at room temperature, any time, any season.

Salads made with potatoes, beans, pasta, or rice and other grains are especially good when served warm or at room temperature. Usually we prepare such salads by tossing the warm, just-cooked main ingredients with chilled raw vegetables. Leftovers, of course, should be refrigerated, but remember to let them stand at room temperature to take the chill off before serving. Most important, take a taste

salad

sings

and correct the seasonings to brighten the flavor.

Once upon a time our supermarket produce sections only had two or three types of lettuce to choose from. Now in addition to the ever popular iceberg, romaine, and Boston lettuce, there is a startling array of fresh salad greens, many of them grown by local farmers, some of them organic. Many markets even stock mixed baby greens, all trimmed and washed and ready to serve.

Salads are inherently healthful; the downfall is in the dressing. Not only do dressings add calories and fat but too much dressing can overwhelm the delicate flavor of the greens. We've come up with several light dressings; use just enough to coat the greens or vegetables.

The chapter opens with "A Guide to Salad Greens," followed by a few very simple to make, good tasting, lowfat dressings, which can be used on a mixture of any of the greens. The rest of the salad recipes all include their own dressings, formulated with an eye to eliminating excess calories without sacrificing taste.

We both like main dish salads. We like the philosophy, the esthetics, and the efficiency of mixing two courses—on one plate. Starting with a bed of leafy greens, we might add wedges of crisp vegetables and juicy tomatoes, chunks of roasted chicken or grilled fish, and on and on until we have put together a platter that is as pleasing to the eye as it is to the palate.

a guide to salad greens

MILD SALAD GREENS

BIBB A type of butterhead lettuce with loosely furled dark green leaves, Bibb lettuce is somewhat crunchy in texture. It is rather sweet and is best with mild, light dressings.

BOSTON Also a type of butterhead, it has medium-size, loosely furled green leaves, which form a tight core as the leaves reach the center. The leaves are pale green (almost white near the center rib) and are soft and delicate. They have a smooth consistency. Boston lettuce is best with a very light vinaigrette dressing.

CORN SALAD OR MÂCHE A dark green very small leaf shaped like a teaspoon, this lettuce grows in a cluster of leaves from a small center stem. This green is a specialty item, very expensive when available. It is also highly perishable. It has a mild, sweet flavor and is often added to other greens or served solo with a mild vinaigrette.

CURLY LEAF OR RUBY LETTUCE A very pretty, veritable wedding bouquet green, this loose leaf lettuce with frilly edged leaves is relatively new in supermarket produce sections. The leaves can be pale green or red tipped. Like Boston and Bibb, these lettuces are best with a mild, light dressing.

ICEBERG Appreciated primarily for its crunchy texture, iceberg has an insipid flavor that has made it the object of much scorn, but it stands up very well to heavy, full-flavored dressings such as Green Goddess (page 97) or Buttermilk-Herb Dressing (page 85). It also adds a nice crisp touch to a mixed salad of more strongly flavored greens, such as arugula, escarole, or chicory.

OAK LEAF This lettuce has a large leaf shaped like an oak leaf. The leaves are loosely arranged around a central core. It Is a delicately flavored, pretty lettuce with a sweet, mild flavor. Available in both a red leaf (also called ruby) and pale green leaf. Best with light dressings.

ROMAINE **Also called Cos, this lettuce has crisp, oblong leaves that are dark green with a rather thick white rib down the center. The inner leaves, or heart, are usually paler and more tender than the outer leaves. The flavor is slightly more pronounced than the other mild greens in this list, but it is still considered a mild or sweet green. Romaine stands up well to fuller flavored salad combinations, like the cheese and anchovies in our Chicken Caesar Salad (page 102). It also adds interest to a mixed salad of other sweet and bitter greens. The dark green outer leaves can be cooked, as in Braised Romaine with Red Wine Vinegar (page 181).**

FULL-FLAVORED OR BITTER GREENS

ARUGULA **Also known as rocket, this small, tender, pungent green adds a decidedly spicy taste to a mixed green salad. The elongated, smooth, dark green leaves have fairly long tender stems.**

BELGIAN ENDIVE **Belgian endive come in small compact heads with very pale, almost white, spear shape leaves, which are light yellow at their slightly ruffled edges. The leaves are crisp and pleasantly bitter. Belgian endive pairs well with other bitter greens, such as watercress or radicchio. It stands up to full-bodied dressings, especially sweet mixtures that help to balance its slightly bitter edge. It is also delicious braised in broth.**

CHICORY OR CURLY ENDIVE **This bitter salad green has large lacy, almost prickly, dark green outer leaves with tender, pale green leaves toward the center of the head. The outer leaves can be blanched and served, either warm and cold, with olive oil and a dash of lemon juice or vinegar. The inner leaves are used in salads. Frisée is a variety of chicory that is all pale green and curly and more tender. Good with robust dressings and when paired with other bitter greens.**

ESCAROLE Also a member of the chicory family, escarole has loosely packed, slightly furled leaves, dark green on the outside, pale green and tender at the heart. It can be prepared like curly endive by blanching the outer leaves and saving the inner leaves for salad. The flavor is bitter with just a slight sweet edge. Escarole is excellent in salads of mixed bitter and sweet greens. It makes a good soup (page 59) and is assertive enough to stand up to other strongly flavored ingredients.

MESCLUN A mixture of several baby greens, including spinach, oak leaf, chicory, arugula, fresh herbs, and sometimes edible flowers.

RADICCHIO A relatively new face on the American salad scene, radicchio is another member of the chicory family. The leaves can be bright red to a dark maroon; they are beautifully veined with white. Radicchio is best served in a mixture of other bitter greens and dressed with a full-flavored extra virgin olive oil. It can also be served braised, grilled, or wilted with a splash of vinegar and oil.

WATERCRESS Usually sold in bunches of about six ounces each, watercress has crisp succulent stems five to six inches long with tender dark green leaves attached. It has a distinctively peppery flavor. Watercress is often used as a garnish as well as an ingredient in salads of other bitter greens.

NEITHER SWEET NOR BITTER

SPINACH This versatile green is fairly mild tasting. Available in both curly and flat varieties, spinach has a tender dark green leaf. It is sold loose, by the bunch, or in convenient ten-ounce cellophane bags. It can be used raw in salads or for stir-fries and other cooked dishes. It stands up well to other assertively flavored ingredients.

WASHING AND DRYING SALAD GREENS

If the greens are very sandy, plunge them into a large bowl or sink filled with *warm* water.

The water relaxes the leaves so the sand or grit rinses off easily. Lift the leaves to a colander and drain. Crisp the leaves in several changes of very cold water. Otherwise, just rinse very well in a colander, separating the leaves to be sure you wash away all traces of dirt.

Drying salad greens properly is as important as washing them. Not only will damp, watery greens dilute the flavor of a carefully prepared dressing, it will end up in a puddle in the bottom of the bowl rather than clinging to the leaves.

The salad spinner is a brilliant invention. It spins the greens dry and keeps refrigerated greens fresh and crisp. The next best thing is to drain washed greens thoroughly in a colander and then wrap them in several clean dish towels. Step out in the backyard and, holding all the ends tightly so the greens won't go flying, spin the greens over your head helicopter style. If you don't have a backyard, shake the colander over a sink, then lay the greens out on several layers of paper towels and carefully blot each leaf. Crisp the greens in the refrigerator wrapped in a clean dish towel. We have a friend who uses a chef's toque to store washed salad greens. You can also use a cloth salad bag designed especially for drying and storing salad until ready to serve.

Buttermilk-Herb Dressing

½   cup (packed) flat-leaf parsley leaves
¼   cup (packed) dill sprigs, including a few stems, cut up
1   scallion, cut into ½-inch lengths
1   small garlic clove, chopped
1   tablespoon fresh lemon juice, or to taste
½   teaspoon salt
⅔   cup buttermilk
2   tablespoons olive oil

1. Combine the parsley, dill, scallion, garlic, lemon juice, and salt in a food processor or blender and process until chopped fine. Add the buttermilk and olive oil and blend until thoroughly emulsified.

2. Pour dressing into a pint jar or other container, cover tightly, and refrigerate several hours or overnight. Correct seasonings and stir well before serving.

This tangy dressing is excellent on everything from a plain green salad to steamed vegetables to pasta, chicken, and shrimp salads. It thickens nicely and the flavors develop on standing, so for best consistency make it at least one day before serving. We've used a small amount of olive oil for flavor and consistency, rather than omitting it entirely. The dressing will keep well for about three days refrigerated.

Makes about 1 cup

Bonaventure Spa House Dressing

This dressing is good on all sorts of salads. It is also excellent as a dip with fresh vegetables. Depending on the use, you may need to thin the dressing with buttermilk. This is from the Bonaventure Spa in Fort Lauderdale, Florida.

Makes about 1 ½ cups

½ cup nonfat yogurt
½ cup reduced-calorie mayonnaise
1 tablespoon horseradish, drained if very watery
1 tablespoon Dijon mustard
1 tablespoon chopped parsley
1 teaspoon minced dill
¼ teaspoon celery seed
¼ to ½ cup buttermilk, as needed

1. Whisk the yogurt, mayonnaise, horseradish, mustard, parsley, dill, and celery seed in a mixing bowl. Gradually whisk in the buttermilk to bring dressing to desired consistency.
2. Refrigerate until ready to serve. Dressing will thicken slightly upon standing.

Low-Calorie Vinaigrette

2   tablespoons extra virgin olive oil
2   tablespoons red wine vinegar
2   teaspoons balsamic vinegar
1   tablespoon water
    Pinch of salt
½   garlic clove, crushed (optional)

Whisk the olive oil, red wine vinegar, balsamic vinegar, water, salt, and garlic, if using, in the bottom of a large salad bowl. Add the salad greens and toss to coat. Serve at once on individual salad plates.

Traditionally the ratio for vinaigrette dressings has been three or even more oil to one acid. We've adjusted it to equal proportions of oil and acid and then added water, a tablespoon at a time, to increase the volume. To add flavor now that the fat has been decreased, we've added minced herbs, and used two vinegars. Combining red wine vinegar with balsamic vinegar brings depth of flavor and a touch of sweetness to the dressing. It is especially good with a mix of greens, such as Boston lettuce, arugula, and radicchio, or a pre-mixed mesclun blend.

Makes about ¼ cup

Tomato-Basil Dressing

In this dressing, the tomato is the dressing. Surprisingly, it has only one tablespoon of olive oil, but it seems much richer than it is.

Makes about 1 cup

1   ripe tomato, coarsely cut up (about 1 cup)
¼   cup (packed) coarsely chopped fresh basil
1   small garlic clove, crushed
¼   teaspoon salt, or to taste
1   tablespoon olive oil, preferably extra virgin
     Freshly ground black pepper

Combine the tomato, basil, garlic, and salt in a food processor. With the motor running, gradually add the oil until the mixture is finely chopped. Add pepper to taste.

Yogurt, Honey, and Lime Dressing

½ cup nonfat yogurt
1 tablespoon honey
1 tablespoon lime juice

Just before serving, combine the yogurt, honey, and lime juice in a small bowl. Whisk until blended.

A creamy, tangy dressing with a slightly sweet edge, this is good on fruit as well as mixed greens. If you make it with non-fat yogurt, it will be absolutely fat free.

Makes about ²/₃ cup

buttermilk

Contrary to its name, buttermilk does not contain butter. It is a thick, tangy, lowfat drink rich in calcium, phosphorus, and protein and often enriched with vitamins A and D. There are only 87 calories and 4 g of fat in an 8-ounce glass of buttermilk.

Two-Tone Slaw with Lemon-Buttermilk Dressing

We have created a half mayonnaise and half buttermilk dressing for this version of cole slaw. We recommend using reduced calorie or so-called light mayonnaise instead of real mayon-naise. Either will cut the fat and calories by about half. Many light versions are cholesterol free as well.

Makes 4 servings

Lemon-Buttermilk Dressing

⅔ cup buttermilk

⅔ cup reduced-fat or light mayonnaise

1 tablespoon fresh lemon juice

1 teaspoon finely shredded lemon zest

¼ cup chopped dill

¾ cup thin diagonal slices scallions

Red Cabbage Slaw

½ head red cabbage, cored and finely sliced (about 3 cups)

½ green bell pepper, stemmed, seeded, and cut into thin slivers

Salt

Green Cabbage Slaw

½ head green cabbage, cored and finely sliced (about 3 cups)

½ red bell pepper, stemmed, seeded, and cut into thin slivers

Salt

4 large lettuce leaves

1 tablespoon chopped parsley

1. Whisk the buttermilk, mayonnaise, lemon juice, and zest until blended. Add the dill and ¹/₂ cup of the scallions and stir to blend. Divide the dressing between 2 bowls.

2. Add the shredded red cabbage and green bell pepper to one bowl, toss, add salt to taste, and set aside. Add the shredded green cabbage and red bell pepper to the other bowl, toss, add salt to taste, and set aside. Cover each bowl with plastic wrap and refrigerate until ready to serve.

3. For each serving, spoon about ¹/₂ cup of the red slaw on a lettuce leaf and ¹/₂ cup of the green slaw next to it. Garnish with remaining scallions and the chopped parsley and serve.

Potato, Green Bean, and Feta Salad with Yogurt Dressing

¾ pound small (about 1 inch) yellow Finn or red new
potatoes, scrubbed and halved, or larger potatoes cut into
1-inch cubes

½ pound tender green beans, trimmed and cut into 1-inch
lengths

⅓ cup plain lowfat or nonfat yogurt

1 tablespoon chopped dill, including stems

3 to 4 cups torn salad greens, such as tender chicory, red
leaf lettuce, watercress, Boston lettuce, and/or radicchio

1 ounce feta cheese, rinsed, dried, and crumbled

2 tablespoons slivered red bell pepper
Freshly ground black pepper

1. Place the potatoes on a steaming rack set over 1 inch of gently boiling water. Cover tightly and steam for 8 minutes. Uncover and spread the green beans over the partially cooked potatoes. Cover and continue steaming until the potatoes and beans are both tender, about 5 minutes.

2. Meanwhile, stir together the yogurt and dill in a large bowl. Add the potatoes and beans while still warm. Stir to coat with dressing.

3. Arrange the greens on the salad plates. Spoon the potato mixture into the center of each plate, dividing it evenly. Garnish with the feta and red pepper slivers. Season with black pepper, grinding it coarse.

We like cooked potatoes so much we add them to tossed green salads as readily as some people do wedges of tomato.

Steaming the potatoes and green beans in the same pot saves time and clean-up. The beans must be young and tender to steam as soft as they would cook in a pot of boiling water. The recipe calls for fresh dill; or try basil, flat-leaf parsley, or summer savory.

If you buy packaged feta, remove it from the package, rinse it well, and store it in a jar of water or lowfat milk. Use within three or four days.

Makes 4 side dish or 2 main dish servings

Streamlined Classic Potato Salad

An old-fashioned, all-American potato salad streamlined by using part lowfat yogurt and part reduced-fat mayonnaise, and three hard-cooked egg whites and one yolk. Who says we can't have our old favorites?

Makes 4 servings

1½ pounds small potatoes, peeled
3 eggs
½ cup lowfat yogurt
½ cup reduced-fat mayonnaise
2 teaspoons Dijon mustard
½ cup 1 × ⅛-inch pieces green or red bell pepper
⅓ cup chopped dill pickle
⅓ cup thinly sliced celery
2 tablespoons finely chopped dill
Freshly ground black pepper

1. In a large saucepan, cook the potatoes, covered, in boiling water 12 minutes. Using a large spoon, carefully lower the eggs into the water. Cover and cook over medium heat 12 minutes more. Drain in a colander and rinse with cold water. Carefully peel eggs and separate the whites and yolks. Discard two of the yolks. Set aside the remaining yolk. Coarsely chop the egg whites. Quarter the potatoes. Cool at room temperature.

2. Stir the yogurt, mayonnaise, and mustard together in a large serving bowl until blended. Add the potatoes, egg whites, bell pepper, pickle, celery, dill, and a grinding of black pepper. Toss to coat. Finely chop the yolk and sprinkle on top of the salad. Serve at room temperature or refrigerate until ready to serve.

Potato Salad with Tomato Salsa

Potatoes

2   pounds russet (baking) potatoes, peeled

Quick Tomato Salsa

2   cups diced ripe tomato, half red and half yellow if available

½   cup diced (¼ inch) yellow or green bell pepper

¼   cup finely chopped red onion

2   tablespoons chopped cilantro

1   tablespoon seeded and minced jalapeño

1   tablespoon extra virgin olive oil

    Salt

2   or 3 scallion greens, sliced thin on the diagonal

½   cup cilantro leaves

1. Place the potatoes in a large saucepan and cover with cold water. Cover, bring to a boil, and reduce the heat. Simmer until the potatoes are tender when pierced with a fork, 20 to 25 minutes. Do not overcook.

2. Combine the tomatoes, bell pepper, onion, chopped cilantro, jalapeño, oil, and salt to taste in a small bowl. Set aside at room temperature until ready to serve.

3. Drain the potatoes and rinse with cold running water. When they are cool enough to handle, halve lengthwise and cut each half into $1/2$-inch slices. Spread half the potatoes in a broad shallow serving bowl.

4. Spoon half the salsa evenly over the potatoes. Add half the scallion tops and half the cilantro leaves. Top with the remaining potatoes, salsa, scallions, and cilantro leaves. Serve warm or at room temperature.

This is a bright, pretty, practically fat-free summery dish. Great for a picnic or with grilled foods.

Makes 6 servings

Warm White Bean Salad
with Gremolata Dressing

Because we prefer a firm bean in salads our first choice is dried beans that we've cooked ourselves rather than canned beans, even though canned beans are quicker. If dried cannellini beans are not available, use any oval-shaped white bean. Great Northern, baby limas, or navy beans are all good choices.

Makes 8 servings

1½ cups dried cannellini beans, rinsed (see Note)
1 cup diced (¼ inch or about same size as beans) red onion
1 cup diced (¼ inch or about same size as beans) celery
¼ cup chopped leafy celery tops
½ cup (packed) coarsely cut flat-leaf parsley, including stems
2 strips (2 × ½ inches) lemon zest, coarsely chopped
2 garlic cloves, coarsely chopped
½ cup extra virgin olive oil
⅓ cup red wine vinegar
3 tablespoons fresh lemon juice
Freshly ground black pepper
Ripe plum tomato wedges, for garnish

1. Soak the beans overnight or use a quick soak as described on page 204. Drain beans. Add 2 quarts fresh water and simmer beans, covered, until tender but not mushy, 1½ to 2 hours. Drain.

2. Add the onion, celery, and celery leaves to the hot beans. Combine the parsley, lemon zest, garlic, and olive oil in a food processor and process, pulsing, until the mixture is very finely chopped but not pureed. Transfer to a saucepan, add the vinegar, and bring to a boil over low heat, stirring. Remove from the heat and add to the beans. Add the lemon juice and pepper and toss to blend. Transfer the bean salad to a large shallow serving bowl.

3. Garnish the salad with plum tomatoes and serve while still warm or at room temperature.

Note: You can substitute 2 large cans of cannellini beans. Empty the cans in a strainer, rinse the beans with cold water, and drain them well before using.

Crisp Marinated Cucumbers

2   large cucumbers, preferably seedless, peeled and
    sliced very thin

1½ teaspoons coarse (kosher) salt

½   cup rice wine vinegar

¼   cup fresh lemon juice

1   garlic clove, crushed through a press

⅛   teaspoon freshly ground white pepper

2   tablespoons minced dill and/or mint (see Note)

1. Layer the cucumbers and salt in a colander and weight the cucumbers with a saucer and something heavy like a can. Let stand at room temperature for at least 1 hour. Drain off all liquid and squeeze cucumbers dry.

2. Combine the vinegar, lemon juice, garlic, pepper, and dill or mint in a glass serving bowl. Add the cucumbers. Refrigerate. When cucumbers are cold and crisp, drain some of the liquid and serve.

Note: If fresh herbs aren't available, use ½ teaspoon dried mint or dillweed. Finely chop the herbs together with a stem of fresh parsley, which will help rehydrate the dried herbs and bring out their flavor.

Richard brought this recipe back from a visit to Budapest, and it has since become a mainstay at his place, particularly with broiled salmon. Salting cucumber slices removes excess liquid, making them crisp and translucent.

Makes 4 servings

Spinach, Tomato, and Country Bread Salad

A wonderful first course salad spooned over toasted Italian bread. Use tender flat spinach leaves or substitute arugula or a mixture of tender greens including red leaf or Bibb lettuce.

Makes 4 servings

2 or 3 ripe plum tomatoes, cored and cut into thin lengthwise wedges (about 1 cup)
2 tablespoons extra virgin olive oil, plus more for bread
1 tablespoon (packed) finely shredded basil leaves
Salt and freshly ground black pepper
4 large slices (about ½ inch) Italian whole wheat or other crusty peasant-style bread
½ garlic clove
6 cups (packed) torn trimmed spinach leaves

1. In a large bowl combine the tomatoes, 2 tablespoons olive oil, basil, and salt and pepper to taste. Toss to coat. Set aside.

2. Heat broiler or grill. Rub each slice of bread generously with the cut side of the garlic. Discard garlic or reserve for another use. Brush bread with a light film of olive oil. Grill or broil on both sides until lightly toasted.

3. Add the spinach to tomato mixture. Toss to coat. Place a slice of toasted bread in the bottom of each of 4 shallow bowls. Top each with the salad, dividing evenly. Serve as a first course.

Mixed Greens with Green Goddess Dressing and Croutons

Croutons

2   slices (½-inch) day-old whole grain crusts, trimmed

1   teaspoon extra virgin olive oil

Green Goddess Dressing

1   cup lowfat or nonfat yogurt

1   cup (packed) watercress, thick stems removed

2   tablespoons chopped dill

2   tablespoons chopped basil leaves

1   teaspoon chopped mint leaves

1   tablespoon thinly sliced scallion

1   teaspoon sugar

½   teaspoon salt, or to taste

    Hot pepper sauce

Salad

4   cups (packed) washed and trimmed spinach

4   cups torn romaine or other lettuce

1   cup (packed) watercress, thick stems removed

½   cup 1-inch dill sprigs

½   small red onion, cut into thin rings

½   ripe avocado, pit and peel removed, cut into thin wedges

1   cup thin cucumber slices

A completely new take on an old favorite. The dressing is slimmed down with lowfat yogurt; the croutons, made from whole grain bread, are nutty and crunchy. The salad is a wonderful mix of greens, cucumber, and avocado.

Makes 6 servings

1. Heat the oven to 350°F. Lightly brush bread with olive oil. Cut into ½-inch squares and spread out on a baking sheet. Bake 10 minutes. Turn the croutons with a spatula and toast the other side, about 5 minutes. Cool.

2. Combine the yogurt, watercress, dill, basil, mint, scallion, sugar, salt, and a dash of hot pepper sauce in a food processor.

3. Combine the spinach, romaine, watercress, dill, onion, avocado, and cucumber in a large serving bowl. Pour the dressing over the salad and toss. Top with the croutons.

Mild Greens with Strawberries and Fresh Goat Cheese

This salad is a departure from our usual style, but one summer day an abundance of strawberries forced Marie to look beyond the dessert course for ways to use them up. She sliced them into a green salad and crumbled some goat cheese on top. It was surprisingly good. Farmer's cheese, a dry version of cottage cheese, can be substituted for the goat cheese.

Makes 4 servings

1   pint strawberries, rinsed, hulled, and sliced
3   tablespoons fresh orange juice
1   tablespoon fresh lemon juice
1   tablespoon mint leaves
1   teaspoon sugar
4   cups (packed) torn mild salad greens, such as Boston, Bibb, romaine, oak leaf, or other loose leaf lettuce or a combination
½   cup thinly sliced scallion greens
2   ounces fresh goat cheese or farmer's cheese, crumbled
¼   cup alfalfa sprouts (optional)

1. Stir the strawberries, orange juice, lemon juice, mint, and sugar together in a bowl. Let stand at room temperature 10 minutes.

2. Combine the salad greens and scallions in a large bowl. Add half of the strawberry mixture and toss. Divide among 4 salad plates. Scatter the crumbled goat cheese over each salad, dividing evenly. Top each salad with alfalfa sprouts, if desired. Serve at once.

Roast Beef and Beet Salad
with Horseradish Dressing

3   or 4 medium beets, tops trimmed to within 1 inch, tender
    greens reserved (about 1 pound)

1   tablespoon cider vinegar

1   teaspoon capers, rinsed and drained

⅓   cup lowfat yogurt

1   tablespoon bottled horseradish or 2 teaspoons grated fresh
    horseradish, or to taste

½   teaspoon sugar
    Salt and freshly ground black pepper

4   cups (packed) greens, such as torn arugula or spinach leaves
    and tender beet greens, if available

½   pound (about two ¼-inch-thick slices) rare roast beef,
    cut into ½-inch-wide strips

4   paper-thin slices sweet onion, separated into rings

1. Cook the beets in water to cover over medium heat until tender when pierced with a fork, about 40 minutes. Drain. When cool enough to handle, slip off and discard the skins. Cut the beets into ¼-inch rounds. Place the sliced beets, vinegar, and capers in a small bowl and stir to combine.

2. Stir the yogurt, horseradish, and sugar together in a large bowl and season with salt and pepper to taste. Add the greens and strips of beef and toss to coat. Arrange the greens on a large platter. Top with the beet mixture and onion rings. Serve at room temperature.

This salad is a great way to integrate small amounts of red meat into a lighter eating style. The emphasis here is on beets and greens with a wallop of flavor from capers, horseradish, and onion. Convenience is also key here. Although the beets need to be cooked and peeled (this can be done up to two days ahead), the remaining ingredients—including the roast beef—can come from the store right before serving time.

Makes 4 servings

Black-Eyed Pea, Green Pea, and Rice Salad

This is sort of a free-form salad version of hoppin' John, the Carolina low-country dish of black-eyed peas and rice. We've added green peas and left out the smoked pork. For this salad, we prefer frozen black-eyed peas to the canned ones. Because frozen peas are fresh peas that have been flash-frozen, while canned peas are reconstituted dried peas, the frozen are firmer and have a less starchy taste.

Makes 6 servings

1½   cups water
1   package (10 ounces) frozen black-eyed peas
1   cup long-grain white rice
1   cup diced (¼ inch) carrots
1   cup fresh or frozen tiny green peas, thawed if frozen

Dressing
¼   cup mild olive oil
3   tablespoons fresh lemon juice
2   tablespoons cold water
1   teaspoon prepared grainy mustard, or to taste
¼   teaspoon hot pepper sauce
½   teaspoon salt

½   cup diced (¼ inch) celery
½   cup diced (¼ inch) red onion
½   cup diced (¼ inch) green or yellow bell pepper
¼   cup finely chopped parsley
2   teaspoons thyme leaves (optional)
     Freshly ground black pepper

1. Heat water to a boil in a medium saucepan. Stir in the black-eyed peas, cover, and cook over medium-low heat until tender but not soft, about 40 minutes. Drain and rinse with cold water. Set aside.

2. Meanwhile, cook the rice in a large pot of boiling salted water, as you would cook pasta. When tender, usually 13 to 15 minutes, drain well and cool to room temperature.

3. Heat a medium saucepan half filled with water to a boil. Stir in the carrots and boil, uncovered, for 2 minutes. Immediately add the green peas to the carrots and boil, uncovered, 1 minute. Immediately drain and rinse with cold water. Set aside.

4. Whisk the oil, lemon juice, water, mustard, hot pepper sauce, and salt until blended. Set aside.

5. Combine the black-eyed peas, rice, carrots, peas, celery, onion, bell pepper, parsley, and thyme, if using, in a large serving bowl. Add the dressing and a generous grinding of black pepper and toss to blend. Let stand 20 minutes before serving. Taste and add more lemon juice, salt, or pepper, if needed. Serve at room temperature.

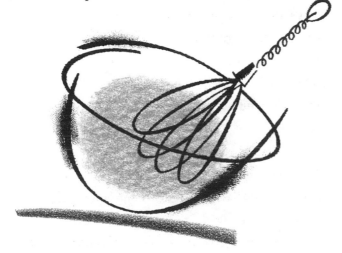

Chicken Caesar Salad

We both love Caesar Salad, but the creamy dressing, usually made with a coddled or raw egg (now possibly unsafe), parmesan, and lots of oil can be a healthy-eating disaster. This main dish salad with a twist is adapted from one of Frank Stitt's. He is chef-owner of The Highlands Bar & Grill and Bottega, two fine restaurants in Birmingham, Alabama.

Makes 4 servings

2   boneless and skinless chicken breasts, cut in half

Marinade

1   tablespoon olive oil

1   tablespoon chopped parsley, preferably flat-leaf

1   garlic clove, minced
    Salt and freshly ground black pepper

Croutons

1   tablespoon olive oil

1   small garlic clove, crushed

2   cups cubed (½ inch) day-old whole wheat Italian or other whole grain bread

Dressing

2   anchovy fillets, drained and blotted dry, chopped

½   garlic clove, minced

2   tablespoons fresh lemon juice

1   tablespoon red wine vinegar

¼   cup olive oil
    Salt and freshly ground black pepper

1   large head romaine lettuce, torn into bite-size pieces

2   tablespoons freshly grated parmesan cheese

12 ripe cherry tomatoes, halved, for garnish (optional)

1. Place chicken on a plate or pie dish and drizzle with olive oil. Sprinkle with parsley, minced garlic, salt, and pepper. Rub seasonings into the chicken, coating evenly. Refrigerate, covered, for 1 hour.

2. Heat the oven to 350°F.

3. To make the croutons, place the olive oil and crushed garlic in a small bowl. Add bread cubes and toss to coat. Spread on a baking sheet. Bake until lightly toasted, turning once, about 15 minutes. Set aside.

4. Puree the anchovy and garlic with the lemon juice and vinegar in a blender. With the motor running, gradually add the oil until dressing is blended. Season to taste with salt and pepper. Set aside.

5. Heat a large nonstick skillet over medium-high heat until hot enough to evaporate a drop of water upon contact. Add the chicken breasts and cook until golden, about 3 minutes per side. When cool enough to handle, cut into long strips about $1/4$ inch wide.

6. Toss the romaine with the dressing, the croutons, and 1 tablespoon of the parmesan. Mound the mixture on 4 large serving plates. Arrange warm chicken strips on top. Sprinkle with remaining cheese and garnish with cherry tomatoes, if using. Serve at once.

Thai-style Squid Salad

With squid, you either have to cook it in a flash—for less than a minute—or else simmer or braise it slowly, for about forty-five minutes. This is a good example of the flash-cooking method, which results in tender, fresh-tasting squid.

Makes 4 servings

1   pound cleaned squid
½   onion
1   bay leaf
    Salt to taste
1   cucumber, peeled, halved lengthwise, seeded, and sliced crosswise
3   ripe plum tomatoes, cored, seeded, and cut into strips
2   scallions, trimmed and thinly sliced on a sharp diagonal
¼   cup (loosely packed) basil leaves, roughly torn
¼   cup (loosely packed) cilantro leaves, roughly torn or separated into individual leaves
1   lime, peeled in vertical strips and sectioned (optional)

Dressing
    Juice of 2 limes
1½ tablespoons rice wine vinegar
1   teaspoon sugar
½   jalapeño pepper, trimmed and minced, or to taste

Cilantro sprigs, for garnish

1. Bring a saucepan of water to a boil. Cut the squid into rings and cut the tentacles into bite-size 2- or 3-tentacle pieces. Add the onion, bay leaf, and salt to the water and simmer for 5 or 10 minutes. Add the squid and cook for 45 seconds (the water will probably not even return to a boil). Drain and refresh under cool water. Drain well and transfer to a bowl, discarding the onion and bay leaf. Add the cucumber, tomato, scallions, basil, cilantro, and lime, if using.

2. Stir together all dressing ingredients. Pour the dressing over the salad and toss to combine. Cover and refrigerate for at least ¹/₂ hour, preferably longer. Taste and correct seasonings. Serve cold, garnished with cilantro sprigs.

Tuna and Two-Bean Salad
with Mustard Vinaigrette

1	large tuna steak, about ¾ inch thick (about ¾ pound)
	Salt and freshly ground black pepper
2	cups ½-inch pieces trimmed green beans
3	tablespoons red or white wine vinegar
1	tablespoon olive oil
1	teaspoon prepared mustard
2	cups cooked or rinsed and drained canned cannellini beans
¼	cup chopped red onion
2	tablespoons chopped dill
4	or 5 large romaine or other lettuce leaves
1	medium tomato, cored and cut into wedges
½	cup dill sprigs
1	lime, cut into wedges

Canned tuna and white beans are a classic combination in Tuscany in northern Italy. We've borrowed the idea and made a salad with fresh tuna, white beans plus green beans, and salad greens.

Makes 4 servings

1. Heat the broiler or grill. Season the tuna with salt and pepper and broil or grill until browned on outside and pale pink in center, about 3 minutes per side. Remove from grill and cut into 1/2-inch pieces. Set aside at room temperature.

2. Cook the green beans in boiling salted water until crisp tender, about 4 minutes. Drain and rinse with cold water. Set aside.

3. Whisk the vinegar, oil, mustard, and salt and pepper to taste in a large bowl until blended. Remove 1 tablespoon and set aside for the fish.

4. Add the green beans, beans, onion, and dill to the dressing in the bowl. Toss to coat. Line a large plate with the lettuce leaves and spread the bean mixture evenly on top. Spoon the reserved dressing over the fish and arrange on top of the beans. Garnish with tomato wedges, dill sprigs, and lime. Serve cold or at room temperature.

Fresh Corn and Seafood Salad

This salad is wonderful made with freshly picked corn cut right from the cobs without cooking. If fresh corn is unavailable, thawed but uncooked frozen corn can be used instead. The salad can be made entirely with shrimp, but we strongly recommend the combination of shrimp and scallops.

Makes 4 servings

6   ounces bay or calico scallops
6   ounces medium shrimp, peeled and deveined
    Salt and freshly ground black pepper
2   cups fresh corn kernels, cut from 3 ears of corn, or thawed frozen corn kernels
½   cup diced red bell pepper
½   cup thinly sliced scallions
¼   cup (packed) chopped cilantro leaves
3   tablespoons fresh lime juice
1   tablespoon vegetable oil
1   teaspoon seeded and minced fresh jalapeño or other chili pepper
    Lettuce leaves
    Cilantro sprigs
    Lime wedges

1. Wipe the scallops and shrimp dry with a paper towel and sprinkle lightly with salt and pepper. Heat a large nonstick skillet over medium-high heat until hot enough to evaporate a drop of water upon contact. Add the scallops and shrimp, a few at a time, and toss just until cooked through, about 2 minutes. Transfer to a plate. Cool to room temperature.

2. Combine the corn, red pepper, scallions, cilantro, lime juice, oil, and jalapeño in a large bowl. Add the scallops and shrimp. Stir to blend. Season to taste with salt.

3. Line a shallow bowl with lettuce leaves. Add the salad and garnish with cilantro sprigs and lime wedges. Serve cold or at room temperature.

Sardine, Potato, and Egg Salad
with Mustard Dressing

1½   pounds potatoes, scrubbed

3   eggs

½   cup thinly sliced half circles of seedless cucumber

½   cup thin slivers red onion

¼   cup (lightly packed) dill sprigs

Dressing

3   tablespoons fresh lemon juice

2   tablespoons cold water

2   tablespoons extra virgin olive oil

1   tablespoon Dijon mustard

1   tablespoon chopped dill

½   teaspoon salt

   Freshly ground black pepper

2   cans (1½ ounces each) sardines, rinsed and drained

1. Place the potatoes in a saucepan filled with water. Cook, covered, until the potatoes are almost cooked, about 25 minutes. Add the eggs and cook with the potatoes, 12 minutes longer. Drain in a colander. When cool enough to handle, peel the skins from the potatoes, halve, and cut into ¼-inch slices. Place in a large bowl. Peel the eggs and separate the whites and yolks. Discard two of the yolks. Set aside the remaining yolk. Coarsely cut up the whites and add to the potatoes. Add the cucumber, onion, and half the dill sprigs to the potatoes.

2. Whisk the lemon juice, water, olive oil, mustard, chopped dill, salt, and pepper until blended. Add to the potatoes. Toss just until coated.

3. Cut sardines into ½-inch pieces. Spread the potato mixture in a shallow bowl. Arrange the sardines evenly on top. Top with the remaining dill sprigs. Place the reserved egg yolk in a small strainer and press the yolk directly over the salad.

Sardines are an oily fish, but the fats are primarily the Omega-3 variety, which research has linked to lowering LDL, the "bad" cholesterol in the blood. We have cut the fat and cholesterol in this salad by using one whole hardcooked egg and two hardcooked egg whites and by rinsing the oil from the canned sardines. Sardines packed in water are available, but for flavor reasons we prefer to use the oil-packed variety, draining and rinsing off most of the excess oil.

Makes 4 servings

Salmon and Vegetable Salad
with Lemon-Dill Dressing

All of the components of this salad can be prepared in advance. Then when you're ready to serve, line up the dinner plates and start building the salad. First the lettuces, then the marinated vegetables, next the salmon, and finally the dressing, the garnishes, and feathery dill sprigs.

Makes 4 servings

1   small head cauliflower, cut into florets (about 4 cups)
¾   pound slender green beans, stem ends trimmed

Dressing

½   cup lowfat or nonfat yogurt
2   tablespoons olive oil
2   tablespoons fresh lemon juice
2   tablespoons chopped dill
½   teaspoon sugar
    Salt and freshly ground pepper

1   cup sliced seedless cucumber, slices halved
1   cup quartered small white mushrooms
2   scallions, sliced ⅛ inch thick on a diagonal
1½   pounds salmon steak, about 1 inch thick
1   head radicchio, leaves separated
1   head Bibb or Boston lettuce, leaves separated
12   small radishes, scrubbed and trimmed, with ½ inch of leaves
2   small ripe tomatoes, cored and quartered
¼   cup small dill sprigs, for garnish

1. Set up a steamer in a wide shallow saucepan, placing the rack over simmering water. Add the cauliflower and green beans and steam, tightly covered, until vegetables are just tender, 5 to 7 minutes. Transfer to a colander and rinse with cool water to stop the cooking. Drain. Set aside.

2. In a food processor, blend the yogurt, oil, lemon juice, dill, sugar, and salt and pepper until well combined. Transfer to a small bowl.

3. Toss the cauliflower, green beans, cucumber, mushrooms, and scallions with half the dressing in a mixing bowl. Cover and refrigerate for at least 1 hour. Refrigerate remaining dressing separately.

4. Just before serving, set up a steamer in a wide pan. Steam the salmon on a rack over simmering water until just cooked through, about 10 minutes. Lift the rack from the pan and cool salmon briefly. When cool enough to handle, remove skin and bones. Carefully divide the salmon into 12 evenly sized chunks.

5. Line 4 large serving plates with alternating leaves of radicchio and lettuce. Spoon the vegetables over the lettuce. Nestle 3 pieces of salmon between the vegetables. Spoon the remaining dressing over the salmon. Garnish each plate with 3 radishes and 2 tomato wedges. Sprinkle with dill sprigs and serve.

Pas

ta

IT'S FUNNY HOW WE GREW UP thinking of pasta, potatoes, and bread as "bad foods"—starches that we thought were fattening. Today we realize that pasta is a great source of complex carbohydrates and a good protein. It has only a fraction of the fat of animal protein sources, without cholesterol.

Pasta is quick, lends itself to endless variation, and is perennially satisfying. While freshly made pasta can be one of the most ethereal food experiences, most of the time both of us use a good brand of dried pasta.

As with baked potatoes topped with butter and sour cream, it's not the pasta itself that is the problem—it's what you put on it. Focus on ingredients that add flavor instead of fat. Dress your pasta with plenty of fresh vegetables and herbs with just a little olive oil, or tomato-based sauces, or sauces made with seafood or small amounts of meat.

STRANDS

SPAGHETTI
VERMICELLI

Tomato sauces, olive oil and garlic, pesto, clam and seafood sauces

ANGEL HAIR
SPAGHETTINI

Delicate, not-too-chunky sauces that don't overwhelm thin pastas. Cut vegetables and other solid ingredients into thin strips.

LONG, FLAT NOODLES

FETTUCCINE
LINGUINE

Butter and Parmigiano-Reggiano cheese, cream-based sauces, clam and seafood sauces

SHORT PASTA SHAPES

CONCHIGLIE
FARFALLE
FUSILLI
ORECCHIETE
PENNE
RADIATORE
RIGATONI
ROTELLE
ZITI

Chunky sauces, whose bits are caught by the pasta, including vegetable-based sauces and meat sauces

TINY SHAPES

CONCHIGLIETTE
DITALINI
FARFALLINE
ORZO
TUBETTI

Sauces with ingredients cut to same size as pasta. Can also be added to soups and stews.

which shape for which sauce?

Basic Chunky Tomato Sauce

1½ teaspoons olive oil

1 medium onion, coarsely chopped

2 garlic cloves, minced

3 pounds (5 to 6) ripe tomatoes, peeled, seeded, and
    coarsely chopped, or 1 can (28 ounces) canned tomatoes,
    or a combination of canned and fresh

1 teaspoon salt, or to taste

1 bay leaf

    Pinch of dried thyme or oregano (optional)

    Freshly ground black pepper

2 tablespoons chopped parsley

1. Heat the olive oil in a heavy saucepan, preferably nonstick, over medium heat. Add the onion and sauté until wilted, about 5 minutes. Add the garlic and sauté 2 minutes longer.

2. Add the tomatoes, salt, bay leaf, and thyme, if using. Boil over medium-high heat, uncovered, until the liquid has reduced to a thick sauce that binds the chunks of tomato, 15 to 20 minutes. Stir often to prevent scorching. Remove and discard the bay leaf.

3. Just before serving, add pepper to taste and parsley. Add more salt if needed.

Tomato Sauce with Mushrooms: Sauté 1 to 1½ cups sliced mushrooms in 1 tablespoon of olive oil in a nonstick skillet over medium-high heat for 5 to 8 minutes. Add to the pasta sauce as it is finished.

Tomato Sauce with Capers and Olives: Add 2 tablespoons capers, rinsed and drained, and 2 tablespoons slivered black (Kalamata) olives to the sauce when it is done.

For quick pasta dinners, tomato sauces are among the best. They can be made with either fresh or canned tomatoes, or with a combination of the two, and with just a trace of olive oil.

This sauce is cooked very briefly. We often prepare a big batch in late summer, buying a bushel of overripe tomatoes at the farmers' market at giveaway price. The sauce can then be canned or frozen in meal-size containers. Do the same, and you'll enjoy the fresh taste of summer all through the fall and winter.

If fresh basil is available, add a few leaves, finely shredded, as you remove the sauce from

continued

the heat. Cooking fresh herbs too long causes them to lose their bright green color.

Makes 2 ½ to 3 cups

Tomato Sauce with Dried Tomatoes: Mince 3 dried tomato halves and add to the sauce near the end of the simmering time in Step 2.

Red Clam or Mussel Sauce: Steam well-washed clams or mussels in the thickened sauce (don't add too much salt, as the shellfish may be salty), tightly covered, just until the shells open. Finish seasoning as described in Step 3.

lighter, quicker, better pasta

Here are a few tips for keeping down the fat in your favorite pasta dishes:

◆ Think lean. Choose tomato- and vegetable-based sauces with just a little olive oil.

◆ Sweat vegetables. Cook vegetables in a minimal amount of olive oil in a nonstick pan to start.

◆ Keep pasta moist. Ladle out a little of the cooking liquid just before you drain the pasta. Add a splash of the pasta cooking liquid when tossing the pasta with a sauce. The starchy liquid binds with a small amount of grated cheese and what Italians call a "thread" of olive oil, forming a light sauce, with minimal fat.

◆ Use small amounts of flavor-packed cheese. One or 2 tablespoons per serving of freshly grated Parmigiano-Reggiano cheese—the real thing— provide more flavor than larger amounts of reduced-fat cheeses.

Summer Salad Bowl Pasta

1½ cups ripe red cherry tomatoes, halved

1½ cups ripe yellow pear or cherry tomatoes, halved

     Kosher or sea salt

2 tablespoons olive oil

1 medium red onion, finely chopped

2 large garlic cloves, bruised

4 scallions, sliced on a sharp diagonal, white and green parts separated

     Freshly ground black pepper

1 pound conchigliette (tiny shells) or other very small pasta, such as ditalini, tubetti, cavatelli, or small elbow macaroni

5 or 6 ounces ricotta salata, cut into very small dice, or firm goat cheese or mild feta

¼ cup finely shredded basil leaves, or more to taste

½ to ⅔ cup freshly grated Parmigiano-Reggiano cheese

     Olive oil, for serving (optional)

     Freshly grated Parmigiano-Reggiano cheese, for serving (optional)

1. Place the red and yellow tomatoes in a colander in the sink or over a plate, sprinkle lightly with salt, and set aside for about ½ hour. Bring a large pot of water to a boil.

2. Heat 1 tablespoon of the olive oil in a nonstick skillet over medium heat. Add the onion, garlic, and white parts of scallion, and sprinkle with salt and pepper. Cook, tossing, just until the onion begins to wilt but is still crunchy, 7 or 8 minutes. Remove from heat, discard garlic cloves, and set aside.

3. Add salt to the boiling water and cook the pasta until al dente. Set aside a ladleful of the pasta cooking liquid. When the pasta is done, transfer the tomatoes from the colander to the skillet with the vegetable mixture. Drain pasta well.

continued

In summertime in Italy, hot pasta is tossed with chunks of raw dead-ripe tomatoes, olive oil, and sometimes little cubes of mozzarella and slivers of black olive. This sort of dish, quick and light, offers the flavor complexity of a sauce without the work of cooking one, plus the clean refreshment of a salad. If summer's peak corn is available, cut the kernels from one ear and toss them in with the cheese in Step 4.

S e r v e s 6

4. Return the pasta to the pot in which it was cooked and place over medium-low heat. Add the vegetable mixture, scallion greens, ricotta salata, basil, remaining 1 tablespoon olive oil, $\frac{1}{2}$ cup of the Parmigiano-Reggiano, and about $\frac{1}{4}$ cup reserved pasta cooking liquid. Sprinkle with freshly ground pepper.

5. Toss everything together with 2 large spoons, heating the mixture through. As you toss, add a little more of the cooking liquid and Parmigiano-Reggiano if needed. The pasta should be just moistened with a light sauce, neither dry nor soupy; the diced ricotta salata cheese should warm through but not melt.

6. Correct seasonings and serve immediately, drizzling each portion with a little more olive oil at the table if you like. Pass a pepper mill and grated Parmigiano-Reggiano separately, if desired.

Pasta with Marinated Tomatoes and Three Cheeses

2½ pounds ripe tomatoes, cored, seeded, and cut into
   ¾-inch cubes
½ cup shredded basil leaves
   Salt
1 cup part-skim ricotta cheese
2 tablespoons milk
   Freshly ground pepper
   Freshly grated nutmeg
2 ounces fresh mozzarella cheese, cut into small cubes
2 ounces Italian fontina cheese, cut into small cubes
1 pound rigatoni or other tubular pasta
   Freshly grated Parmigiano-Reggiano cheese, for serving

1. Combine the tomatoes, basil, and a sprinkling of salt in a colander. Place in the sink or over a plate. Let stand at room temperature for about 1 hour.

2. Combine the ricotta, milk, pepper, and nutmeg in a large serving bowl and mix with a wooden spoon until fluffy. Stir in the mozzarella and fontina. Let stand at room temperature.

3. Bring a large pot of water to a boil and add salt. Cook pasta until al dente, or firm-tender. Drain well and add to the ricotta mixture. Toss until cheeses begin to melt.

4. Spoon the tomato mixture on top and serve immediately, passing Parmigiano-Reggiano and a pepper mill.

Don't even think about making this unless you can get the reddest, the ripest, the juiciest summer tomatoes. The heat of the pasta turns the cheese into a creamy no-cook sauce.

If you can get freshly made ricotta, available in cheese shops and Italian markets, this dish will have an especially sweet, rich flavor. Fresh ricotta, however, is usually made with whole milk. It's worth it.

Serves 4 to 6

Ditalini with Garden-Fresh Summer Salsa

This sparkling uncooked sauce works best with very small pasta shapes, which catch all the fresh vegetable bits.

Makes 4 servings as a first course

2	cups diced (¼ inch) ripe tomatoes
½	cup fresh corn kernels, cut from 1 ear of corn
½	cup diced (¼ inch) peeled Kirby or seedless cucumber
½	cup thinly sliced scallion
¼	cup finely diced green bell pepper
2	tablespoons chopped cilantro or basil
½	teaspoon salt, or to taste
5	tablespoons extra virgin olive oil
2	tablespoons fresh lime juice
1	small garlic clove, crushed
	Freshly ground black pepper
¾	pound ditalini, farfalline, conchigliette, or other small pasta

1. Bring a large pot of water to a boil.

2. Combine the tomatoes, corn, cucumber, scallion, green pepper, and cilantro in a large serving bowl and sprinkle with salt. Add the olive oil, lime juice, and garlic and toss to blend. Add pepper to taste. Set aside at room temperature.

3. Salt the water and cook the pasta until al dente. Drain. Add the pasta to the sauce, toss, and serve at once.

Rotelle with Provençale-style Pasta Sauce

2 cups diced ripe tomatoes

5 tablespoons extra virgin olive oil

½ cup diced roasted red pepper, jarred or homemade (page 10)

1 tablespoon torn flat-leaf parsley leaves

8 brine-cured black olives, pitted and cut up

1 teaspoon fresh thyme leaves, stripped from stems

1 teaspoon tiny capers, rinsed and drained

1 anchovy fillet, rinsed, patted dry, and finely chopped

1 small clove garlic, crushed

1 pound rotelle (wheels) or other short pasta
  Salt

2 tablespoons pine nuts, toasted in a dry skillet until lightly golden

1. Bring a large pot of water to a boil.

2. Combine the tomatoes, olive oil, roasted pepper, parsley, olives, thyme, capers, anchovy, and garlic; and stir to blend in a large serving bowl. Set aside.

3. Add salt to the water and cook the pasta until al dente, or firm-tender, and drain.

4. Add the hot pasta to the sauce and toss to blend. Sprinkle with pine nuts and serve at once.

The salty Provençale elements (olives, capers, anchovies) are used in very discreet amounts in this uncooked sauce. If tomatoes aren't at their peak, use ripe plum tomatoes or cherry tomatoes, now available year round. This sauce is served without grated cheese.

Serves 4

Penne with Cauliflower, Tomatoes, and Basil

To save trouble, we cook the cauliflower right in the pasta water. This is a good trick whenever you're combining pasta with a vegetable that needs to be boiled or blanched. Combining sundried with fresh plum tomatoes reinforces the tomato flavor.

Makes 4 servings

2 cups finely chopped ripe plum tomatoes (about 1½ pounds) or a combination of fresh and canned plum tomatoes
2 tablespoons olive oil
¼ cup chopped basil leaves
1 small sweet onion, cut into lengthwise slivers (about ½ cup)
2 tablespoons diced sundried tomato
1 garlic clove, crushed
Salt
½ pound penne or other short tubular pasta
2 cups sliced (⅜ inch) cauliflower florets, about ½ medium head
Wedge of Parmigiano-Reggiano cheese, at room temperature (see Note)

1. Bring a large pot of water to a boil.

2. Combine the tomatoes, 1 tablespoon of the oil and 2 tablespoons of the basil, the onion, sundried tomato, and garlic in a large bowl and stir to blend. Set aside.

3. Add salt to the boiling water. Stir in the pasta and cook 8 minutes, or until just slightly underdone. Stir in the cauliflower and cook, stirring occasionally, until cauliflower is tender and the pasta is al dente, 5 to 7 minutes longer. Drain.

4. Add the penne and cauliflower to the tomato mixture and toss to coat. Sprinkle with the remaining olive oil and basil. Transfer the mixture to 4 warm bowls. With a vegetable peeler, shave curls of Parmigiano-Reggiano cheese over each serving. Pass a pepper mill at the table.

Note: It's easiest to shave Parmigiano-Reggiano when the cheese is at room temperature.

Fusilli with Broccoli Rabe and Spicy Olive Oil

3   tablespoons olive oil
2   garlic cloves, peeled and halved lengthwise
½   cup strips (1 to 2 inches) red bell pepper
½   teaspoon crushed red pepper
    Salt
1   pound fusilli, penne, or other tubular pasta
10 ounces broccoli rabe, escarole, or broccoli, stems trimmed, cut into 1-inch lengths (about 6 cups)

1. Bring a large pot of water to a boil.

2. Meanwhile, heat the olive oil in a medium skillet over medium-low heat. Add the garlic and cook, stirring occasionally, until the garlic is light golden and soft, about 6 minutes. Transfer garlic to a saucer; mash to a paste with a fork and set aside.

3. Add the red pepper strips and crushed red pepper to the hot oil. Sauté over medium heat, stirring occasionally, until the edges of the peppers brown slightly. Remove the skillet from heat.

4. Add salt to the boiling water, add the fusilli, and boil for 8 minutes, or until slightly undercooked. Stir in the broccoli rabe and cook, stirring often, until fusilli and greens are tender, 2 to 3 minutes longer.

5. Drain fusilli and greens, shaking the colander over the cooking pot, so that about ¼ cup of the cooking liquid drains into the pot. Transfer the pasta and greens to a serving dish and add the reserved cooking liquid, the mashed garlic, and the oil-pepper mixture. Toss and serve immediately.

Pasta and fresh greens with lively seasonings make a quick, easy supper. If broccoli rabe isn't available, use an equal amount of other bitter greens, such as chard, escarole, kale, or a combination.

Serves 4 as a main course or 6 as a first course

Penne with Potatoes, Green Beans, and Herbs

Pasta with potatoes and green beans is typical of Genoa, where the dish is tossed with pesto. We've used lots of fresh herbs instead. For the right balance of textures, the beans should not be undercooked.

Makes 4 servings

¼ cup (packed) flat-leaf parsley leaves
1 tablespoon oregano leaves, stripped from stems
1 teaspoon thyme leaves, stripped from stems
1 pound small red-skinned potatoes, scrubbed
  Salt
2 tablespoons olive oil
¼ cup slivered red bell pepper
1 garlic clove, crushed
¼ teaspoon freshly ground black pepper
¾ pound penne or other tubular pasta
1 pound green beans, ends trimmed, cut to same length as penne (about 1¼ inches)
  Freshly grated Parmigiano-Reggiano cheese

1. Bring a large pot of water to a boil.

2. Finely chop the parsley, oregano, and thyme together. Set aside. Cook the potatoes in boiling salted water until tender, 15 to 20 minutes. Drain and let stand until cool enough to handle. Halve the potatoes and slice into ¼-inch-thick half-moon shapes.

3. Meanwhile, heat the oil in a large skillet, preferably non-stick, over medium heat. Add the red pepper and sauté 1 minute. Add the garlic and sauté 30 seconds longer. Add the potatoes, herb mixture, ½ teaspoon salt, and the pepper.

4. Add salt to the pasta water. Cook the penne for 5 minutes; add the green beans and cook until the penne is al dente and the beans are tender, about 8 minutes. Ladle out ⅓ cup pasta cooking liquid. Drain the pasta.

5. Toss together the pasta and green beans, pasta cooking liquid, and potato mixture. Correct seasonings and serve at once. Pass freshly grated Parmigiano-Reggiano cheese at the table.

Linguine with Parsley Pesto and Toasted Walnuts

2　cups (packed) flat-leaf parsley

½　cup (packed) basil leaves

¾　cup Chicken Broth (page 42) or reduced-sodium canned broth, fat skimmed

¼　cup plus 2 tablespoons broken walnuts, toasted until fragrant

2　tablespoons freshly grated Parmigiano-Reggiano cheese

1　garlic clove, chopped

5　tablespoons extra virgin olive oil

　　Salt

1　pound linguine or spaghetti

　　Freshly grated Parmigiano-Reggiano, for serving (optional)

We've substituted chicken broth for some of the olive oil traditionally (and copiously) used in making pesto. This is a parsley and walnut variation on the Genovese original, which is made with fresh basil.

Serves 4

1. Bring a large pot of water to a boil.

2. Combine the parsley, basil, broth, ¼ cup of the toasted walnuts, Parmigiano-Reggiano, and garlic in a blender or food processor. Puree until smooth. With the motor running, add the olive oil in a slow steady stream. If made in advance, keep at room temperature.

3. Add salt to the water and cook pasta until al dente. When the pasta is almost finished, ladle out about ⅓ cup of the pasta cooking liquid and set aside. Drain the pasta.

4. Combine the drained pasta, the parsley pesto, and the reserved pasta cooking liquid in a large serving bowl. Toss to coat. Garnish with the remaining 2 tablespoons toasted walnuts and serve, sprinkled with a little more grated cheese, if you like.

Fettuccine with Creamy Red Pepper Sauce

We developed this recipe when we were first starting our Bon Appétit *column. We concocted a whole series of dishes called "Taking the Cream out of Creamy." Pureeing roasted peppers with a little lowfat milk approximates the texture of a cream-based sauce with very little fat.*

Serves 4

1½ pounds red bell peppers, roasted (page 10)
1 yellow bell pepper, roasted (page 10)
½ cup dry white wine, preferably Chardonnay
½ cup chopped sweet onion
1 garlic clove, minced
½ cup lowfat (1%) or skim milk
1 teaspoon thyme leaves, stripped from stems
    Salt and freshly ground black pepper
1 pound fresh fettuccine, preferably a combination of spinach and plain egg pasta, or 12 ounces dried fettuccine
    Thyme sprigs, for garnish

1. Bring a large pot of water to a boil for the pasta.

2. Peel and cut the peppers into strips ¼ inch wide over a bowl to catch the juices. Set aside red and yellow pepper strips separately. Strain contents of the bowl, discarding solids and reserving pepper juices. You should have ¼ to ½ cup juices.

3. Combine the red pepper strips, white wine, onion, and garlic in a 10-inch heavy skillet, preferably nonstick. Cook, covered, until the onions are very tender, about 20 minutes. Transfer the mixture to a food processor. Add the reserved pepper juices and puree until smooth. Return the puree to the skillet.

4. Stir in the milk and heat puree to a boil. Boil, uncovered, stirring, until mixture has reduced slightly to about 1 cup. Stir in the yellow pepper strips, thyme, and salt and pepper to taste.

5. Salt the pasta water and cook the fettuccine until al dente. Fresh pasta will be done in 2 minutes, dried pasta in about 8 minutes. Drain. Toss the pasta with half of the sauce and spoon onto warm plates. Spoon the remaining sauce over the pasta, garnish with a sprig of thyme, and serve immediately.

Soup Bowl Lasagna

2½ cups tomato sauce, homemade (page 113), or storebought
    Salt
¾ pound large spinach leaves, stems trimmed
8 lasagna noodles, half spinach lasagna if available
1¼ cups part-skim ricotta cheese
4 ounces coarsely shredded part-skim mozzarella cheese
    Freshly ground black pepper
    Freshly grated nutmeg
    Freshly grated Parmigiano-Reggiano cheese

This is a new take on old-fashioned lasagna. The noodles and sauce are layered with less— and lowfat—cheese, plus fresh spinach for color and flavor.

Makes 4 servings

1. Bring a large pot of water to a boil. Warm the sauce in a saucepan.

2. Add salt to the boiling water and blanch the spinach for 1 minute. Lift out the leaves with a skimmer or large strainer, shaking hard to release excess moisture. Set the strainer over a saucepan half-filled with hot water to keep warm.

3. Break the lasagna noodles in half crosswise. Cook the noodles until al dente. Drain.

4. While the noodles are cooking, heat the ricotta in a saucepan. Stir constantly over low heat until warm. Do not overheat. Stir in the mozzarella until almost melted. Do not overheat. Remove from heat. Sprinkle generously with pepper and nutmeg.

5. Line up 4 wide-rimmed soup bowls. Working quickly, assemble the lasagna as follows: Using half of the sauce, spoon a pool of hot sauce in the bottom of each bowl. Top with 2 pieces of lasagna noodles set side by side. Arrange a single layer of spinach over the noodles. Top with cheese, dividing it evenly among the plates. Top with a second layer of lasagna noodles. Top with the remaining sauce, dividing it evenly Sprinkle lightly with grated cheese and serve at once.

Lighter Macaroni and Cheese

In this update of maca-roni and cheese, we use ricotta cheese flavored and moistened with a little tomato sauce. If subjected to long baking, the cheese would tighten up, so the macaroni and cheese is run quickly under the broiler to brown the surface while keeping the interior creamy. We also add plenty of vegetables for color, flavor, and fiber.

Makes 4 servings

2   teaspoons olive oil

1   small red onion, chopped

3   scallions, white parts thinly sliced, green parts sliced on a diagonal about ½ inch wide

1   large garlic clove, minced

6   mushrooms, thickly sliced
     Salt

½   pound rigatoni or elbow macaroni

1   cup thinly sliced carrots, cut on a sharp diagonal

1   cup broccoli florets (¾ inch), including peeled and diced (½ inch) stems

½   red bell pepper, cut into short thin slivers

1   cup ricotta cheese, preferably freshly made

½   cup finely grated sharp cheddar cheese (about 2 ounces)

½   cup tomato sauce, homemade (page 113), or storebought
     Hot pepper sauce
     Freshly grated nutmeg
     Freshly ground black pepper

2   tablespoons freshly grated Parmigiano-Reggiano cheese

1. Bring a large pot of water to a boil.

2. Meanwhile, heat 1 teaspoon of the olive oil in a large non-stick skillet over medium heat. Add the onion, white parts of scallion, and garlic and sauté, tossing, until the onion has soft-ened slightly, about 6 minutes. Add the remaining teaspoon of oil and the mushrooms. Sauté, tossing, for about 3 minutes longer.

3. Add salt to the boiling water. Cook the pasta until partial-ly cooked, 4 or 5 minutes. Add the carrots and cook 2 minutes longer. Add the broccoli and cook 3 minutes longer.

4. Spray a 10- to 12-inch oval gratin dish or 9-inch square pan with nonstick cooking spray. Adjust the broiler rack so that the top of the dish will be 2 to 3 inches from heat source. Preheat the broiler.

5. Drain the pasta and vegetables and return to the pot. Add the mushroom mixture, scallion greens, and red pepper, tossing gently to combine. Stir in the ricotta, 5 tablespoons of the cheddar, the tomato sauce, a few drops of hot pepper sauce, a pinch of nutmeg, and a pinch of pepper. Transfer to the baking dish. Combine the remaining cheddar with the Parmigiano-Reggiano and scatter the mixture evenly over the surface.

6. Broil, watching carefully, until the surface of the pasta is nicely glazed and golden brown, usually 3 to 5 minutes. Let rest briefly, then serve hot.

Roasted Vegetables with Rigatoni

Although tossing pasta with roasted vegetables is not traditional, it's an inspired solution for a last-minute dinner.

Makes 4 servings

1 medium eggplant, cut into ¾-inch cubes (about 3 cups)
1 cup quartered white button mushrooms
1 cup diagonally sliced (about ¼ inch) carrots
1 medium red onion, cut into 1-inch chunks
1 cup cubed (¾ inch) peeled potatoes
1 pint cherry tomatoes, stems removed
3 garlic cloves, bruised
¼ cup extra virgin olive oil
2 cups broccoli florets with tender stems (about 1-inch pieces)
¼ teaspoon dried oregano
¼ teaspoon dried thyme
¼ teaspoon dried rosemary
Salt and freshly ground black pepper
1 pound rigatoni or other short pasta
3 tablespoons freshly grated Parmigiano-Reggiano cheese, or more to taste

1. Heat the oven to 425°F.

2. Place the eggplant, mushrooms, carrots, onion, potatoes, tomatoes, and garlic in a roasting pan. Drizzle with the olive oil.

3. Roast the vegetables, stirring often, until the edges begin to brown and vegetables are tender, about 45 minutes. Add the broccoli and sprinkle with the dried oregano, thyme, rosemary, and salt and pepper. Stir to blend. Roast until the broccoli is crisp-tender, about 12 minutes longer. Remove from the oven.

4. Meanwhile, cook the pasta in a large pot of boiling salted water until al dente. Ladle out ½ cup of the pasta cooking liquid and add to the vegetables, scraping the browned bits from the bottom of the pan. Drain the pasta and add it to the vegetables. Stir, until the ingredients are tossed well. Transfer to a serving dish and sprinkle with the cheese before serving.

Spaghetti and Little Herbed Meatballs

1 pound ground turkey

1 garlic clove, minced

2 tablespoons chopped parsley

1 teaspoon chopped fresh thyme or ⅛ teaspoon dried thyme

1 teaspoon chopped fresh oregano or ⅛ teaspoon
dried oregano
Salt and freshly ground black pepper

2 teaspoons olive oil

2 cups Basic Chunky Tomato Sauce (page 113)

2 tablespoons chopped parsley

1 pound spaghettini or spaghetti

¼ cup freshly grated Parmigiano-Reggiano cheese
Flat-leaf parsley sprigs, for garnish

Ground turkey is still fairly new in supermarkets; it allows you to make meatballs with all the old-fashioned flavor, but very little fat.

Makes 4 servings

1. Place ground turkey in a bowl. Lightly mix in garlic, parsley, thyme, oregano, and salt and pepper to taste. Form ³/₄-inch meatballs, moistening your palms with cold water, and place the meatballs on a plate lined with wax paper. Chill for ¹/₂ hour.

2. Heat the olive oil in a large nonstick skillet over medium-high heat. Working in batches, brown the meatballs, rolling and turning them for 5 or 6 minutes. Pour off the fat, leaving the browned bits in pan.

3. Add tomato sauce to the skillet and bring to a simmer. Add meatballs and any juices to sauce. Cover and simmer about 3 minutes, stirring gently, until the meatballs are just cooked through. Stir in chopped parsley and correct the seasonings.

4. Meanwhile, boil the spaghettini in salted water until tender. Drain. Arrange in 4 shallow bowls, spoon the meatballs and sauce over, sprinkle with Parmigiano-Reggiano, and garnish each bowl with a parsley sprig.

Rigatoni with Sliced Steak and Tomato-Vegetable Sauce

This substantial dish is a good example of how a small amount of beef can be used to flavor plenty of vegetables, tomatoes, and pasta. If you have fresh herbs on hand, add a little fresh thyme or oregano.

Makes 4 servings

½ pound boneless sirloin steak, well trimmed, about ¾ inch thick

½ cup diced (¼ inch) onion

½ cup diced (¼ inch) carrot

½ cup diced (¼ inch) celery

½ cup thinly sliced green beans

¼ cup water or reduced-sodium canned beef broth, fat skimmed

1 garlic clove, crushed

1 can (28 ounces) Italian-style plum tomatoes with basil, with juice

1 bay leaf

¼ teaspoon crushed red pepper

½ teaspoon salt

⅛ teaspoon freshly ground black pepper

½ pound rigatoni, ziti, or penne

1 tablespoon finely chopped parsley

Freshly grated Parmigiano-Reggiano cheese (optional)

1 teaspoon fresh thyme or oregano leaves (optional)

1. Heat a heavy nonstick skillet over medium-high heat until a drop of water evaporates instantly upon contact. Add the steak; brown quickly on both sides, shaking the pan occasionally. Set steak aside on a plate.

2. Add the onion, carrot, celery, green beans, and water to the skillet, stirring to combine ingredients. Cover and cook over low heat until the vegetables are tender but not brown, about 12 minutes.

3. Stir in the garlic and cook, stirring, for 1 minute longer. Add the tomatoes, bay leaf, and red pepper. Cook over medium heat, uncovered, stirring and breaking up the tomatoes, until the sauce has thickened, about 20 minutes. Put a large pot of water on to boil.

4. Put the steak and any juices that accumulated into the sauce. Season with salt and pepper and spoon the sauce over the steak. Cover and simmer over medium-low heat for 10 minutes. Transfer the meat to a cutting board and let stand while cooking the pasta.

5. When the water comes to a boil, add salt. Cook the rigatoni until al dente. Drain.

6. Cut the steak into very thin slivers of random lengths. Briefly reheat the sauce. Stir in the steak and any juices and correct the seasonings. Spoon half of the sauce into a serving bowl or dish, top with the pasta, then with the remaining sauce. Toss. Sprinkle with parsley and serve at once, passing a pepper mill, grated Parmigiano-Reggiano cheese separately, and fresh thyme or oregano leaves, if desired.

Shells with Roasted Chicken, Escarole, and Roasted Garlic

A great supper dish on a cold night. The combination of pasta with chicken, greens, and garlic is wonderfully hearty. It's the ideal dish to make when you have a piece or two of leftover roast chicken.

S e r v e s   4

4   large garlic cloves

1½   teaspoons plus 1 tablespoon olive oil

2   cups (about 12 ounces) roasted chicken, fat and skin removed

1   head escarole, trimmed and torn into large pieces (about 1½ pounds)

1   tablespoon red wine vinegar
  Salt and freshly ground black pepper

¾   pound shells, orecchiete, penne, or other tubular pasta

2   plum tomatoes, halved, seeded, and cut into ½-inch strips, or 6 cherry tomatoes, halved

½   cup (packed) basil leaves, torn into pieces

1. Bring a large pot of water to a boil. Heat the oven to 375°F.

2. Peel the garlic, leaving a thin layer of skin on each clove. Place in a pie plate or other shallow baking dish and drizzle lightly with 1½ teaspoons olive oil. Roast the garlic until soft when pierced with a small knife but not yet browned, 12 to 15 minutes. Set aside to cool.

3. Peel the skins from the garlic and cut each clove in half. Place in a heatproof bowl. Cut the chicken into wide strips and add to the garlic. Cover with foil and place in a warm oven until ready to serve.

4. Rinse the escarole and place it with just the water clinging to its leaves in a large shallow saucepan or deep sauté pan. Cook, covered, over low heat until the leaves are wilted and tender, 10 to 15 minutes. Uncover and cook over medium heat, pressing on the greens with the back of a spoon to extract moisture and cook off excess liquid. Drizzle with remaining 1 tablespoon oil and vinegar and sprinkle with salt and pepper. Set aside.

5. Add salt to the boiling water and cook the shells until al dente. Ladle out $1/3$ cup of the pasta cooking liquid. Drain the pasta.

6. Quickly reheat the escarole, about 30 seconds. Return the pasta to the cooking pot over low heat. Add the reserved pasta cooking liquid, escarole, chicken and garlic mixture, tomatoes, and basil, tossing until combined and heated through. Correct seasonings and serve at once.

Tomato-steamed Seafood Stew over Green Linguine

This zesty seafood stew is lavish but low in calories. It works equally well as the centerpiece of a dinner party or a meal for family or friends. You can prepare the tomato base mixture in advance. Then at serving time, all you have to do is reheat the sauce and drop in the seafood while the pasta cooks. In keeping with Italian tradition, cheese is not served with seafood sauces.

Makes 4 servings

1 tablespoon olive oil
1 medium red onion, coarsely chopped
1 small red bell pepper, trimmed and chopped
1 small green bell pepper, trimmed and chopped
2 or 3 garlic cloves, thinly sliced
Pinch of dried oregano
Pinch of crushed red pepper
1 bay leaf
1 strip orange zest
1 tablespoon water
⅔ cup dry white wine
1 can (about 1 pound) tomatoes in puree
1 bottle (8 ounces) clam juice or ¾ cup water
Salt
1 pound spinach linguine
1 dozen littleneck or other small clams or ½ pound sea scallops, cut into 2 or 3 pieces each if very large, or a combination of scallops and clams
¾ pound thick fish fillets, such as cod, scrod, or haddock, cut in 1-inch chunks
¾ pound medium shrimp, peeled and deveined
2 tablespoons chopped parsley
2 tablespoons chopped basil
Fresh lemon juice
Freshly ground black pepper
Small basil or parsley sprigs, for garnish

1. Heat the oil in a large nonstick skillet or deep sauté pan over medium-high heat. Add the onion, bell peppers, garlic, oregano, red pepper, bay leaf, orange zest, and water, tossing to

134

coat. Cover and cook, stirring, until the vegetables begin to wilt, 3 or 4 minutes. Uncover and sauté, tossing, for 3 minutes longer.

2. Add the wine and cook until nearly evaporated, about 3 minutes. Add the tomatoes. Rinse out the can with a little water and add that. Cook, breaking up the tomatoes, for about 8 minutes. Add the clam juice and simmer until the sauce has thickened lightly, 6 to 8 minutes. Remove the bay leaf and orange peel. *(The recipe can be prepared in advance to this point.)*

3. Bring a large pot of water to boil for the pasta and add salt. Return the tomato mixture to a simmer, if necessary. Boil the pasta just until al dente. While the pasta is cooking, place the clams in the simmering tomato mixture and cover tightly. Simmer gently, adjusting the heat if necessary, for about 3 minutes, or until the shells are just beginning to open. Stir in the chunks of fish and shrimp. Cover tightly and simmer until the fish is just opaque and the clams have opened, 4 or 5 minutes. Timing may vary; do not overcook.

4. Turn off the heat. Add the parsley, basil, a few drops of lemon juice, pepper, and a little salt, if needed. When the pasta is ready, drain it in a colander, leaving it slightly moist. Arrange the pasta in 4 shallow bowls. Spoon the seafood stew over the pasta, using tongs to arrange the pieces quickly and attractively. Garnish with basil or parsley sprigs and serve immediately. Pass a pepper mill at the table.

Sand

pizz

and eggs

wiches

a BOTH OF US LOVE SANDWICHES. We love pizza. And we have no shame in saying that we love eggs, which have become, more than just about any other food, the great forbidden favorite of the food police. The surprise is that while these foods can be nutrition disasters, sandwiches, pizza, and eggs, when prepared right, can also fit nicely into a healthier approach to eating.

Like pasta and potatoes, sandwiches are a misunderstood food. Remember the time when if you were watching your weight, you'd have a roast beef sandwich without the bread? Mistakenly, we'd consume up to a quarter pound of fat- and cholesterol-laden beef, while avoiding the bread, which itself offers beneficial carbohydrates with very little fat. And if that bread is whole wheat or other whole grain, there are additional nutrient benefits, along with a healthy dose of fiber.

As with baked potatoes and pasta, the sandwich itself is not the problem—it's what you put on it. Slathering on mayonnaise, Russian dressing, or butter is where the trouble comes in. If, instead, you choose mustard, horseradish, or a blend of yogurt and reduced-calorie mayo, you can enjoy a custom-made sandwich any time you like.

Stick with lower-fat meats like turkey breast or lean ham rather than corned beef or salami; use a moderate amount of cheese, and lowfat spreads. Then add flavor enhancers that add crunch but not fat. We love roasted vegetables splashed with a tangy vinaigrette, raw tomatoes, and cucumbers; lettuces, salsa, relish, even pickle slices with fresh vegetables, relishes, and other crunchy flavor-enhancers.

Pizzas, surprisingly, can be a wonderfully healthful way to enjoy a high-carbohydrate, home-baked meal with all sorts of toppings—fresh vegetables, herbs, seafood. Our quick pizza dough, made with part whole wheat flour and a trace of olive oil, is a snap in the food processor. Throw a batch together in the morning before you leave the house and put it in the refrigerator, or do it when you get home from work. Then go about your business as the dough rises, scatter on a few topping ingredients, and twenty minutes later, enjoy a fresher, tastier pizza than you can get anywhere except from a rare wood-burning oven.

For toppings, accentuate those ingredients that carry flavor in a lowfat way—fresh vegetables, greens, mushrooms, herbs, tomatoes, seafood. Use cheese sparingly, but don't leave it out. A drizzle of olive oil—what Italians call "a thread"—and you're in pizza heaven. A leftover slice of pizza, in fact, is not a bad way to start the day: The bread dough is fairly lean, and the cheese offers some protein (albeit with some fat, too).

With eggs, you either love them or loathe them. If you love them, there's no reason to go without; the thing to keep in mind is to stay away from too many yolks. The traditional breakfast of two or three eggs fried in butter, rashers of bacon, buttered toast, and coffee with cream—just thinking about it makes our blood pressure rise. But you don't have to go on an austerity regime, either. Even the American Heart Association allows three to four eggs per week in its recommended diet for healthy Americans.

A mixture of whole eggs and whites—we use two whole eggs plus two whites for our souffléed omelet—has enough yolk to provide flavor and tenderness but cuts back on the fat and cholesterol found in three whole eggs. If you go too far in the low-fat direction, and make eggs and omelets with egg whites alone, the results can be tough as rubber. A nonstick pan is the key to making a reduced-yolk omelet work.

In a frittata and a strata that's a perfect brunch main course, we combine eggs with plenty of colorful vegetables so that the eggs are used as a binder. As always, the point is not to eliminate eggs completely but to figure out ways to enjoy them while keeping fat to a minimum.

how nutritious is bread?

	Fiber g	Protein g	Fat g	Carbohydrates g	Calories
Bagel (one 3 ounce)	1.5 to 2	9	1	46	230
English muffin (1)	2	4	1	25	130
Rye bread (2 slices)	3	6	2	32	152
Seven-grain bread (2 slices)	2–3	5	2	36	180
White bread (2 slices)	2	7	2	38	190
White pita bread (one, 6½ inches)	2	3	.5	16	79
Whole wheat bread (2 slices)	3	5	1.4	20	96
Whole wheat pita bread (one, 6½ inches)	.7	6	2	28	150

Tuna Salad on Whole Wheat Toast

Tuna, egg, and chicken salad sandwiches account for a major portion of the American consumption of mayonnaise. By using a mixture of yogurt and reduced-fat mayo, the fat usually lurking in these sandwiches can be cut back tremendously. We've added plenty of vegetables for crunch, too. Chicken salad can be made the same way, adding celery if you like.

**M a k e s 2
g e n e r o u s
s a n d w i c h e s**

2   tablespoons nonfat yogurt
2   tablespoons reduced-calorie mayonnaise
1   tablespoon fresh lemon juice
¼   teaspoon grated lemon zest
1   can (6½ ounces) white tuna packed in water, drained well
⅓   cup diced (¼ inch) unpeeled seedless or seeded cucumber
⅓   cup diced (¼ inch) red onion
¼   cup finely chopped red bell pepper
1   tablespoon minced parsley
    Salt and freshly ground pepper
4   thin slices whole wheat bread, toasted
    Romaine lettuce leaves
4   thin rings green bell pepper
    Cherry tomatoes

1. Combine the yogurt, mayonnaise, lemon juice, and lemon zest in a small bowl. Add the tuna, cucumber, red onion, red pepper, and parsley. Stir to blend, gently breaking up the tuna into large flakes. Season with salt and pepper to taste.

2. Place two slices of the whole wheat toast on serving plates. Top with a layer of romaine leaves, then with the tuna salad, dividing it evenly. Place two green pepper rings on top of each sandwich and close the sandwiches with the remaining toast. Pressing down and holding the sandwich together, cut each diagonally in two. Serve garnished with more romaine leaves and cherry tomatoes.

Warm Open-Face Curried Egg Salad Sandwiches

4   warm hardcooked eggs
¼   cup lowfat (1%) cottage cheese, stirred to blend
½   teaspoon curry powder
⅓   cup chopped celery
¼   cup chopped sweet onion
1   tablespoon minced chives or scallion tops
    Salt and freshly ground black pepper
2   thick slices seven-grain bread or other whole-grain loaf,
    toasted
1   tablespoon chutney
    Red leaf lettuce leaves
4   thin slices ripe tomato
⅓   cup (loosely packed) alfalfa sprouts (optional)
    Chives or thinly sliced scallion greens, for garnish

We've used only two of the egg yolks in four hardcooked eggs to cut back on fat and cholesterol. The salad served on a cracker instead of bread makes a good snack or hors d'oeuvre.

Makes 2 sandwiches

1. Peel the eggs under lukewarm running water while still warm. Quarter two of the eggs and cut crosswise into ¹/₂-inch chunks. Halve the remaining two eggs and remove and discard the yolks. Cut the whites into ¹/₂-inch pieces and combine with the whole eggs in a bowl.

2. Add the cottage cheese, curry powder, celery, onion, chives, and salt and pepper to taste. Stir to blend.

3. Place the toasted bread on 2 plates. Spread each with a layer of chutney; add a lettuce leaf and 2 tomato slices. Add a mound of egg salad, dividing it evenly. Garnish with alfalfa sprouts, if using, and a few pieces of chive. Sprinkle with pepper and serve.

Chef's Salad in Pita Bread

A chef's salad is a great way to eat a little of everything. Here we offer a light variation on an old theme, made with plenty of vegetables and a light vinaigrette, all packed into a pita pocket.

Makes 5 sandwiches

Dressing

2   tablespoons red wine vinegar

1   tablespoon olive oil

1   tablespoon cold water

¼   teaspoon paprika

¼   teaspoon salt

½   small garlic clove, crushed

    Pinch dried thyme leaves

    Pinch dried oregano

    Freshly ground black pepper

5   large pita breads, preferably whole wheat

Salad

4   cups (loosely packed) mixed salad greens, such as curly leaf lettuce, romaine, red oak leaf lettuce, and fresh spinach leaves, torn into bite-size pieces

1   cup small (½ inch) broccoli florets, steamed until crisp-tender, rinsed, and cooled

½   cup unpeeled julienned (2 × ⅛ × ⅛ inch) seedless or seeded cucumber

½   cup slivered red onion, cut vertically

½   cup coarsely shredded carrot

½   cup halved cherry tomatoes

2   ounces (4 thin slices) baked or cured ham, fat trimmed, cut into 2 × ¼ × ¼-inch strips

2   ounces (4 thin slices) Swiss cheese, cut into 2 × ¼ × ¼-inch strips

1. Whisk all the dressing ingredients together in a bowl. Set aside.

2. Wrap the pita breads in foil and place in a 350°F oven until warm, about 5 minutes.

3. Combine the salad greens, broccoli, cucumber, red onion, carrot, cherry tomatoes, ham, and cheese in a large bowl. Toss gently.

4. Just before serving, whisk the dressing again and add to the salad mixture and toss. Slice about 1 inch off one edge of each pita bread, or slit about ⅓ of the edge open and open up the bread to form a pocket. Stuff the salad into the pockets, dividing it evenly. Serve immediately.

Chick Pea Salad in Pita Bread

Canned chick peas are the basis of a quick Middle Eastern-style salad, which can be stuffed into pita bread and moistened with seasoned yogurt. The yogurt dressing stands in for the fat-rich tahini usually included in hummus.

**M a k e s   4
g e n e r o u s
s a n d w i c h e s**

1	can (19 ounces) chick peas, drained and rinsed
½	cup finely chopped parsley
3	tablespoons fresh lemon juice, or more to taste
1	tablespoon extra virgin olive oil
½	garlic clove, crushed
	Salt and freshly ground pepper
4	cups mixed salad greens, torn into bite-size pieces
½	cup thinly sliced seedless or seeded cucumber
½	cup slivered red onion
½	cup diced ripe tomato
4	whole wheat pita breads, 1 edge slit and pockets opened
½	cup lowfat yogurt
½	garlic clove, crushed
	Pinch ground cumin
	Hot pepper sauce

1. Combine the chick peas, parsley, lemon juice, olive oil, and garlic, and salt and pepper to taste in a large bowl. Stir to blend. *(The chick pea mixture can be prepared 1 day ahead.)*

2. Just before serving, add the salad greens, cucumber, red onion, and tomato to the chick peas and toss to combine. Correct the seasonings, adding more lemon juice and/or salt and pepper to taste. With tongs, stuff the mixture into each pita.

3. Stir the yogurt, garlic, cumin, and a dash of hot pepper sauce together in a small bowl. Drizzle a little into each sandwich and serve.

Tofu, Avocado, and Tomato Salad with Tahini in a Pita Pocket

4   large whole wheat pita breads, 1 edge slit and
    pockets opened
½   pound tofu, preferably soft, drained and cut into
    eight ⅛-inch slices
4   ripe tomato slices, ¼ inch thick
4   thin slices red onion
4   large lettuce leaves
1   cup alfalfa sprouts
1   large ripe avocado, halved, pitted, peeled, and cut
    into thin wedges
Tahini Sauce
1   cup nonfat yogurt
2   tablespoons tahini
½   clove garlic, crushed
1   teaspoon fresh lemon juice
    Salt
    Hot pepper sauce

1. Carefully open the pita breads. Slip a slice of tofu, tomato, onion, and a lettuce leaf into each one. Add some of the alfalfa sprouts. Divide the avocado slices among the sandwiches.
2. Combine the yogurt, tahini, garlic, lemon juice, salt, and a dash of hot pepper sauce in a small bowl. Drizzle 2 or 3 tablespoons of the dressing into each sandwich and serve at once.

This is a great combination, especially when summer tomatoes are at their peak. Tahini, made from ground sesame seeds, is very high in fat. Because it's concentrated in flavor, it can be stretched with yogurt, extending its flavor while cutting way back on fat. Though sprouts are almost synonymous with health food, they are not especially nutrient-packed. But they are a good way to add crunch to a sandwich.

Makes 4 sandwiches

Roasted Vegetable Pan Bagna

Pan Bagna *means "bathed bread"—bathed in plenty of olive oil, that is—in Provençal. You see it sold on the streets, everywhere you turn in and around Nice. Pan Bagna is a round loaf, split and piled with tomatoes, olives, sometimes artichokes, olive oil, and anchovies, then weighted down so the flavors combine. This roasted vegetable version works year round. It has just enough olive oil to flavor the mixture. In summer, use the juiciest tomatoes you can find, sliced but not roasted.*

Makes 4 sandwiches

2 plum tomatoes or 6 cherry tomatoes, cored and halved
2 garlic cloves, bruised
1 zucchini, cut lengthwise into ¼-inch slices
1 red bell pepper, quartered, stems and seeds removed
1 medium red onion, halved lengthwise, cut into ½-inch half-moons
½ eggplant cut into ¼-inch half-moons (about 12 ounces)
2 tablespoons extra virgin olive oil
2 tablespoons finely chopped parsley
½ teaspoon dried rosemary
¼ teaspoon dried thyme
   Salt and freshly ground black pepper
4 Italian hero rolls or small semolina loaves
1 can (2 ounces) anchovy fillets, drained and rinsed
2 cups trimmed arugula leaves

1. Heat the oven to 400°F.
2. Combine the tomato, garlic, zucchini, red pepper, onion, eggplant, and olive oil in a large roasting pan or jelly-roll pan. Toss to coat with oil. Bake, turning often, until the vegetables are browned and tender, about 45 minutes.
3. Meanwhile chop the parsley, rosemary, and thyme together. Stir into the vegetables during the last 15 minutes of baking. Remove from the oven and add salt and pepper to taste.
4. Preheat the broiler or a toaster oven. Split the rolls open like a book and toast until the cut sides are lightly golden. Divide the warm vegetables among the rolls. Top each with 2 or 3 anchovy fillets. Scatter the arugula on top. Fold the top of the roll over the filling and serve.

Toasted Healthy Hero

Marinated Mushrooms

1 cup thinly sliced mushrooms

1 tablespoon balsamic or red wine vinegar

1 tablespoon olive oil

½ garlic clove, crushed

   Pinch dried oregano

   Pinch salt

   Freshly ground black pepper

1 cup trimmed arugula leaves

1 long loaf (12 inches) French baguette or Italian hero bread, split lengthwise, soft inside of top half pulled out, bottom half reserved for another use

6 to 8 thin slices turkey breast, preferably smoked (about 4 ounces)

1 medium-size ripe tomato or 2 plum tomatoes, cored and sliced

1 medium green or red bell pepper, stem and seeds removed, sliced in thin rings

2 ounces part-skim mozzarella, coarsely shredded

This is a far cry from the mile-long Italian hero, piled high with fatty, salt-cured meats and cheeses and oily dressing. But the fun of eating a hero is still there. We've used lowfat smoked turkey and mozzarella with fresh vegetables and marinated mushrooms.

Makes 2 sandwiches

1. Combine the mushrooms, vinegar, oil, garlic, oregano, salt, and pepper in a small bowl, stirring to blend. Let stand for 10 minutes. Add the arugula and toss to combine.

2. Preheat the broiler. Spoon the mushroom and arugula mixture into the top half of the loaf of bread. Fold the slices of turkey to fit the bread and arrange them, overlapping slightly, over the mushroom-arugula mixture. Top with a row of overlapping tomato slices; place a row of overlapping pepper rings on top. Sprinkle with the mozzarella.

3. Broil just until the cheese has melted. Cut the hero in half crosswise and serve warm with a knife and fork.

Café Kula Grilled Chicken Sandwich With Onion, Tomato, and Arugula

This recipe is from spa chef Kathleen Daelemans of the Grand Wailea Resort in Maui. Café Kula is her dazzling spa restaurant. Kathleen was new to spa cooking when she was hired away from Zuni Café in San Francisco to open this spectacular resort. As with many innovative chefs, her inspiration was the produce available to her from local farmers.

"The first time I visited Robbie Friedlander's organic farm," she says, "I wrote my whole menu from what he had there." Kathleen makes this sandwich with sweet Maui onions and local tomatoes.

Makes 4 sandwiches

8   thin slices large ripe tomato
    Salt (optional)
2   tablespoons finely chopped basil leaves
2   tablespoons finely chopped opal basil or green basil leaves
    Freshly ground black pepper
4   thick slices Maui onion or other sweet onion
4   boneless and skinless chicken breast cutlets
    (about 3 ounces each)
8   thick slices whole-grain round Italian loaf
1   garlic clove, halved
2   cups (packed) trimmed arugula leaves
4   teaspoons fresh lime juice

1. Arrange the tomatoes on a platter. Sprinkle lightly with salt, if desired, then with the 2 types of basil and a grinding of black pepper. Set aside at room temperature for about 1 hour, or until ready to serve.

2. Preheat the grill. Skewer the onion slices through the rings so they won't separate when grilled. Grill the onions until golden and tender, about 10 minutes per side. Do not overcook. Cool. Remove the skewers.

3. Season the chicken with pepper. Grill just until golden, about 5 minutes per side. Grill the bread until toasted on both sides, about 5 minutes per side. Rub 1 side of each slice of bread with the cut side of the garlic clove. Discard the garlic.

4. Place 2 slices of bread on each of 4 plates. On 1 side of the bread arrange a bed of arugula and place the chicken breast on the arugula. Sprinkle the chicken breast with lime juice. On the other slice of bread arrange 2 overlapping slices of tomato. Top with a slice of onion, separating it into rings. Serve hot.

Deluxe Steak Sandwich,
The Healthy Way

1	teaspoon olive oil
1	slice (6 ounces) filet mignon, well trimmed
	Salt and freshly ground black pepper
½	small onion, cut into slivers
6	large mushrooms, sliced
2	French rolls or an 8-inch length French or Italian bread, split
1	garlic clove, halved
	Dijon mustard
1	tablespoon chopped parsley
½	cup water
	Watercress or arugula sprigs

Here's a way to enjoy an old-fashioned steak sandwich. Use a little bit of steak from the lean and tender fillet and top it with sautéed onions and mushrooms.

Makes 2 sandwiches

1. Heat the olive oil in a nonstick skillet over medium-high heat. Sprinkle both sides of the steak with salt and pepper. Place the steak in the pan and lower the heat to medium. Sauté the steak until well browned, 6 to 9 minutes, adjusting the heat if necessary to maintain a steady sizzle. Turn the steak and brown the second side, about 5 minutes.

2. Transfer the steak to a plate, cover loosely with foil to keep warm, and set aside to rest. Add the onions to the skillet. Cook tossing, until slightly softened, about 4 minutes. Add the mushrooms and cook, tossing, for 3 minutes.

3. Meanwhile, toast the cut sides of the rolls or bread in a toaster oven or broiler. Rub the cut sides of the bread with the cut surface of the garlic clove. Spread with a little mustard. Arrange the bread on 2 serving plates, toasted sides up.

4. Slice the steak and arrange the slices, overlapping, over the toast. Stir the parsley and any steak juices into the mushroom mixture, adding salt and pepper to taste. Spoon this mixture over the beef. Add the water to the pan over medium-high heat, scraping up any browned bits in the pan and letting the sauce boil slightly until reduced by half. Pour the sauce over the steak, so that it moistens the toast. Garnish with watercress or arugula and serve at once.

hold the mayo

Reduced-fat mayonnaises, some of which taste fine, have recently become available. This reduced-fat mayo can be combined with plain yogurt to reduce the fat even further. There is even no-cholesterol mayonnaise made without egg yolks. Instead of mayonnaise, you can also use condiments that add flavor punch without any fat:

◆ **Prepared horseradish, alone or stirred into a little yogurt**

◆ **Dijon mustard, smooth or grainy, as well as other mustards**

◆ **Salsa**

◆ **Pickles and relishes**

Basic Quick Pizza Dough

1	cup lukewarm water
1	tablespoon honey
1	teaspoon olive oil, or more as needed
2	teaspoons dry yeast
½	cup whole wheat flour
½	teaspoon salt
1½	cups unbleached all-purpose flour
	Cornmeal
	Topping (see Variations)

1. Place the warm water, honey, and olive oil in a cup and sprinkle with the yeast. Let stand for 10 minutes.

2. Place the whole wheat flour, salt, and 1 cup of all-purpose flour in a food processor. Process for about 10 seconds, or until combined. Add the yeast mixture, pulsing to combine. Add enough of the remaining flour to form a soft, slightly moist dough. If the mixture is too sticky, sprinkle with a little more flour and process it in; if it is too dry, add a little more water. Process the dough for 45 seconds.

3. Turn out the dough onto a lightly floured work surface and knead until smooth, about 1 minute. Transfer the dough to a bowl. Drizzle with a little olive oil and turn the dough over to coat lightly with oil. Cover the bowl with plastic wrap and let the dough rise until doubled in bulk, about 1 hour. *(If you are not baking the pizza right away, refrigerate the dough after it rises. It can be kept overnight.)*

4. When ready to bake, heat the oven to 450°F. Lightly oil a heavy 12- to 14-inch round pan or 15 × 10-inch jelly-roll pan and sprinkle with cornmeal.

5. Punch down the dough and place it in the pan. Stretch the dough to fit the pan, building up the edges slightly. Cover with

Homemade pizza dough can be made in a couple of minutes. It takes 45 minutes or so to rise, but you can throw the dough together the night before or earlier in the day, refrigerate it, and let it rise slowly until you're ready to bake. If you have tomato sauce on hand, you can assemble a pizza and have it hot on the plates by the time you set the table and pour a glass of wine or beer.

For a crisp brown crust, bake pizza on a heavy round pizza pan. If you don't have one, use a jelly-roll pan. Have the oven very hot, and spray with water to create steam that will help crisp the crust. Begin to watch after about fifteen

minutes. In any case, get to know your oven and your pan.

Makes one 12- to 14-inch pizza

topping and bake until the pizza is browned and crusty, usually 15 to 25 minutes. Spray the bottom of the oven with water 3 times during the first 5 or 10 minutes of baking time.

Broiled Eggplant Pizza: Broil thin eggplant slices as described on page 167. Arrange on the crust, sprinkle lightly with fresh herbs and a little freshly grated parmesan. Drizzle with olive oil and bake until done.

Braised Escarole Pizza: Braise escarole as described on page 181. Sprinkle lightly with fresh herbs, a little freshly grated parmesan, and freshly ground black pepper. Drizzle with olive oil and bake until done.

Mushroom Pizza: Sauté 10 ounces sliced white button mushrooms or a mixture of cultivated and shiitake and/or cremini mushrooms, in olive oil with a little garlic until lightly golden, about 8 minutes. Scatter over the crust. Sprinkle with fresh herbs, a little freshly grated parmesan, and freshly ground black pepper. Drizzle with olive oil and bake until done.

Ricotta and Fresh Herb Pizza: Spoon dabs of ricotta cheese, fresh if available, over the crust, using about 1 cup. Scatter shredded basil leaves or oregano over and top with a little freshly grated parmesan and freshly ground black pepper. Drizzle with olive oil and bake until done.

Tomato and Fresh Herb Pizza: Scatter thinly sliced ripe beefsteak or plum tomatoes over the crust or use 1$^1/_2$ cups thick tomato sauce. Sprinkle with shredded basil leaves and/or oregano. Top with shaved parmesan, coarsely shredded Italian fontina, or mozzarella, and freshly ground black pepper. Drizzle with olive oil and bake until done.

Red Onion and Vegetable Pizza

1 recipe Basic Quick Pizza Dough (page 151)

1 small red bell pepper, stemmed, seeded, and cut into long slivers

1 small yellow bell pepper, stemmed, seeded, and cut into thin slivers

1 teaspoon fresh thyme and/or oregano leaves or pinch dried thyme and/or oregano

2 teaspoons olive oil, or more as needed
Freshly ground black pepper

1 pound red onions, halved and thinly sliced (3 or 4 onions)
Salt

2 tablespoons water

¾ cup drained canned tomatoes or tomato sauce

1 tablespoon balsamic vinegar

⅓ cup grated fresh or part skim mozzarella cheese

¼ cup freshly grated parmesan cheese

⅓ cup shredded basil leaves (optional)

Makes 4 servings

1. Prepare the dough as directed and place it in the pan, stretching the dough to fit the pan and building up the edges slightly. Set aside.

2. Place oven rack in the lowest position. Heat the oven to 450°F for at least 15 minutes.

3. Toss the red and yellow pepper slivers in a small bowl with half of the herbs, 1 teaspoon olive oil, and a generous grinding of black pepper. Set aside.

4. Heat the remaining teaspoon of olive oil in a wide skillet over medium heat. Add the onions, remaining herbs, and salt and pepper to taste. Toss to coat. Add the water, cover, and cook, tossing occasionally, until the onions are softened, about 8 minutes. Uncover and cook, tossing occasionally, until the onions are soft but not limp, about 3 minutes longer. Add the tomatoes and cook, crushing them, until the mixture has thickened. Stir in the vinegar and simmer briefly. Transfer the mixture to a plate to cool slightly. *(This mixture can be prepared in advance and refrigerated overnight.)*

5. Scatter the onion mixture over the crust, leaving the edges uncovered. Scatter half the pepper mixture over, then top with ⅓ of the mozzarella. Top with the remaining peppers, remaining mozzarella, the parmesan, basil, if using, and a few grindings of black pepper. Drizzle with olive oil.

6. Bake the pizza on the lower rack and spray the bottom of the oven with water 3 times during the first 5 or 10 minutes of baking time. Bake until the crust is crisp and well browned, usually 15 to 25 minutes. Cut the pizza into wedges and serve.

Streamlined Cheese Soufflé

1   cup lowfat (1%) milk
1   tablespoon cornstarch
½   teaspoon dry mustard
½   teaspoon salt
2   large eggs, separated
4   ounces gruyère or Swiss cheese, finely shredded
    (about 1 cup)
    Pinch cayenne
    Freshly grated nutmeg
1   large egg white
⅛   teaspoon cream of tartar

1. Place the rack in the lower third of the oven and heat the oven to 350°F. Brush the bottom of a 1½-quart soufflé dish with vegetable oil. Fold a long 6-inch wide piece of wax paper for a 3-inch collar to go above the rim of the soufflé dish. Brush 1 side of the folded paper lightly with vegetable oil. Tie or tape the collar around the soufflé dish, overlapping the edges slightly, with the folded edge on top. Heat a kettle of water to a boil for the water bath.

2. Scald ¾ cup of the milk in a small saucepan. Meanwhile, whisk the remaining ¼ cup cold milk, cornstarch, dry mustard, and salt in a small bowl until smooth. Whisk into the hot milk until blended. Cook the mixture over low heat, whisking, until it has thickened and come to a boil.

3. Whisk the egg yolks in a bowl. Gradually whisk in the thickened milk until blended. Stir in the cheese and cayenne. Set aside.

4. With clean beaters, beat the 3 egg whites in a large clean bowl until foamy. Add the cream of tartar and beat until stiff but not dry peaks form. Pour the cheese mixture over the

Soufflés can fit in a healthy lifestyle, and aren't nearly the difficult culinary bugaboo they've been made out to be. The classic recipe for cheese soufflé is made with a butter-and-flour roux, whole milk, and three or four whole eggs. We've replaced one of the eggs with an egg white and used lowfat milk thickened with a cornstarch slurry, which makes it possible to omit the butter entirely. The soufflé is baked at a low temperature in a water bath.

Makes 4 servings

155

whites. Gently fold together just until blended. Spoon into the soufflé dish. Smooth the top gently with a spatula. If you'd like the soufflé to form a high hat as it bakes, run your thumb around the rim of the batter, about $1/2$ inch in from the edge.

5. Place the soufflé dish in a shallow baking pan and place on the oven rack. Add enough boiling water to the baking pan to come halfway up the sides of the soufflé dish. Bake until the top is well browned, 50 to 60 minutes. Serve at once, spooning some of browned top and creamy interior for each portion.

Souffléed Omelet with Fresh Tomatoes and Basil

1	tablespoon olive oil
½	cup chopped sweet onion
1	cup cubed (½ inch) ripe tomatoes
½	garlic clove, minced
2	tablespoons torn basil leaves
1	tablespoon grated parmesan cheese
	Salt and freshly ground black pepper
2	large eggs
2	large egg whites

1. Heat 2 teaspoons of the oil in a medium nonstick skillet. Add the onion and sauté over low heat, stirring, until tender, about 5 minutes. Add the tomatoes and garlic and sauté until heated through, about 2 minutes. Scrape onto a plate and sprinkle the vegetable mixture with half of the basil and half of the parmesan. Season with salt and ground pepper. Set aside.

2. Wipe out the skillet. Whisk the whole eggs and remaining basil in a small bowl until frothy. In a separate bowl, whisk the egg whites and a pinch of salt until soft peaks form. Gently fold the whites into the beaten eggs.

3. Heat the remaining teaspoon of oil in the skillet over medium-low heat until hot. Pour in the eggs and cook, covered, for 2 minutes. Spoon the tomato mixture in a line, just off the center of the omelet. Cover and cook until the egg has set to the desired doneness, 1 to 2 minutes longer. Carefully lift the edges of the omelet and fold it in half over the filling. Place a serving plate on top of the skillet and invert the omelet onto the plate. Sprinkle with remaining parmesan and serve hot.

By using four eggs, but only two of their yolks, we've cut back considerably on fat and cholesterol, without sacrificing flavor or texture. If you'd like to make this a plain omelet instead of a puffy one, use the same ingredients but beat the whole eggs and whites together. Consider this recipe a basic method. Play with other fillings: chopped ham and a little cheese, sautéed mushrooms, cooked spinach, ratatouille, or any leftover vegetable, meat, or fish mixture.

Serves 2

Potato and Cheddar Frittata

A frittata can be served warm or at room temperature, as a main dish for supper, lunch, or brunch. It's ideal picnic fare. Be sure not to overcook, or the frittata will be tough.

Serves 2 as a main dish or 4 as an appetizer

2 teaspoons olive oil

1 small onion, cut into short slivers

2 scallions, cut on a diagonal, whites in ¼-inch lengths, greens in ½-inch lengths

6 cooked new potatoes, peeled but not rinsed and sliced (about ¾ pound)

3 large eggs

2 large egg whites

2 tablespoons lowfat milk
  Salt and freshly ground pepper

3 tablespoons grated sharp cheddar cheese

1. Heat 1 teaspoon olive oil in an 8- or 9-inch nonstick skillet over medium heat. Add the onion and scallions and cook, stirring occasionally, until onion begins to soften, 5 or 6 minutes.

2. Place the broiler rack so that the top of skillet will be about 1 inch from the heat source. Preheat the broiler.

3. Add the potatoes to the skillet, spreading them to cover bottom of pan. Toss once or twice.

4. Meanwhile, whisk together the eggs, egg whites, milk, and salt and pepper in a mixing bowl. Reduce the heat to low and pour the remaining olive oil into the pan. Pour the egg mixture over the vegetables, covering evenly. Cover and cook until the egg mixture has set around the edges but the center is still liquid, usually 6 to 8 minutes. Adjust heat so that mixture sizzles gently but steadily as it cooks.

5. Scatter the cheese over the surface. Place skillet under the broiler and cook until lightly golden, about 1 minute. Move skillet under broiler if necessary to brown surface evenly. Do not overcook, or the egg mixture will toughen. Cut the frittata into 4 wedges and serve hot or lukewarm.

Tomato and Spinach Strata
with Three Cheeses

3 pounds fresh spinach, stems trimmed, or 3 packages
(10 ounces each) frozen spinach, thawed and squeezed dry

2 tablespoons olive oil

2 medium-large onions, coarsely chopped (3 to 3½ cups)
Salt and freshly ground black pepper

10 to 12 ounces mushrooms, sliced ⅛ inch thick (5 to 6 cups)
Freshly grated nutmeg

1 pound part-skim ricotta cheese

6 cups skim milk, or as needed

2 loaves day-old Italian bread, with crust, preferably whole
wheat, sliced ⅛ inch thick (32 to 40 thin slices)

1 recipe Basic Chunky Tomato Sauce (page 113)

¾ pound fresh or part-skim mozzarella cheese, sliced very thin

1½ tablespoons chopped thyme leaves

1½ tablespoons chopped basil leaves

1½ tablespoons chopped parsley

5 large eggs

4 large egg whites

⅓ cup freshly grated parmesan cheese

An old-fashioned egg dish, a strata is a baked, layered pudding of bread, eggs, and flavorings. This one is flavored with a chunky tomato sauce, spinach, and mild cheeses. You can assemble this the night before a brunch and pop it in the oven in the morning. Add 5 to 10 minutes to the baking time if it is cold when it goes into the oven.

**Serves
about 12**

1. The strata can be made in a 13 × 9-inch baking dish, two 2-quart soufflé dishes, or a deep oval 13-inch gratin dish and 1 soufflé dish. Spray the baking dish or dishes with nonstick cooking spray; set aside.

2. If using fresh spinach, cook it in 2 batches. Cook each batch in a large saucepan with just the water that clings to the leaves, stirring it over medium-high heat until wilted but still bright green. Drain in a colander and cook the remaining spinach. When the spinach is cool enough to handle, gently press out excess liquid. If using frozen spinach, simply thaw and squeeze as dry as possible.

3. Heat 1½ teaspoons of the olive oil in a large nonstick skillet over medium-high heat. Add the onions, season lightly with salt and pepper, and cook, tossing. After 2 or 3 minutes, lower the heat to medium and cook until the onions are softened but not browned, 5 or 6 minutes longer. Transfer the onions to a plate.

4. Add 1½ teaspoons oil to the pan and raise the heat to medium-high. Add the mushrooms, season lightly with salt and pepper, and toss until heated, 5 to 8 minutes. Transfer to the plate with the onions.

5. Add 1½ teaspoons oil to the pan and add the spinach. Season with salt, pepper, and nutmeg. Cook, stirring constantly, just until the spinach has dried out, about 4 minutes. Transfer the spinach to a mixing bowl. In a small bowl, combine the ricotta cheese with 2 tablespoons skim milk or slightly more if needed to bring the ricotta to a creamy consistency. Stir the ricotta into the spinach until combined. Correct seasonings.

6. In a shallow dish, soak 8 to 10 slices of bread in the milk until bread has absorbed the milk and is quite moist but not limp. (Work in batches, a few slices at a time, as you layer the ingredients as explained below. Also, note that white Italian bread is somewhat more fragile, once soaked, than whole wheat.)

7. Spoon a small amount of the tomato sauce in the bottom of a casserole. Arrange a layer of bread slices in the casserole, draining off excess milk as you do so. Put 8 to 10 more bread slices in milk to soak. Spoon the spinach mixture over the layer of bread. Top with the bread and scatter the onion-mushroom mixture over the bread. Top with half the slices of mozzarella cheese, partially covering the vegetables. Add a layer of bread and put the rest in to soak. Spoon most of the tomato sauce over the bread. Sprinkle with the herbs. Top with the remaining mozzarella. Finally, top with another layer of bread, arranging the slices neatly and spoon a thin layer of tomato sauce on top.

8. Beat the eggs and egg whites until well combined. Pour the egg mixture slowly over the casserole, poking the bread gently with a knife until the eggs have been absorbed. The amount of egg used can vary with the shape and depth of the casserole. The eggs should come up almost to the top layer of bread. Sprinkle the top with the parmesan and drizzle with the remaining 1½ teaspoons of olive oil. Let stand while you preheat the oven, to allow the eggs to soak into the bread.

9. Preheat the oven to 375°F.

10. Bake until the strata has set and is puffed and golden brown, usually about 50 minutes. Let stand for about 5 minutes, then cut into large wedges or squares and serve hot.

Veget

WHILE VEGETABLES MAY NOT BE the first thing we reach for when famished, put a serving of perfectly cooked and well-seasoned vegetables in front of us, and we'll scarf them down.

We now realize how fortunate we are that our mothers were (and are) good cooks. Marie was raised on steamed escarole in olive oil and Richard on fresh-picked Jersey corn on the cob. Coming from a childhood where vegetables were considered good food, we learned as adults and culinary students to respect and admire their simplicity.

ables

163

Vegetables are nature's gift to the busy cook. Throughout this chapter we use cooking techniques—roasting, stir-frying, steaming, and braising—that are fast and that bring out the natural flavor of the vegetable. We treat vegetables with a light hand and let their own fresh flavors shine through.

More and more research data indicate that a diet rich in vegetables (plus fruits, grains, and legumes) is not only healthful but could thwart obesity, prevent heart disease, and perhaps even hinder the growth of some types of cancer. The bottom line is that vegetables are an extremely important food for good health. So important that such agencies as the U.S. Department of Agriculture, the Department of Health and Human Services, and the National Cancer Institute, among others, have come forward to recommend that Americans eat three to five servings of vegetables every day. (The new food pyramid recommends five to nine servings of fruits and vegetables.)

Five vegetables a day sound like a lot, but it really isn't that big a deal. One serving can be as little as half a cup of a cooked vegetable, one potato, one cup of salad greens, one small carrot or half a stick of celery, or six ounces of vegetable juice (a small glassful). If counting cups and servings is a nuisance, the National Cancer Institute suggests what we think is an easy way to keep track. The institute suggests eating at least one fruit or vegetable high in vitamin A, one high in Vitamin C, one high in fiber, and one member of the cabbage family every day. We have grouped these vegetables and fruits into the easy-to-read chart on page 165.

how to eat five
to nine servings
of fruits and
vegetables daily

EAT 1 SERVING OF A VITAMIN-A RICH FOOD EVERY DAY bok choy, broccoli, kale, carrots, swiss chard, collards, mustard, beet, or turnip greens, red bell pepper, romaine lettuce, spinach, winter squash, sweet potatoes, and tomatoes. Apricot, cantaloupe, mango, and papaya are also rich in vitamin A.

EAT 1 SERVING OF A VITAMIN-C RICH FOOD EVERY DAY Asparagus, bok choy, broccoli, brussels sprouts, cabbage, cauliflower, green bell pepper, and tomatoes. Orange, grapefruit, kiwi, raspberries, strawberries, watermelon, cantaloupe, honeydew, papaya, and mango are also rich in vitamin C.

EAT 1 SERVING OF A FOOD HIGH IN FIBER EVERY DAY All fresh fruits and vegetables as well as dried peas and beans and dried fruit.

EAT 1 SERVING FROM THE CABBAGE FAMILY EVERY OTHER DAY Bok choy, broccoli, brussels sprouts, cabbage, cauliflower, kale, mustard, turnip, and beet greens, swiss chard, and watercress.

Asparagus and New Potatoes with Dill

Both these spring vegetables are usually boiled in water, a technique that works fine, but once you try them roasted, you'll never go back. Roasting seems to intensify the flavor of the asparagus. The potatoes get slightly browned, which adds a subtle sweetness. If dill is not available, use tarragon, basil, thyme, or a combination of other fresh herbs.

Makes 4 servings

1   pound small red or white new potatoes, scrubbed and halved or quartered
1   tablespoon extra virgin olive oil
¾   pound asparagus, trimmed and cut into 1-inch diagonal pieces
     Salt and freshly ground black pepper
2   tablespoons chopped dill

1. Heat the oven to 400°F.
2. Place the potatoes in a large roasting pan or baking dish, about 13 × 9 inches. Drizzle with olive oil and toss to coat.
3. Roast 20 minutes and turn with a spatula. Roast 20 minutes more, or until potatoes are beginning to brown. Add the asparagus, sprinkle with salt and pepper, and toss to combine.
4. Roast potatoes and asparagus together until vegetables are tender, 15 to 20 minutes. Sprinkle with dill and serve warm or at room temperature.

Eggplant, Red Bell Pepper, and Garlic

1 medium eggplant, trimmed, peeled, halved lengthwise, and cut into ½-inch slices (about 1 pound)

1 red bell pepper, quartered, seeds, stem, and white membranes removed

8 garlic cloves, peeled, stem end trimmed, and bruised lightly with side of knife

1 tablespoon extra virgin olive oil
Salt and freshly ground black pepper

2 tablespoons thinly slivered basil

2 teaspoons red wine vinegar, or to taste (optional)

1. Heat the oven to 400°F.

2. Place the eggplant, bell pepper, and garlic in a large roasting pan, drizzle with oil, sprinkle with salt and pepper, and stir to coat.

3. Roast vegetables until browned and tender, stirring often with a spatula, about 50 minutes. Move the garlic from the edges of the pan to the center to prevent overbrowning. Sprinkle with basil and add vinegar, if desired. Serve warm or at room temperature.

Brushing eggplant slices with a thin film of olive oil and roasting them is a terrific alternative to the old way of frying eggplant in lots of oil. We combine the eggplant with a compatible summer vegetable—red bell pepper—and lots of garlic.

Makes 4 servings

Onions and Jerusalem Artichokes with Sage

Onions are usually thought of more as a flavor enhancer than a main event. But whole roasted onions are something very special. As the onions cook, their natural sugars surface and the sharp raw onion is converted to a sweet and creamy consistency. In this recipe we mix three types of onions and roast them together with Jerusalem artichokes.

The Jerusalem artichoke is a member of the sunflower family. These knobby tubers are a good source of iron. If they are not available, prepare this dish with just onions.

M a k e s 6 s e r v i n g s

6   ounces shallots, peeled and trimmed (6)
¾   pound small white boiling onions, peeled and trimmed (8 to 10)
¾   pound small red boiling onions, peeled and trimmed (8 to 10)
1½   pounds Jerusalem artichokes, scrubbed and left whole
2   tablespoons extra virgin olive oil
1   tablespoon fresh sage leaves, cut into small pieces
     Salt and freshly ground black pepper

1. Heat the oven to 350°F.
2. Place the shallots, onions, and Jerusalem artichokes in a single layer in a large shallow baking dish. Drizzle with the oil and half the sage leaves. Cover with foil and bake 30 minutes.
3. Using a spatula, carefully turn the onions and artichokes over. Bake, uncovered, until browned and tender, 20 to 30 minutes more. Add the remaining sage and salt and pepper to taste. Serve immediately.

Sweet Potatoes with Mushrooms, Onion, and Thyme

2   large sweet potatoes, peeled and cut into
    1-inch cubes (about 1 pound)
1   large sweet onion, cut into ½-inch chunks (about ½ pound)
1   10- to 12-ounce package white button mushrooms,
    wiped clean, halved or quartered
2   tablespoons extra virgin olive oil
1   teaspoon fresh thyme leaves or ½ teaspoon dried thyme
    Salt and freshly ground black pepper

1. Heat the oven to 400°F.

2. Arrange the sweet potatoes, onion, and mushrooms in a large roasting pan or baking dish, about 13 × 9 inches. Drizzle evenly with olive oil, sprinkle with thyme, salt, and pepper, and stir to coat vegetables.

3. Roast vegetables until golden and tender, turning occasionally with a spatula, about 45 minutes. Serve immediately.

Roasting sweet potatoes with onions accentuates the natural sweetness of both. The mushrooms add an earthy, rounded flavor, making this dish perfect winter comfort food.

Makes 4 servings

beta-carotene and vitamin a

WHAT: Beta-carotene is a pigment found naturally in fruits and vegetables, especially those that are yellow-orange and dark green, such as apricots, cantaloupes, acorn squash, spinach, and sweet potatoes. It is converted into vitamin A in the body. The importance of beta-carotene was once obscured by vitamin A, but research now indicates that beta-carotene has antioxidant properties (along with vitamins C and E), which may protect against cancer.

WHERE: Each of the following fills the USRDA for beta-carotene:

◆ ½ cup cooked cubed acorn squash

◆ 1 medium carrot

◆ ½ cup cooked spinach

◆ 1 baked sweet potato

Spinach with Black Beans, Ginger, and Almonds

The joy of stir-frying is that it's so quick. And it leaves greens brightly colored, with their nutrients intact. Use a light hand with the almonds; although almonds are good for you, they are high in fat, like all nuts.

Makes 4 servings

Seasoning mixture

1   tablespoon dried fermented black beans (see Note)
2   tablespoons low-sodium soy sauce
1   teaspoon Chinese black vinegar or red wine vinegar
½   teaspoon oriental sesame oil, or to taste

1   tablespoon unblanched sliced almonds
1   tablespoon peanut oil
1   tablespoon minced fresh ginger
2   pounds spinach, long stems trimmed

1. Place the black beans in a small strainer and rinse under cold water. Drain on paper towels, then chop into smaller pieces. Combine the beans with the soy sauce, vinegar, and sesame oil in a small bowl. Set aside.

2. Heat a large heavy nonstick skillet over high heat until a drop of water evaporates on contact. Add the almonds and stir constantly until they are fragrant and the edges begin to turn golden, about 45 seconds. Transfer to a small plate. Set aside.

3. Add oil to skillet. When hot enough for a pinch of ginger to sizzle, add remaining ginger and stir-fry until fragrant, about 30 seconds.

4. Add spinach and stir-fry until leaves are limp and just tender, about 3 minutes. Drizzle with the black bean mixture and toss well. Serve immediately, sprinkled with the almonds.

Note: Dried fermented black beans, Chinese black vinegar, and oriental sesame oil are available in Asian markets.

Broccoli with Fried Shallots

1   bunch broccoli, washed
1   tablespoon olive oil
½   cup thinly sliced shallots
    Salt

1. Trim about 1 inch from the stems of the broccoli and discard. Cut tops into florets leaving about 1 inch of the stalks attached. Using a vegetable peeler, remove the tough outer layer from the remaining stalks, especially near the bottom. Cut the stalks into 2-inch lengths and then trim to ½-inch-thick sticks.

2. Place a steaming basket over 1 inch of boiling water and add the broccoli. Cover and cook until crisp tender, 6 to 8 minutes. Lift the basket from the saucepan.

3. Meanwhile, combine the oil and shallots in a medium nonstick skillet over medium-high heat. Cook, stirring, until shallots are well browned, about 5 minutes.

4. Add the broccoli and stir-fry 1 minute, just until blended. Sprinkle with salt and serve at once.

Broccoli might be considered the near-perfect vegetable. A half cup of steamed broccoli contains only 20 calories. It is low in sodium and is an excellent source of vitamins A and C, as well as calcium and potassium.

Makes 4 servings

Dry-fried Green Beans

As opposed to deep-frying, dry-frying requires very little oil. Organize the preparation of this dish so that the beans are parboiled and the seasonings measured out ahead of time. Then all you have to do at serving time is heat the oil, add the seasonings, and give the beans a quick toss over high heat.

**M a k e s   4
s e r v i n g s**

Salt
1 pound thin green beans, stem ends trimmed
2 teaspoons low-sodium soy sauce
2 teaspoons dry sherry
½ teaspoon sugar
½ teaspoon oriental sesame oil
1 tablespoon peanut or other vegetable oil
1 garlic clove, thinly sliced

1. Bring a large saucepan of water to a boil and add a pinch of salt. Add the beans and cook, uncovered, 5 minutes. Drain and rinse under running water. Spread beans out on a clean dish towel and pat dry.

2. Stir together the soy sauce, sherry, sugar, and sesame oil in a small bowl. Set aside.

3. Heat a large heavy nonstick skillet over high heat until hot enough to evaporate a drop of water upon contact. Add the oil and garlic and stir-fry just until garlic sizzles, about 30 seconds.

4. Gradually add the beans, a handful at a time, to the hot skillet. Stand back to avoid splatters. Stir-fry just until the beans begin to blister, about 3 minutes. Add the soy mixture and stir to coat, about 1 minute. Serve immediately.

Brussels Sprouts Leaves with Dry-roasted Peanuts

1   pint brussels sprouts, bottoms trimmed, quartered
¼   cup dry-roasted peanuts, coarsely chopped
¾   teaspoon oriental sesame oil
    Salt and freshly ground black pepper

1. Steam the brussels sprouts on a rack over about 1 inch of boiling salted water, covered tightly, until just tender but with a hint of crispness, 6 to 8 minutes. Rinse the sprouts under cold water and drain well.

2. Toast the peanuts in a dry large nonstick skillet over medium heat, tossing, until starting to brown, about 3 minutes. Add the sprouts, sesame oil, and a sprinkling of salt and pepper. Cook, tossing gently to combine the ingredients, until the sprouts are heated through, about 5 minutes. Serve immediately.

Brussels sprouts are available in supermarkets pretty much year round, but each fall we look forward to seeing entire stalks of the brussels sprouts plant at the farmers' market.

This recipe treats brussels sprouts as miniature cabbages; instead of being cooked whole, they are trimmed so that they break up into little cups as they cook, and stay bright green. Sesame oil gives the brussels sprouts a nice nutty taste and brings out the flavor of the peanuts.

Makes 4 servings

a guide to greens

TYPES OF GREENS

BEET GREENS Tender green leaves with fine purple veins. Preparation: Follow directions for chard. Cooking: Place 1 cup water in a large pot, bring to a boil, add the leaves, cover, and cook 10 minutes, or until tender. Very tender, young leaves can be steamed on a rack over boiling water just until limp, about 4 minutes. Tiny young beet leaves can be eaten raw, but full-size leaves should be boiled or braised.

CHARD Floppy large dark green or red leaves; mild, almost sweet flavor. Swiss chard has thick white stems. Preparation: Separate leaves from stems; cut up leaves. Cut stems into 1-inch lengths. Cooking: Place 1 cup water in a large pot; bring to a boil. Cook leaves until tender, 10 minutes. Add the stems, cover, and cook 4 minutes, then add the leaves.

COLLARD GREENS Dark green, tough, almost leathery leaves. Preparation: Cut or tear dark green leafy part away from the tough stems and center rib; discard stem and rib. Cut leaves into 1-inch pieces. Cooking: Place 2 cups water in a large pot and bring to a boil. Add the collards, cover, and cook over medium heat until tender, 15 to 20 minutes. Drain and season to taste.

DANDELION GREENS Long, slender, pointed leaves, with toothed edges; moderately sharp flavor. Follow guidelines for mustard greens.

ESCAROLE Pale green, sturdy leaves with wide ribs. Preparation: Trim and discard stem; separate head into leaves. Rinse well; drain and tear leaves into 1-inch pieces. Cooking: Follow directions for collard greens.

KALE Curly, blue-green leaves; mild, cabbagelike flavor. Preparation: Strip leaves from stems; tear leaves into 2-inch pieces. Cooking: Follow directions for collard greens. Tender leaves can be braised in a skillet in a small amount of broth or water.

MUSTARD GREENS Oval, frizzy-edged leaves, often bright green; peppery flavor. Smaller leaves are less bitter. Very young, tender leaves can be eaten raw. Preparation: Trim the long stems; cut leaves into 1-inch pieces. Cooking: Older mustard greens should be cooked by boiling or braising.

SORREL Long, delicate leaves; tart, sour flavor. Preparation: Strip stems from leaves and shred leaves. Cooking: Sauté sorrel in a nonstick skillet with a little butter.

SPINACH Dark green, tender leaves; sweet/mild but distinctive flavor. Preparation: Remove tough stems. Cooking: Small tender leaves can be cooked with the water that clings to the leaves in a dry pot. Or steam on a rack set over ½ inch of boiling water.

WASHING GREENS

Don't wash before storing—added moisture can cause decay.

Wash greens in at least 2 changes of water. Immerse greens in lukewarm water, then rinse in a colander with cold water. Repeat if needed.

An easy way to clean arugula, spinach, and other gritty greens is to place them in a salad spinner, fill with water, and swish the leaves around. Lift out basket, discard water, and rinse leaves. Repeat procedure several times.

SEASONING COOKED GREENS

Cooked greens need little more than a pinch of coarse salt and a grinding of black pepper, a drizzle of olive oil, and/or a splash of red wine or cider vinegar to season them. A squeeze of fresh lemon juice is also delicious.

NUTRITION

Dark green leafy greens are an excellent source of vitamin A, vitamin C, and calcium. Generally speaking, 2 pounds of fresh greens will serve 4 people.

Creamy Garlic Mashed Potatoes without Cream

No milk or cream and little or no butter—yet these mashed potatoes are creamy and intense with fresh potato flavor. The secret is to reserve the cooking water, and use it to lighten the mashed potatoes. Instead of mashing a big lump of butter into the potatoes, we melt a small pat (about a teaspoon) on top of each serving. This small pool of pure melted butter gives instant gratification.

Makes 4 servings

4 russet (baking) potatoes, peeled and cut into chunks
2 garlic cloves
   Salt and freshly ground black pepper
   Freshly grated nutmeg (optional)
4 teaspoons cold butter

1. Place the potatoes and garlic into water to cover in a saucepan. Bring to a boil, covered, add salt, reduce heat and simmer, covered, until the potatoes are very tender, about 30 minutes.

2. Drain the potatoes well, reserving cooking liquid. Pass the mixture through a food mill or with a large wooden spoon, press it through a coarse strainer back into the pan over low heat. Gradually add ½ to 1 cup reserved liquid, or enough to make a creamy consistency. Season with salt, pepper, and nutmeg, if using. Serve piping hot with a thin slice of butter on top of each serving.

Pureed Potatoes with Celery Root

1½ to 1¾ pounds whole celery root, peeled, washed, quartered, and sliced thin
1 bay leaf
1 garlic clove
½ teaspoon salt
1 pound all-purpose potatoes, peeled, quartered, and sliced thin
Freshly grated nutmeg
1 tablespoon extra virgin olive oil (optional)

1. In a large saucepan combine the celery root, bay leaf, and garlic, add enough water to cover the celery root by 2 inches, and add salt. Bring to a boil, reduce heat, cover, and simmer over medium heat until the celery root is almost tender, about 15 minutes.

2. Add the potatoes. Cover and cook until potatoes and celery root are very tender, 15 to 20 minutes. Drain vegetables, reserving about 1 cup of the cooking water. Remove and discard the bay leaf.

3. Pass the vegetables through a food mill. Add small amounts of the reserved cooking water as needed to keep vegetables moist. Add grated nutmeg to taste. Stir the pureed vegetables and add more cooking water for desired consistency. Drizzle the olive oil over the surface, if using.

Celery root, sometimes called celeriac, is about the size of a softball, gnarled and ugly. It has an intense but mellow celery flavor. Puree it with potatoes; it's a haunting combination.

Makes 4 servings

One-Step Browned New Potatoes

These potato wedges cook in shallow water until tender. Once the water boils away, the potatoes brown in the pan until golden.

M a k e s   4   s e r v i n g s

2   pounds red new potatoes, scrubbed and quartered lengthwise, or cut into 6 wedges if large
1½   tablespoons olive oil
2   garlic cloves, crushed
   Salt
   Freshly ground black pepper
   Chopped fresh parsley or rosemary (optional)

1. Place the potatoes in a wide heavy nonstick skillet. Add enough cold water to come about two-thirds of the way up the potatoes. Add the olive oil, garlic, and salt to taste. Bring the water to a boil.

2. Adjust the heat to maintain a steady boil. Cook, uncovered, until the water has evaporated, 15 to 18 minutes. Turn the potatoes over with a slotted spoon 2 or 3 times as they cook.

3. When the liquid has evaporated, raise the heat slightly to medium-high. Sauté the potatoes, tossing them frequently or turning with tongs, until golden and crusty, 7 to 10 minutes longer. Remove the garlic, season with pepper, parsley, if using, and more salt, if needed.

Oven-fried Potatoes

4   long russet (baking) potatoes or sweet potatoes,
     scrubbed and patted dry (about 2 pounds)
2   tablespoons vegetable oil
     Coarse (kosher) salt and freshly ground black pepper
¼   cup (packed) parsley leaves, chopped fine (optional)
1   garlic clove, minced (optional)

1. Heat the oven to 425°F.

2. Cut the potatoes into long wedges, rinse with cold water, and drain. Spread on a double thickness of paper towels, top with another double layer of paper towels, and press to dry thoroughly.

3. Place the potatoes in a bowl, add the oil, and toss to coat evenly. Spread in a single layer on a large heavy nonstick baking sheet or jelly-roll pan.

4. Bake 20 minutes. Remove pan from oven and carefully turn and rearrange potatoes. Sprinkle with salt and pepper. Bake 15 to 20 minutes longer, or until golden, turning the baking sheet once to ensure even browning. While hot, sprinkle with more salt, parsley and garlic, if using.

American-style fried potatoes and classic french fries are deep-fried, sometimes twice, in beef fat, lard, or oil. Here, we cut the fat down to only two tablespoons for four large potatoes. This oven version has been adapted for scrubbed russet or sweet potatoes. The potatoes are turned often as they cook, so all sides brown evenly. It takes a while, but it's time well spent.

Makes 4 servings

Grilled Sweet Potato Slices

Like many other Americans, for years we ate sweet potatoes only on Thanksgiving and other holidays. Sweet potato slices can be baked as well as grilled.

Makes 4 servings

3   or 4 sweet potatoes, peeled and cut into ¼-inch slices (1½ to 2 pounds)
1   tablespoon olive oil
     Salt

1. Place the sweet potato slices in a large bowl and drizzle with the olive oil. Toss to coat evenly.

2. Arrange the slices in a grill basket or place on a fine mesh sheet designed to keep small pieces of grilled foods from falling into the fire. Grill until browned on 1 side, turn, and grill the other side until potatoes are tender. It will take 20 to 25 minutes total cooking time, depending on the heat of the fire. Sprinkle with salt and serve.

Variation: Heat the oven to 400°F. Spread the potatoes in a single layer on a heavy nonstick baking sheet. Bake until browned on 1 side, about 15 minutes. Using a spatula, carefully turn the potatoes over and bake the other side until browned and potatoes are tender, about 10 minutes.

Braised Romaine with Red Wine Vinegar

1   large head romaine lettuce (about 2 pounds)
½   garlic clove
1   tablespoon olive oil
2   teaspoons red wine vinegar, or more to taste
    Pinch of salt
    Freshly ground black pepper

1. Pull the dark green outside leaves from the romaine, leaving the pale green heart intact. Reserve the heart for a salad. Stack the outer leaves in manageable bundles. Starting at the stem end, cut leaves crosswise 1 inch wide. Gradually increase the width to about 2 inches at the tips. Wash in plenty of cool water. Place in a colander and drain. You should have about 12 cups of packed greens.

2. Place the romaine in a large heavy saucepan, with just the water that clings to the leaves. Cover and cook over medium-high heat until leaves have cooked down, about 5 minutes. Stir. Continue to cook, covered, until leaves are tender, stems are crisp-tender, and some of the liquid in the bottom of the pan has cooked down slightly, 2 or 3 minutes longer.

3. Rub a serving bowl with the cut side of the garlic, then discard it. Add olive oil, vinegar, salt, and pepper, whisking to blend. Transfer the romaine to a serving bowl, toss, and serve immediately. This is also good at room temperature.

This dish is made with cooked romaine lettuce, a green usually seen only in salads. Since only the dark outer leaves are used, the pale heart can be saved for a salad at another meal. The dish is especially good with broiled or baked fish. Escarole can be cooked the same way.

Makes 4 servings

Greens with Garlic and Hot Pepper Oil

This quick method works with just about any kind of greens—spinach, esca-role, chicory, kale, col-lards, beet greens, even outer romaine lettuce leaves. Adjust the amount of hot red pepper flakes to taste.

Makes 4 servings

2 pounds spinach or other greens, stems and thick ribs trimmed, leaves cut crosswise into bite-size pieces, washed
1 tablespoon olive oil
1 garlic clove, cut into thin slivers
¼ to ½ teaspoon crushed red pepper
Salt

1. If using spinach, place in large heavy saucepan with just the water that clings to leaves. For other tougher greens, bring 2 cups water to a boil and then add greens. Cover and cook over medium-high heat, stirring leaves once or twice, until leaves are wilted and tender. Spinach will take only 2 or 3 minutes; other greens will take up to 15 minutes. Drain off excess liquid.

2. Meanwhile, place olive oil, garlic, and red pepper in a small skillet. Heat over low heat, stirring, just until the garlic begins to sizzle. Remove from heat and set aside.

3. When the greens are cooked, remove from saucepan with tongs, drain off excess water, and transfer to a serving bowl. Add the reserved oil and salt to taste. Toss and serve immediately.

Kale with Potatoes and Bacon

1 pound kale, trimmed, stems removed

Salt

1 pound russet (baking) potatoes, peeled and cubed (½ inch)

1 thin slice bacon

½ cup chopped onion

2 teaspoons vegetable oil

Freshly ground black pepper

1. Heat 2 cups water in a large pot, add kale and a pinch of salt, and boil, covered, stirring occasionally, until tender, about 15 minutes. Drain and cool slightly. Squeeze the excess liquid from the kale and finely chop it. Set aside.

2. Meanwhile, cook the potatoes in boiling salted water to cover until tender, about 15 minutes. Drain and set aside.

3. Fry the bacon in a heavy nonstick skillet over medium heat until crisp. Remove bacon and drain on a paper towel; discard drippings. Crumble the bacon and set aside. Add the onion and oil to the skillet and cook until tender, about 5 minutes.

4. Add the potatoes to the skillet. Stir to blend over low heat, breaking the potatoes into small pieces with a wooden spoon or spatula. Add the kale and stir to blend. Add salt and pepper to taste. Sprinkle with crumbled bacon before serving.

This makes a hearty side dish with roasted meats; it's also suitable as a main dish for a light meal. Notice how just a single slice of bacon imparts a subtle smoky flavor without loading up on fat and calories.

Makes 6 servings

Mom's Baked Stuffed Artichokes

Some families ate canned peas; Marie's family ate artichokes. Often they were simply steamed until tender and then served plain with little bowls of oil and vinegar for dipping the leaves before eating. Or they were baked. First the artichokes were simmered until almost tender, then drained and the chokes removed. Seasoned crumbs (homemade from yesterday's bread) were stuffed down between the leaves and the artichokes were baked until the crumbs were browned.

Makes 4 servings

4	medium artichokes
	Juice of 1 lemon

Bread stuffing

2	tablespoons chopped onion
2	tablespoons extra virgin olive oil
1	garlic clove, finely chopped
1½	cups coarse bread crumbs made from day-old Italian bread (see Note)
½	cup grated Parmigiano-Reggiano
2	tablespoons chopped flat-leaf parsley
1	tablespoon minced prosciutto or salami (optional)
	Salt and freshly ground black pepper

1. Use a large knife to cut artichoke stem flush with the base. Pull off small leaves from around base. Using scissors, trim off the prickly tips of the leaves. Lay artichoke on its side and use the knife to slice off the tip of the artichoke about ¹/₂ inch down. Rub cut edges with lemon to prevent darkening.

2. Fill a wide saucepan halfway with water and bring to a boil. Add the artichokes and cook, covered, over medium heat, until tender, about 45 minutes or longer. A leaf should pull out easily when done. Lift from water with a slotted spoon and invert on a folded kitchen towel. Drain until cool enough to handle. To remove the choke, spread the leaves and reach down into the center. Pull out the purple tipped leaves. Using the tip of a teaspoon, scoop out the fuzzy part from the heart.

3. Combine the onion and 1 tablespoon of the oil in a medium skillet. Cook, stirring, over medium-low heat, until onion is sizzling, about 5 minutes. Add the garlic and crumbs and cook, stirring, until they are lightly browned, about 3 minutes.

184

Transfer to a bowl and add the cheese, parsley, prosciutto, if using, and salt and pepper to taste.

4. Heat the oven to 350°F. Arrange the artichokes, cut side up, in a baking dish. Spread the leaves at even intervals and stuff the bread crumbs between the leaves. Drizzle the remaining olive oil evenly over the tops of the stuffed artichokes.

5. Bake, uncovered, until the crumbs are browned, about 25 minutes. Serve warm or at room temperature.

Note: To make coarse bread crumbs, cut the tough crusts from day-old bread. Cut the center part into medium dice (¼ to ½ inch). Process in a food processor until coarse crumbs form. If the bread is very dry and hard, grate it by hand on the coarse holes of a four-sided grater.

taking a new look at vitamin c

Vitamin C is getting more attention now than ever since scientists are looking at its antioxidant properties, which may protect the body against cancer.

Each of the following fills the USRDA for vitamin C:

◆ 6 ounces grapefruit juice

◆ 1 kiwifruit

◆ 1 orange

◆ ½ cup chopped red bell pepper

One cup of broccoli, brussels sprouts, cauliflower, or kohlrabi contains as much or more vitamin C as an orange.

Oven-roasted Asparagus with Parmesan Curls

This easy method comes courtesy of old friends Johanne Killeen and George Germon of Al Forno restaurant in Providence, Rhode Island. You could omit the cheese and instead sprinkle the asparagus with a teaspoonful of fresh thyme leaves stripped from the stems.

Makes 4 servings

1¼ pounds asparagus, trimmed and rinsed
1 tablespoon extra virgin olive oil
   Freshly ground black pepper
6 curls Parmigiano-Reggiano, shaved from a wedge with a vegetable peeler or cheese server

1. Heat the oven to 500°F.

2. Spread the asparagus in a shallow 13 × 9-inch baking dish. Drizzle with the oil and sprinkle with pepper to taste.

3. Bake until crisp-tender, about 8 to 10 minutes for thin asparagus, stirring once halfway through the baking time. Remove dish from oven and arrange curls of cheese on top of the asparagus. Place back in the oven and bake until the cheese melts, 3 to 4 minutes. Serve immediately.

Baked Beets with Balsamic Vinegar

4   medium-size fresh beets, tops trimmed to within
    ½-inch, scrubbed
¼   cup balsamic vinegar, or more as needed
    Salt and freshly ground black pepper

1. Heat the oven to 400°F.

2. Place each beet on a square of aluminum foil and wrap tightly. Place the beets on a baking sheet.

3. Bake until the beets are tender when pierced with a wooden toothpick or the tip of a paring knife, usually 1 to 1½ hours. Poke holes in the foil to let steam escape and carefully unwrap. When the beets are cool enough to handle, slip off the skins.

4. Slice the beets and place them in a bowl. Add the vinegar and salt and pepper to taste. Toss to combine, adding a little more vinegar if needed to moisten. Let stand at least 15 minutes before serving. Serve at room temperature.

Baked this way, beets become incredibly sweet. They take time, so bake them when you have the oven going for something else.

Makes 4 servings

Savoy Cabbage Agrodolce

Agrodolce *in Italian means sweet and sour, and is usually prepared with sugar and vinegar and often with raisins and pine nuts as well. The cabbage is roasted with a few strips of orange zest for added flavor. This dish is excellent with grilled fish, especially salmon, swordfish, halibut, or cod. Use regular cabbage if the crinkly savoy is not available.*

Makes 4 servings

1 small head savoy cabbage, outer leaves trimmed, halved, cored, and cut into ¾-inch squares (about 6 cups)
1 large sweet onion, halved lengthwise and cut into ¾-inch squares
2 strips orange zest
1 tablespoon extra virgin olive oil
  Salt and freshly ground black pepper
3 tablespoons apple cider vinegar
2 teaspoons sugar

1. Heat the oven to 400°F.

2. Combine the cabbage, onion, and orange zest in a shallow 13 × 9-inch baking dish. Drizzle with olive oil and sprinkle with salt and pepper. Stir to blend.

3. Cover dish tightly with aluminum foil and bake 20 minutes. Remove from the oven and stir thoroughly. Replace foil and bake until cabbage is very tender and lightly browned at the edges, 10 to 15 minutes longer.

4. Uncover, turning foil away from you, and drizzle with vinegar and sprinkle with sugar while still piping hot. Serve hot.

Honey and Lemon-glazed Carrots

1   pound carrots, cut diagonally into ¾-inch lengths

1   strip lemon zest

1   tablespoon honey

    Ground cumin (optional)

¼   teaspoon salt, or as needed

    Juice of 1 lemon

    Freshly ground black pepper

1   tablespoon finely chopped flat-leaf parsley or

    1 teaspoon thyme leaves, stripped from stems

1. Place carrots, lemon zest, honey, pinch of cumin, if using, and salt in a medium skillet. Add enough cold water to not quite cover the carrots. Bring to a boil.

2. Boil, uncovered, over medium-high heat, stirring occasionally, until carrots are tender but not mushy and liquid has nearly evaporated, about 15 minutes.

3. Lower heat and toss the carrots gently until coated with a light glaze. Season with lemon juice, pepper, and more salt, if needed. Add parsley. Serve hot.

Mothers used to say, "Eat your carrots; they'll make your eyes bright." Today, we're finding out that there are scientific reasons behind much of the folk wisdom of the past. The beta-carotene in carrots is being studied for its cancer-preventing properties. Fortunately, carrots are easy to like. In this recipe the natural sweetness of carrots is intensified with honey. A squeeze of lemon at the end offsets it.

Makes 4 servings

Cauliflower with Indian Spices

Heating spices brings out their flavor in unexpected ways. In this recipe, the curry powder and cumin seeds are heated in oil for the sauce. This is definitely a dish for curry fans. Serve it as a side dish or spooned over rice as a main course.

Makes 6 servings

1	head cauliflower, broken into florets
1	carrot, sliced thin on the diagonal
¾	cup lowfat yogurt, at room temperature
1	tablespoon all-purpose flour
1	tablespoon vegetable oil
½	teaspoon cumin seeds
2	teaspoons curry powder, or more to taste
½	cup chopped onion
1	garlic clove, finely chopped
	Salt
	Cayenne
2	tablespoons chopped fresh cilantro (optional)

1. Steam the cauliflower and carrot on a rack over about 1 inch of boiling water, covered, until tender, about 6 minutes. Lift basket from pan and set aside.

2. Combine the yogurt and flour in a small bowl, stirring to blend. Set aside. Combine the oil and cumin seeds in a large nonstick skillet over medium heat. Heat, stirring, until the cumin sizzles, stir in the curry powder, and heat for 20 seconds. Add the onion and garlic. Cook, stirring, over low heat until the onion is tender, about 5 minutes. Remove from heat and gradually stir in the yogurt mixture.

3. Add the cauliflower and carrot and stir over low heat until warmed. Season with salt and cayenne to taste. Add cilantro, if using.

Baked Fennel with Melted Parmigiano-Reggiano

2 large fennel bulbs

¼ cup Chicken Broth (page 42) or reduced-sodium canned chicken broth, fat skimmed

8 thin curls or slivers Parmigiano-Reggiano, shaved from a room-temperature wedge with a vegetable peeler or a cheese server

Freshly ground black pepper

1. Trim the base of the fennel bulb. Cut across the top to remove the darker green portion of the ribs and the fernlike tops. Cut the fennel lengthwise into quarters. Place it in a large bowl and cover with water and ice. Let stand 30 minutes before cooking.

2. Heat oven to 400°F.

3. Drain the fennel and arrange in a 10 × 8-inch or other shallow baking dish. Add the broth. Cover with foil and bake until fennel is tender when pierced with a fork, 30 to 35 minutes. Remove the foil.

4. Arrange the cheese evenly over the fennel. Bake until cheese melts, about 5 minutes. Add black pepper to taste.

Cooked fennel is soft and almost silky. Top baked fennel with slivers of imported Parmigiano-Reggiano and let the cheese melt.

Makes 4 servings

Oven-braised Leeks

Leeks are sometimes very sandy. Make sure to rinse them thoroughly in several changes of water. If they are large, partially slit them lengthwise so the rinse water can reach between the leaves to clean them thoroughly; this will also hasten the cooking. Rinsing in warm water helps to remove grit from between the layers.

Makes 4 servings

8   medium leeks, roots, green tops, and outside leaves trimmed, thoroughly rinsed in warm, then cold water
1   tablespoon olive oil or 2 tablespoons reduced-sodium canned chicken broth, fat skimmed
1   strip lemon zest
    Fresh thyme sprig or pinch dried thyme (optional)
    Salt and freshly ground pepper

1. Heat the oven to 350°F.

2. Arrange leeks in 1 layer in a shallow baking dish. Drizzle with the oil or broth. Add the lemon zest and thyme, if using.

3. Cover with foil and bake until the leeks are fork-tender, 25 to 30 minutes. Season with salt and pepper to taste. Serve warm as a side dish or serve chilled as a first course or a salad.

Baby Limas with Red Onion and Fresh Oregano

3   tablespoons finely chopped red onion

1   teaspoon olive oil

1   package (10 ounces) frozen baby lima beans, slightly thawed

⅓   cup reduced-sodium canned chicken broth, fat skimmed

2   fresh oregano sprigs or a pinch dried oregano
    Salt and freshly ground black pepper

1. Combine the onion and olive oil in a medium nonstick skillet. Heat, stirring, over low heat until onion is tender, about 5 minutes. Stir in the lima beans and the broth. Cook, covered, over low heat until beans are tender, 12 to 15 minutes.

2. Strip the oregano leaves from the stems, finely chop, and stir into the beans. Season with salt and pepper to taste. Serve at once.

Fresh lima beans are a treat, but they are devilish to shell, so we usually resort to the convenience of frozen limas. The quality is excellent. This light treatment brings out their flavor in minutes.

Makes 3 to 4 servings

wild mushrooms

Wild mushrooms can be found in specialty shops during the growing season.

CHANTERELLE Usually golden yellow and almost flowerlike in appearance, with an earthy, fruity flavor, almost nutty with a peppery bite. Available from midsummer through fall. Available dried.

MOREL Ranging in color from light tan to dark brown or black, with a long conical cap resembling an empty corncob and a slightly nutty, slightly earthy flavor. Both caps and stems are hollow and edible; if the morel is large, the stem might be tough. One of the first mushrooms to appear in the spring. Available dried.

Mushrooms with Garlic and Fresh Herbs

Quick and straightforward—use this method for any variety of mushroom or several types combined. Add oyster mushrooms or cremini (similar to the white button mushroom but with a brown cap), if available. Serve the mushrooms as a side dish, over sliced steak, over pasta, in a sandwich, or as an omelet filling.

Makes 4 servings

2   tablespoons olive oil
½   pound white button mushrooms, wiped clean and thickly sliced
6   ounces shiitake mushrooms, stems discarded, caps wiped clean and thickly sliced
    Salt and freshly ground black pepper
1   tablespoon minced garlic
2   tablespoons dry white wine
3   tablespoons chopped parsley
1   teaspoon fresh thyme leaves, stripped from the stems, or ½ teaspoon dried thyme

1. Heat the olive oil in a large nonstick skillet over medium-high heat. Add mushrooms and sprinkle with salt and pepper.

2. Sauté the mushrooms, tossing occasionally, for about 4 minutes. Add the garlic and continue to cook, tossing occasionally, until the mushrooms are tender, about 4 minutes longer. Add the wine, parsley, and thyme. Toss briefly and serve.

Twice-cooked Maple-glazed Pumpkin

1 medium sugar pumpkin (4 to 5 pounds)
2 tablespoons pure maple syrup

1. Cut off the top and bottom of the pumpkin. Quarter the pumpkin and scoop out the seeds and loosen pulp with a large spoon. Peel the pumpkin, cutting strips from top to bottom. Cut the pumpkin into 1½- to 2-inch chunks. You should have about 2½ pounds.

2. Steam pumpkin in a tightly covered steamer basket over simmering water until tender enough to pierce with a small knife, about 10 minutes. Transfer to a deep 2-quart casserole. Drizzle with the maple syrup; toss gently to coat.

3. Heat the oven to 375°F.

4. Bake pumpkin until hot and bubbly, 15 to 20 minutes, and serve.

Make this recipe with pumpkin or any other winter squash. We forgo the spices usually used to season hard squash (cinnamon, allspice, and nutmeg), but flavor it with maple syrup instead.

Makes 6 servings

cultivated exotic mushrooms

CREMINI A cultivated mushroom related to the white button, with a large dark brown cap, very flavorful.

ENOKI Clusters of long thin stems with tiny little caps on top of each. Because it is so delicate in texture and flavor, the enoki is best served raw in a salad or as a garnish or very lightly cooked in a stir-fried dish.

OYSTER (PLEUROTE) Delicate mushrooms with a softly ruffled cap resembling an oyster shell, although it's often argued that the name oyster is derived from its similarity in flavor to a real oyster. The entire mushroom is edible, raw or cooked. Available dried.

SHIITAKE The shiitake has a broad cap, spongy texture, and a woodsy, almost meaty flavor. Remove the tough stems and discard or reserve to flavor stock. Available dried.

Baked Tomatoes with Herb Crumb Topping

Don't peel the tomatoes here. The skins help the tomatoes keep their shape during baking.

Makes 4 servings

Extra virgin olive oil

1   garlic clove, bruised with the side of a knife

2   large ripe tomatoes, cored and halved crosswise
    Salt and freshly ground black pepper

4   basil leaves, torn into small pieces

⅔   cup coarse dry bread crumbs, made from
    day-old Italian bread

1   tablespoon minced oregano leaves

1   teaspoon thyme leaves, stripped from stem

1. Heat the oven to 400°F. Select a 9- or 10-inch pie plate or other small baking dish. Lightly brush with a thin film of olive oil and rub with the garlic. Set aside the garlic.

2. Arrange the tomatoes, cut side up, in the pie plate. Sprinkle lightly with salt and pepper and place pieces of torn basil on top of each. Drizzle each tomato with ½ teaspoon olive oil.

3. Crush the garlic through a press and combine with the bread crumbs, oregano, thyme, and 1 teaspoon olive oil in a small bowl and toss to coat. Carefully spoon the crumbs on each tomato, mounding slightly.

4. Bake until the crumbs brown, about 20 minutes. Serve warm or at room temperature.

Broiled Zucchini with Lemon and Mint

1 tablespoon olive oil

1 garlic clove, crushed

1 teaspoon grated lemon zest

4 medium zucchini, halved lengthwise

Salt and freshly ground black pepper

2 tablespoons chopped mint leaves

2 tablespoons finely chopped red onion

1. Heat the broiler.

2. Combine the olive oil, garlic, and lemon zest on a large serving platter. Add the zucchini and turn to coat, rubbing the oil mixture evenly over the zucchini. Place zucchini, cut side up, on a baking sheet or jelly-roll pan. Sprinkle with salt and pepper to taste. Set aside the platter without wiping it clean.

3. Broil close to the heat source, turning as needed, until the zucchini are lightly browned, 8 to 10 minutes, depending on the heat of the broiler. Remove from the broiler.

4. Transfer the zucchini to the platter and arrange browned side up. Sprinkle evenly with the mint and red onion. Serve warm or at room temperature.

Zucchini is plentiful, low in calories, easy to prepare, and, let's face it, very bland. In this recipe we use fresh mint, minced red onion, and lemon zest to give it a much-needed boost. When you use this broiler method, the zucchini emerges slightly crunchy.

Makes 4 servings

Vegetable Stew Provençale

A wonderful medley of late summer vegetables. Serve this warm or at room temperature as a side dish or on thick slices of toasted Italian bread as a vegetarian or light main course. Don't over-cook the vegetables—they should retain some crunch. If the skin of the eggplant seems tough, peel it. Otherwise, leave it on.

Makes 4 to 6 servings

2	tablespoons olive oil
1	garlic clove, minced
1	tablespoon tomato paste
2	small zucchini, cut into ½-inch cubes
½	pound ripe tomatoes, cored and cut into ½-inch cubes
1	cup sweet onion, cut into ½-inch cubes
1	red bell pepper, stems and seeds removed, cut into ½-inch squares
2	cups cubes (½ inch) eggplant (about ½ pound)
1	cup trimmed and quartered (½ inch) mushrooms
½	teaspoon salt, or to taste
	Freshly ground black pepper
¼	cup chopped flat-leaf parsley
¼	cup chopped basil
1	teaspoon fresh thyme leaves, stripped from stems, or ¼ teaspoon dried thyme, or to taste
½	teaspoon fresh rosemary leaves or pinch of dried rosemary, or to taste

1. Heat olive oil in a large skillet or wide shallow saucepan over low heat. Add garlic and sauté for 1 minute. Stir in the tomato paste.

2. Add the zucchini, tomatoes, onion, pepper, eggplant, and mushrooms and stir to blend. Cover and cook over low heat, stirring occasionally, until the vegetables are tender but not mushy, about 15 minutes.

3. Season the vegetable mixture with salt and pepper. Finely chop together the parsley, basil, thyme, and rosemary. Add to the vegetables. Cook over low heat, uncovered, until some of the juices evaporate, about 5 minutes. Taste and add additional herbs and/or seasonings. Serve warm or at room temperature.

ways to cook vegetables

STEAMING

It takes longer to steam than to boil vegetables, but more of the nutrients are retained. To steam, fit a deep skillet or a wide saucepan with a tight-fitting cover with a steamer, add 1 inch of water, and bring to a boil. Add the vegetable, cover, and cook. Not all vegetables steam well.

Suggested vegetables and times:

Asparagus, whole	4 to 6 minutes
½-inch diagonal slices	2 to 4 minutes
Broccoli, stalks	6 to 8 minutes
½-inch pieces	4 to 5 minutes
Carrots, ¼-inch slices	4 to 5 minutes
Cauliflower, 1-inch florets	5 minutes
Corn on the cob	6 to 8 minutes
Green beans (young and tender)	4 to 6 minutes
Spinach	2 minutes
Sugar snap peas	2 to 4 minutes
Snow peas	3 to 4 minutes
Acorn or other winter squash, 1-inch cubes	5 minutes

BOILING

Boiling is the fastest way to cook large quantities of vegetables. Unfortunately, boiling robs the vegetables of a lot of their nutrients. The only vegetables we recommend boiling are potatoes and mature green beans.

STIR-FRYING

This method is borrowed from Asian cultures where fuel for fires was—still is—in short supply so cooking had to be accomplished quickly. Woks are often used, but since they usually won't heat up sufficiently on home stoves (stir-frying calls for fierce heat), we use a large wide skillet with a nonstick surface.

ROASTING

Vegetables can be cooked in a small amount of fat (preferably extra virgin olive oil) in a hot oven. Because the heat is dry there is no problem with leaching out of nutrients or flavor. To roast vegetables, move the oven racks to the lowest level and set the oven temperature to 400°F to 450°F. Use a nonstick baking sheet or jelly-roll pan, a heavy baking dish, or a roasting pan. This is not a quick method—most oven-roasted vegetables (except asparagus) take at least 30 to 50 minutes to brown—but it is easy and gives great results.

BROILING AND/OR GRILLING

Many vegetables can be broiled or grilled until lightly browned and tender. Use a grilling basket or mesh grill cover so vegetables don't fall through the rack onto the fire. Remember to lightly brush the vegetables with extra virgin olive oil, turn vegetables frequently during cooking, and move vegetables around to ensure even cooking.

Suggested vegetables and times:

Shiitake mushroom caps	2 to 3 minutes per side
Small zucchini, split lengthwise	4 to 5 minutes per side
Small yellow squash, split lengthwise	4 to 5 minutes per side
Eggplant slices, ⅓ inch thick	4 to 5 minutes per side
Onion slices, ½ inch thick	4 to 5 minutes per side

| Quartered bell peppers | 5 to 6 minutes per side |
| Potato slices, ¼ inch thick | 6 to 7 minutes per side |

MICROWAVE

The microwave does a great job of cooking many vegetables, and of all the methods, microwave cooking preserves the most nutrients. "Baked" potatoes (both russet and sweet potatoes) are especially time saving, although the skin won't be crusty. For "baked" potatoes, wash the potatoes, pierce the skin twice with the tip of a knife, and place in the microwave. Two potatoes cook in 7 to 9 minutes; 4 potatoes in 12 to 13 minutes. Wrap in a cloth towel and let stand 5 minutes before serving.

For vegetables, place in a 10-inch glass pie plate or 2-quart microwavesafe casserole, add water, cover with a glass cover or vented plastic wrap, and cook. Let stand 2 to 3 minutes before serving to finish cooking.

Suggested vegetables and times:

Asparagus, 1 pound, trimmed and cut into 1-inch diagonals (¼ cup water)	4 to 5 minutes, stirring
Beets, 3 medium, trimmed and scrubbed (¼ cup water)	15 to 18 minutes
Broccoli, 1 bunch, thick stalks trimmed and cut into 1-inch florets (¼ cup water)	8 to 10 minutes
Corn on the cob, 4 ears, husks on, rinsed with cold water but not dried	5 to 6 minutes
Green beans, 1 pound, trimmed and cut into 1-inch pieces (½ cup water)	10 to 15 minutes

Bean &

PEOPLE MISTAKENLY THINK OF BEANS as time-consuming and bothersome to cook, prosaic and humble fare that is bland and uninteresting to eat. This is simply not true.

While dried beans do take time to soak and cook, they can be almost totally unattended. And if you cook a big batch, you can freeze some in small containers and have them ready in minutes for soups and pasta dishes, main dish stews, and more. In addition, rinsed and drained canned beans can be substituted for cooked dried beans in any of our recipes.

Popular throughout the Old World—the Mediterranean Basin, northern Africa, throughout the Middle East and into Asia—beans and grains are compatible with many flavorful ingredients: olive oil and garlic, curry and cumin, mint and other herbs, lemon, and dried fruits.

Grain

side dishes

The recipes in this chapter are all side dishes designed to round out a meal. Meatless main dishes appear in the next chapter, many of them based on the beans and grains, often in combination.

soaking dried beans

Not all dried beans have to be soaked. Lentils and split peas are never soaked before cooking. Gourmet or heirloom beans (also called "new crop") are usually not soaked before cooking.

To soak other dried beans, place beans in strainer and rinse with cold water. Sort and pick out any discolored beans. Use an overnight soak or a quick soak:

◆ Overnight soak: Place rinsed beans in a large bowl and add cold water to cover by 2 inches. Soak overnight in the refrigerator if your kitchen is very warm. The next day, drain, discarding the liquid, and cook according to the recipe.

◆ Quick soak: Place beans and water to cover by 2 inches in a large saucepan. Heat to boiling; turn heat to medium and simmer, uncovered, for 2 minutes. Cover and let stand for 1 hour. Drain and cook according to recipe.

Unless you are rushed, we recommend soaking beans overnight. The beans tend to retain their shape better and not split or crumble.

nonmeat

protein sources

1 cup (cooked)	Protein g	Calories	Fat g	Carbohydrates g	Fiber g
BEANS					
Black beans	15	225	1	41	7
Chick Peas	15	270	8	90	6
Lentils	16	215	1	38	8
RICE					
Brown Rice	5	230	1	50	5
White Rice	4	164	trace	50	1
Wild Rice	7	166	.6	35	.5
WHEAT					
Bulgur	6	152	.44	34	1
Couscous	3	260	2	55	7
Pasta	7	190	1	39	3
OTHER GRAINS					
Kasha	7	182	1	39	1
Millet	8	287	3	57	3
Quinoa	4	193	.7	44	6

White Lima Beans with Fresh Tomatoes and Basil

We used to cook dried beans on top of the stove in lots of liquid, but then we learned to bake them. Baking is a relatively mindless, labor-free method, for there is no stirring or other atten-tion required. Just place the beans in a baking dish, add seasonings and unsalted broth or water, cover, and bake. We've even baked beans this way without soaking them first. The beans needed about thirty min-utes more baking time, and the results were excellent.

Makes 6 servings

1½ cups dried medium or large white lima beans
1 bay leaf
1 leafy rib celery
1 garlic clove, bruised
2 to 3 cups water or unsalted Chicken Broth (page 42)
1 cup diced (½ inch) ripe tomatoes
¼ cup chopped basil leaves
1 tablespoon extra virgin olive oil
½ teaspoon salt, or more to taste
Freshly ground black pepper

1. Rinse the beans and soak them as described on page 204. Next day drain the beans, discarding the water.

2. Heat the oven to 350°F.

3. Place the beans in a casserole and add the bay leaf, celery, garlic, and enough water or broth to cover the beans. Cover and bake until the beans are tender and most of the liquid is absorbed, about 1½ hours. Cool slightly. As beans cook they will absorb most of the liquid.

4. Combine the tomatoes, basil, olive oil, and salt and pepper in a serving bowl. Add the beans and stir to blend. Taste and add more salt, if desired. Serve warm or at room temperature.

Baked Red and White Kidney Beans

1½ cups dried red kidney beans

1½ cups cannellini beans

3 cups unsalted Chicken Broth (page 42), or water

1 garlic clove, bruised

1 teaspoon crumbled dried sage, rosemary, oregano, or thyme

1 bay leaf

1 leafy rib celery

1 tablespoon extra virgin olive oil

   Salt and freshly ground black pepper

1. Rinse and sort the beans and soak them as described on page 204. Drain and place in a casserole with a lid.

2. Heat the oven to 350°F.

3. Add the broth, garlic, herb, bay leaf, and celery to the beans and stir to blend. Cover and bake until the beans are tender and most of the liquid has been absorbed, about 1½ hours. As mixture cools it will absorb much of the liquid. Drain off any excess.

4. Cool slightly and stir in the olive oil and salt and pepper to taste. Serve warm or at room temperature.

Baking beans in a slow oven produces a soft, almost creamy bean that still holds its shape. Be sure to use unsalted chicken broth because salt has a tendency to toughen the skins. This dish is also good with either all red or all white beans. You can vary the herb flavors to taste, but keep a light touch, especially when using strongly aromatic herbs like sage or rosemary.

Makes 8 servings

Black Beans with Red, Green, and Yellow Peppers

This is an example of how to put together a simple side dish quickly using canned black beans. We liven them up with three colors of bell peppers, tomatoes, and cilantro. The flavors are slightly Southwestern, but the appeal is universal.

Makes 4 servings

2 cups diced (¼ inch) red, yellow, and green bell pepper (½ each color pepper)

½ cup diced (¼ inch) onion

2 garlic cloves, chopped

1 tablespoon olive oil

1 tablespoon water

1 can (16 to 19 ounces) black beans, rinsed and drained

½ cup drained and diced canned plum tomatoes

Salt and freshly ground black pepper

2 tablespoons coarsely cut-up cilantro

1. Combine the peppers, onion, garlic, olive oil, and water in a large nonstick skillet. Cook, stirring, over medium heat until vegetables are crisp-tender, about 5 minutes.

2. Add the black beans and tomatoes. Simmer, uncovered, over low heat until the flavors are blended, about 5 minutes. Add salt and pepper to taste. Spoon into a serving dish and sprinkle with cilantro.

Chick Peas with Zucchini and Tomato

1½ cups diced (½ inch) onion

1 rib celery, diced (½ inch)

1 garlic clove, chopped

1 tablespoon olive oil

1 tablespoon water

1 can (19 ounces) chick peas, rinsed and drained

1 cup cut-up canned Italian plum tomatoes, with juice

¼ cup chopped flat-leaf parsley

1 tablespoon tomato paste

1 teaspoon fresh oregano or thyme leaves or a pinch of
   dried oregano or thyme
   Salt and freshly ground black pepper

2 small zucchini, diced (½ inch)

2 tablespoons chopped pitted green olives

1. Combine the onion, celery, garlic, olive oil, and water in a large nonstick skillet. Cook, stirring occasionally, over medium heat until the onion is tender, about 10 minutes.

2. Add the chick peas, tomatoes, parsley, tomato paste, oregano, and salt and pepper to taste. Cook, covered, 10 minutes. Stir in the zucchini and olives. Cover and cook until zucchini is tender, about 10 minutes. Taste and add more salt and pepper to taste. Serve hot, warm, or chilled.

Marie grew up eating a vegetable side dish of zucchini, onion, celery, and tomato cooked to an almost stewlike consistency that her mother and grandmother called ciambotta, *although, evidently, there are many dialect names and spellings for this dish throughout southern Italy. Marie re-created the dish from memory, adding chick peas and chopped green olives. It's almost hearty enough to be a meal. Serve it with white rice or orzo, the rice-shaped pasta.*

Makes 4 servings

Stir-fried Lentils with Ginger and Soy

Lentils are one of the few legumes that require no presoaking and that are quick cooking. Depending on the variety, age, and dryness, they can cook until firm-tender in as little as twenty minutes.

Makes 4 servings

1 cup brown lentils, rinsed and sorted

6 cups water

½ onion

1 bay leaf

1 slice (¼ inch thick) fresh ginger

1 tablespoon vegetable oil

2 garlic cloves, coarsely chopped

1 tablespoon chopped peeled fresh ginger

¼ cup diced red bell pepper

2 tablespoons thinly sliced scallion, white part only

2 tablespoons reduced-sodium soy sauce

2 tablespoons thinly sliced scallion tops

1. Combine the lentils, water, onion, bay leaf, and ginger slice in a large saucepan. Bring to a boil. Cook, uncovered, over medium heat, stirring occasionally, until the lentils are firm but tender, 15 to 20 minutes. Do not overcook. Drain. Discard the onion, bay leaf, and ginger.

2. Heat a large nonstick skillet over medium heat until hot enough to evaporate a drop of water upon contact. Add the oil, garlic, and chopped ginger and quickly stir-fry until garlic is tender but not browned, 1 minute. Add the red bell pepper and white part of scallion and stir-fry 1 minute.

3. Add the drained lentils and soy sauce. Toss the lentils to coat with soy sauce and to distribute the vegetables evenly. Spoon into a serving dish and sprinkle with scallion tops.

Pilaf with Currants and Cumin

2 teaspoons extra virgin olive oil
1 teaspoon cumin seed
1 cup long-grain basmati rice
1 tablespoon dried currants
2 cups water or 1 cup each water and Chicken Broth
(page 42)
½ teaspoon salt

1. Combine the olive oil and cumin seed in a large wide saucepan. Cook, stirring, over low heat until fragrant, about 1 minute. Stir in the rice and currants until coated. Add the water and salt. Bring to a boil, stirring once.

2. Cook, covered, over low heat until the water is absorbed and the rice is tender, about 18 minutes. Do not stir or uncover during cooking. Let stand, uncovered, for 5 minutes. Correct seasonings and serve hot.

While pilaf, made of long-grain rice, is of Persian origin, the dish is also found in Greek and Indian cooking. Long-grain rice grains elongate, so the rice in a pilaf is separate and dry.

Makes 4 servings

Pilaf with Sunflower Seeds and Raisins

Pilaf is a great way to gussy up rice. Start with a little oil and chopped onion, then add garlic and/or dried spices. Some of the spices typically used are cumin, curry, and turmeric. Often a cinnamon stick or whole cardamom pods are added as well. For sweetness, add a handful of raisins or currants. Add the nuts just before serving; they have a tendency to absorb moisture and lose their crunch when added sooner. Toasted sunflower seeds are nice as are toasted pistachios, walnuts, pine nuts, or almonds.

Makes 4 servings

1	tablespoon extra virgin olive oil
½	cup chopped onion
1	garlic clove, crushed
1	cup long-grain brown rice
⅓	cup raisins or currants
1	piece (1 inch) cinnamon stick
2½	cups water or reduced-sodium canned chicken broth, fat skimmed
	Salt
¼	cup sunflower seeds, preferably unsalted

1. Cook the oil and onion in a large wide saucepan until golden, about 5 minutes. Add the garlic and cook for 1 minute.

2. Stir in the rice, raisins, and cinnamon stick. Cook, stirring, until rice is coated with oil and begins to change color, about 2 minutes. Add the water or broth. Bring to a boil and stir once. Add salt if using water.

3. Cover and cook over low heat, until the water is absorbed and the rice is tender, 45 to 50 minutes. Do not lift cover or stir during cooking time. Just before serving, toast the sunflower seeds in a dry skillet for 1 minute. Sprinkle over the pilaf and serve.

Warm Couscous Salad

1½ cups Chicken Broth (page 42) or reduced-sodium
canned broth, fat skimmed
1 cup couscous
½ cup finely diced radishes
¼ cup thinly sliced scallion tops
1 ripe plum tomato, cored, seeded, and cut into small dice
1 tablespoon olive oil
Salt and freshly ground black pepper

1. Bring the broth to a boil. Place couscous in a medium bowl. Pour broth over couscous without stirring. Cover and let stand for 10 minutes.

2. Add the radishes, scallion tops, tomato, olive oil, and salt and pepper to taste. Fluff with a fork or chopstick. Serve warm.

Couscous is both a grain product and the name of a dish popular in Morocco and throughout North Africa. The product called couscous is made from semolina flour that has been moistened and then rubbed into tiny granules; it is steamed twice until soft and fluffy. The grain is steamed and then served with a savory stew, which may include fish, meat, or vegetables.

This recipe uses a quick method of simply soaking the couscous in boiling liquid to produce a starchy, pleasantly grainy texture. The calories, protein, and fat are all just a little higher than that of pasta.

Makes 4 servings

Kasha with Two Mushrooms

Kasha looks like a grain and tastes like a grain, but it's not. Kasha is toasted buckwheat groats and is a grass, related to rhubarb. Kasha has to be mixed with egg to keep the grains separate while cooking. We substitute an egg white for a whole egg, cutting a little fat and the cholesterol from the dish.

Makes 4 servings

1 tablespoon plus 1 teaspoon olive oil
1 large leek, halved and thinly sliced, white and pale green parts only
1 teaspoon dried thyme
½ pound white button mushrooms, thinly sliced
4 ounces fresh shiitake mushrooms, stems removed, caps thinly sliced
2 tablespoons dry white vermouth or white wine
   Salt and freshly ground black pepper
1 egg white
1 cup medium grain kasha
1 carrot, thinly sliced
2 cups Chicken Broth (page 42) or reduced-sodium canned broth, fat skimmed

1. Heat 1 teaspoon olive oil in a large heavy skillet, preferably nonstick, over medium heat. Add the leek and ½ teaspoon of the thyme and cook, stirring, until leek is tender, but not browned, about 5 minutes. Transfer to a side dish.

2. Add the remaining 1 tablespoon oil to the skillet and heat over medium heat. Add the button and shiitake mushrooms and the remaining thyme. Cook, stirring, over medium to medium-high heat, until mushrooms are tender and begin to brown, about 8 minutes. Stir in vermouth and cook, stirring, until evaporated. Season with salt and pepper to taste. Transfer to the side dish with the leeks. Wipe out the skillet.

3. Beat the egg white in a medium bowl and stir in the kasha until the grains are evenly coated. Heat the skillet over medium-low heat until hot. Add the kasha and stir until the grains are dry and separate. Add the carrot and the broth and bring to a boil. Cover and cook over low heat until the broth is absorbed, about 15 minutes.

4. Add the leek and mushroom mixture. Cover and heat through, about 3 minutes. Spoon into a shallow bowl, stir the mushrooms and leeks into the kasha, and serve.

grain
power

With all grains, buy carefully and check for an off odor, which indicates rancidity. Store them in tightly closed jars, other containers, or plastic bags.

BARLEY

DESCRIPTION: Pearled barley, readily available in supermarkets, undergoes a process much like polished rice. But even though the tough outer hull and germ are removed, barley is still a good lowfat source of fiber, iron, and protein. TASTE AND TEXTURE: Starchy with a mild flavor, slightly chewy. TO COOK: Cook 1 cup barley like pasta in a large pan of boiling salted water until tender, 45 to 55 minutes; drain. SERVING SUGGESTION: Use to thicken soup or stew. Makes a great salad tossed with vinaigrette and chopped fresh vegetables.

BULGUR

DESCRIPTION: Bulgur is wheat berries that have been partially cooked, then cracked. (Cracked wheat is similar except that the berries are cracked without precooking.) TASTE AND TEXTURE: A very nutty whole wheat taste. TO COOK: Stir 1 cup bulgur into 2 cups boiling salted liquid; let stand, covered, 10 to 20 minutes; drain. SERVING SUGGESTION: Serve at room temperature tossed with lemon juice, olive oil, chopped parsley and mint, and sliced scallions.

COUSCOUS

DESCRIPTION: A grain product rather than a grain, couscous is made by mixing semolina flour with salted water to make tiny pellets. Couscous is also the name of a popular Moroccan dish. TASTE AND TEXTURE: Pleasantly grainy with a pastalike taste. TO COOK: Moroccan-style couscous is steamed in a special cooker called a *couscousière.* Quick-cooking precooked couscous can be easily prepared by stirring 1 cup couscous into 1½ to 2 cups boiling water or broth. Let stand, covered, until the water is absorbed, about 10 minutes. Fluff with a fork. SERVING SUGGESTION: Substitute chicken broth for the water and top with a sprinkling of toasted pine nuts.

KASHA

DESCRIPTION: Kasha, or roasted buckwheat, is technically not a grain, but a grass. Sometimes kasha is tossed with an egg or egg white before cooking to keep the grains separate. TASTE AND TEXTURE: A nutty, toasted flavor. TO COOK: Sauté 1 cup kasha in 1 tablespoon olive oil in a hot skillet until toasted. Add 2 cups water or broth; cover and cook about 20 minutes. SERVING SUGGESTION: Add sautéed chopped mushroom, onion, and garlic. Top the dish with a sprinkling of toasted pecans.

MILLET

DESCRIPTION: Possibly the first grain to be cultivated, about 3000 B.C. It is shaped like a tiny bead the color of straw. TASTE AND TEXTURE: Nutty with a slightly sweet edge. TO COOK: Toast in a hot skillet before cooking. Stir 1 cup millet into 1½ to 2 cups water or broth and cook until tender, 20 to 30 minutes. SERVING SUGGESTION: Substitute for rice in soups, or cook as a pilaf.

QUINOA

DESCRIPTION: A high protein grain that originated with the Incas in the Andes. A tiny round seed, pale yellow in color. TASTE AND TEXTURE: Sweet and nutty, soft and slightly chewy. TO COOK: Toast lightly in a hot skillet. Add 2 cups salted water and cook until tender, 12 to 15 minutes. SERVING SUGGESTION: Add stir-fried vegetables to cooked quinoa. Serve with a splash of reduced sodium soy sauce or sprinkle hot cooked quinoa with grated parmesan before serving.

WHEAT KERNELS

DESCRIPTION: Wheat kernels, a.k.a. wheat berries, are unprocessed kernels of wheat.

TASTE AND TEXTURE: Soft wheat berries are small, reddish brown in color; hard wheat berries, including kamut and spelt, are long and golden. TO COOK: Soak overnight and drain. Cook 1 cup wheat kernels in 2 to 3 cups salted water over low heat until tender, about 1½ hours. Make a large batch and freeze leftovers in small portions for later use.

SERVING SUGGESTION: Add cooked wheat kernels to pilaf, salads, and bread doughs. Available in health food stores.

BROWN RICE

DESCRIPTION: Brown rice is unhulled rice, which can be short, medium, or long grain.

TASTE AND TEXTURE: The bran contributes a rich nutty flavor and chewiness to brown rice. Short grain brown rice, although slightly sticky from the high amount of starch, has an especially pleasing chewy texture and nutty taste. TO COOK: Cook 1 cup brown rice in 2½ cups boiling water until rice is tender and water is absorbed, about 45 minutes.

SERVING SUGGESTION: Cook rice with dried currants; top with toasted sunflower seeds before serving.

WHITE RICE

DESCRIPTION: Long-grain rice cooks separate and fluffy. Short-grain is soft and sticky and is also known as sushi rice. Medium-grain rice cooks moist and tender with a slight stickiness, and is used in Spanish paella and Italian risotto. TASTE AND TEXTURE: Depending on the variety, rice has a range of flavors from sweet to nutty. TO COOK: Stir 1 cup rice into 2 cups boiling salted water, reduce heat, cover, and cook until water is absorbed, about 15 minutes. Uncover and let stand 5 minutes before serving. SERVING SUGGESTION: Serve as you would pasta: Spoon onto a platter and top with your favorite "red" sauce. Sprinkle with grated Parmigiano-Reggiano. Or add bits of cooked vegetables and meats and make a quick stir-fry or pilaf.

WILD RICE

DESCRIPTION: Wild rice is actually an aquatic grass and most of what is sold today is cultivated, not wild. TASTE AND TEXTURE: Woodsy in taste with a pleasantly resistant texture. TO COOK: Cook 1 cup wild rice in 3 cups salted water until grain is split and tender, 30 to 50 minutes. Boil, uncovered, until excess liquid evaporates. Do not drain. SERVING SUGGESTION: Add to soups, use in salads, toss with sautéed mushrooms; makes excellent rice pudding.

Meat

main dishes

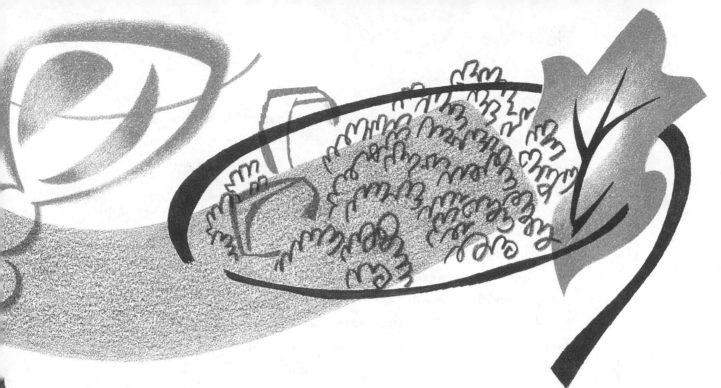

HOW TO GO ABOUT PREPARING meatless main dishes? Everyone knows we should eat less meat, but the idea of a meatless meal usually conjures up visions of plates of pallid steamed vegetables or an assortment of beans, rice, or other grains, none of which seems to add up to a meal.

less

But when you take a look at the peasant cuisines that have nourished people all over the world since time began, you see that they rely chiefly on grains and beans. Meat and fish are added in small amounts. In Asia, the staple is rice; in the Americas, it's often corn and beans; and in the Mediterranean, rice, pasta (from wheat), and beans.

Such grains offer a large amount of protein and fiber, with far less fat than protein from meat sources, and with no cholesterol. Beans and grains are also high in fiber. They are among the least expensive sources of protein, vitamins, minerals (such as calcium), and other nutrients.

In devising meals that don't depend on meat, the first trick is to rethink the plate. Move foods like beans, polenta, rice, and other grains, which are usually thought of as side dishes, over to the center. The American Institute for Cancer Research has a new program called "The New American Plate." Marilyn Gentry, the institute's president, says, "We want to help people think of fruits, vegetables, and grains as the focus of their meals, with that moderate-sized portion of meat, fish, or poultry as the side dish. It's an easy way to eat for good health."

Think of grains as a canvas, on which to paint any number of flavor schemes—fresh vegetable medleys, Italian-style tomato sauces, Indian spices, Thai- and Chinese-style stir-fries, and on and on. These dishes welcome exploration of ethnic influences from all over the world.

Another trick is to punch up the flavor. By combining carbohydrates with plenty of flavorful herbs and fresh vegetables, especially such flavorings as tomatoes, garlic, peppers, chilis, and citrus, you can concoct limitless possibilities for satisfying main courses.

If you don't want to keep dishes completely meatless, add small amounts of slivered cooked meat, poultry, or fish.

Serving complementary proteins in the same dish—combining two nonmeat proteins like rice and beans or pasta and beans—provides all the proteins we need, when either served on its own would not. Dishes like southern Italian *pasta e fagioli*, New Orleans red beans and rice, chick peas with couscous, and black beans with orzo are all good examples of this principle.

These complementary proteins don't even have to be eaten at the same meal for them to work. Rather, think of what you eat during a day or over a period of several days. Some quick and simple menus built around meatless main dishes can be found on the facing page.

meatless
meals

- Sweet Potatoes Topped with Black Bean Chili
- Tossed Green Salad
- Sourdough Bread
- Pears and Gorgonzola

- Chick Peas in Chunky Tomato Sauce over Couscous
- Arugula Salad
- Whole Wheat Italian Bread
- Sorbet or Ice Milk

- Baked Stuffed Poblano Chilies with Salsa
- Crisp Marinated Cucumbers
- Flour Tortillas
- Clementines Poached in Spiced Riesling Syrup

- Brown Rice Pilaf with Spinach, Parmesan, and White Beans
- Ripe Plum Tomato Salad
- Semolina Bread
- Fresh Berries

Barbara Tropp's Recipe
for a Quick Supper

Based on the favorite home supper of old friend Barbara Tropp (Barbara and Richard knew each other in high school in New Jersey, before food was a gleam in either's eye), here is a guide to putting together a healthy dinner in minutes. After feeding other people at her San Francisco restaurant, China Moon Café, this is what Barbara fixes for herself and her husband, Bart, for their own dinner at home.

Makes 2 servings

1	teaspoon vegetable oil
1	large garlic clove, minced
2½	cups cut-up fresh vegetables, such as 1 small red or yellow onion, slivered, 1 red or yellow bell pepper, slivered, 1 carrot, cut on the diagonal, 1 or 2 handfuls cut-up green beans, asparagus, or sugar snap peas, or regular peas
3	cups cooked rice or small pasta
2	teaspoons flavored oil (see Note)
2	scallions, trimmed and sliced thin on a sharp diagonal
1	tablespoon chopped parsley and/or other herbs (optional)
1	plum or small tomato, cored and diced or slivered (optional)
2	tablespoons freshly grated parmesan cheese (optional)
	Salt and freshly ground black pepper

1. Heat the oil in a large nonstick skillet or wok over medium-high heat. Add the garlic and heat, tossing, until fragrant, about 20 seconds. Add the firmer vegetables (onion, pepper, carrot) and cook, tossing, for 3 minutes.

2. Add the quicker-cooking vegetables (green beans, asparagus, peas), plus a spoonful or two of water. Cover and steam for 2 minutes. Uncover and add the rice or pasta. Lower the heat to medium and cook, stirring gently, to combine the ingredients and heat everything through, about 4 minutes. Stir in the oil, scallions, and parsley, tomato, and parmesan, if using. Add salt and pepper and correct the seasonings and serve immediately.

Note: You can use chili oil, basil oil, tomato oil, Szechuan pepper oil, or other herb oil.

Beans and Greens
with Slow-Cooked Garlic

1½   cups dried cannellini beans, soaked (page 204)

2   cups unsalted canned chicken broth plus 2 cups water or
    4 cups Chicken Broth (page 42)

1   bay leaf

1   small onion

1   carrot
    Salt

1   pound fresh broccoli rabe, swiss chard, chicory, or
    escarole, tough stems trimmed

¼   cup olive oil

6   garlic cloves, halved

¼   teaspoon crushed red pepper, or more to taste

1. Combine the beans, broth, bay leaf, onion, and carrot in a large saucepan and bring to a boil. Reduce the heat to low, cover, and cook until beans are tender but not mushy, 45 minutes to 1 hour. Remove the onion and discard. Slice the carrot and return to saucepan. Add salt to taste. *(The beans can be cooked up to 1 day ahead.)*

2. Shortly before serving, stir in the greens. Cook over medium heat, uncovered, stirring occasionally, until the greens are tender, about 20 to 25 minutes.

3. Meanwhile, heat the oil and garlic in a small heavy skillet over low heat, until garlic begins to sizzle. Cook, adjusting the heat so that the garlic simmers but does not brown, until garlic is very soft, about 10 minutes. Stir in the red pepper and cook 1 minute longer. Remove from the heat and mash garlic with a fork. Press the garlic mixture through a small sieve directly into the beans and stir to blend. Serve with additional red pepper, if desired.

A moist, soupy stew, full of flavor and packed with nutrients. Stewing the garlic slowly in olive oil before adding it to the beans mellows its flavor and lets its flavor permeate the oil, which then carries it through the dish.

Makes 4 servings

Black Beans with Saffron Orzo Primavera

Black beans are one of the best vegetable proteins around—one cup has twice the amount of protein as in a glass of milk. The meatiness of black beans makes them ideal for picking up assertive flavorings. In this dish the beans are combined with orzo—complementary proteins—brilliantly colored with saffron and fresh vegetables.

If you're soaking and cooking dried black beans, make a big batch, one and a half pounds or more. You can freeze the cooked beans in two-cup containers, and have them on hand for soups and main-course dishes like this.

Makes 6 servings

Black Beans
1 tablespoon olive oil
1 cup chopped onion
1 garlic clove, chopped
1 teaspoon ground cumin
3½ cups cooked dried black beans or 2 cans (19 ounces each) black beans, rinsed and drained
1 to 1½ cups unsalted or reduced-sodium canned chicken broth, fat skimmed

Saffron Orzo
2½ cups water
Generous pinch of saffron
½ teaspoon turmeric
Salt
1 cup orzo
1 cup coarsely chopped broccoli florets
1 cup diced (¼ inch) zucchini
1 cup sliced (¼ inch) green beans or asparagus
2 tablespoons olive oil
½ garlic clove, crushed
Freshly ground black pepper
¼ cup finely slivered mixed red and green bell peppers

1. Heat the olive oil in a large skillet, preferably nonstick, over medium-low heat. Add the onion and stir to coat with oil. Cover and cook, stirring once or twice, until the onion is very tender and golden, about 10 minutes.

2. Stir in the garlic and raise the heat to medium. Sauté, stirring, until the garlic is cooked, about 2 minutes. Add the cumin and toast, stirring, for 30 seconds. Add the beans and 1 cup of the broth. Cook over medium to medium-low heat, stirring often and crushing some of the beans with the back of a spoon, for 15 minutes. If necessary, add additional broth to keep the mixture moist and saucelike. Cover and keep the beans warm over low heat until ready to serve.

3. *Meanwhile, prepare the saffron orzo.* Bring the water to a boil in a medium saucepan. Stir in the saffron, cover, and remove from the heat. Let stand for 10 minutes. Uncover and bring the water back to a boil. Stir in the turmeric until dissolved. Add ¹/₂ teaspoon salt and the orzo and bring back to a boil. Reduce heat to medium-low and simmer, covered, until the liquid is absorbed, about 15 minutes. Uncover, remove from the heat, stir once, and let stand until ready to serve.

4. Bring water to a boil in a medium saucepan filled halfway. Stir in the broccoli, zucchini, and green beans and boil until tender, about 3 minutes. Drain immediately. Transfer to a large serving bowl and add the 2 tablespoons of olive oil, the crushed garlic, ¹/₄ teaspoon salt, and a generous grinding of black pepper. Toss to blend. Add the orzo and stir gently just to blend.

5. To serve, rewarm the beans if necessary. Mound the orzo and vegetable mixture into the center of 6 dinner plates, dividing it evenly. Make an indentation in the center of each serving of orzo. Add a spoonful of the black beans, garnish with the pepper slivers, and serve at once.

Sweet Potatoes Topped with Black Bean Chili

Chili makes a good topping for vitamin-rich sweet potatoes. The black beans look great on the bright orange sweet potatoes, and the taste is right. The trick of using chipotle chilies to add flavor to a meatless chili was devised by cookbook author Deborah Madison when she was the chef at Greens, the vegetarian restaurant run by the San Francisco Zen Center. It has since been widely copied.

Makes 4 servings

4	large sweet potatoes, scrubbed (about 2½ pounds)
1	tablespoon olive oil
1½	cups chopped onion
1	cup diced (¼ inch) green pepper
1	cup diced (¼ inch) carrot
1	tablespoon finely chopped garlic
1	tablespoon chili powder
1	teaspoon ground cumin
1	can (14½ ounces) Italian-style plum tomatoes, with juice, pressed through a sieve or food mill
½	cup water
1	can (19 ounces) black beans, rinsed and drained, or 2 cups cooked dried black beans
¼	teaspoon dried oregano
	Salt
1	cup diced yellow squash
1	cup diced zucchini
1½	teaspoons chopped chipotle chilies, or 1 tablespoon minced seeded jalapeño, or to taste
4	lime wedges
	Nonfat yogurt, for serving
	Coarsely chopped cilantro, for serving

1. Preheat the oven to 400°F.

2. Pierce the potatoes with the tines of a fork and bake them until tender, about 1 hour.

3. Meanwhile, heat the olive oil in a large nonstick skillet over medium heat. Add the onion, green pepper, and carrot and cook, stirring, until the vegetables are golden, about 10 minutes. Add the garlic and cook, stirring, for 2 minutes longer.

Stir in the chili powder and cumin until blended. Add the tomatoes, water, black beans, and oregano and heat to a simmer. Reduce heat and simmer, covered, over low heat for 20 minutes. Season with salt to taste.

4. Just before serving, add the yellow squash, zucchini, and chipotle. Cover and simmer until the vegetables are crisp-tender, about 5 minutes.

5. To serve, split the sweet potatoes and mash their pulp slightly. Spoon the chili into the center. Add a squeeze of lime juice. Top with yogurt and a sprinkling of chopped cilantro.

a guide to fresh chili peppers

Here are a few of the most commonly found chili varieties:

ANAHEIM Bright green, about 7 inches long. Mildly hot. Used fresh for stuffing.

HABANERO Green or red, small and lantern shaped. Explosively hot.

JALAPEÑO Medium to dark green, red when ripe, about 2 inches long. Hot. Remove veins and seeds to reduce pungency. Smoked and dried jalapeños are called chipotles.

POBLANO Dark green, wide and tapering, about 5 inches long. Excellent for stuffing. Mild to mildly hot. Dried poblanos are called anchos.

SERRANO Dark green, smaller and thinner—and hotter—than jalapeños.

Burritos with Pinto Beans and Cheese

Southwestern food, influenced by the cooking of Mexico, is based on corn or wheat tortillas with beans. Any one of the infinite variations on the tortilla and bean theme—tacos, enchiladas, burritos, tostadas—is an excellent choice for a meatless meal. If you load up the dish with grated cheese, sour cream, and meat, however, it quickly becomes heavy. This lowfat burrito has plenty of flavor with little fat.

Makes 2 servings

Pinto beans

1   teaspoon olive oil
½   cup chopped onion
1   garlic clove, minced
1   can (19 ounces) pinto beans, rinsed and drained, or 2 cups cooked dried pinto or pink beans
    Dash of hot pepper sauce

Salsa

½   cup diced (¼ inch) plum tomatoes
¼   cup chopped, peeled, and seeded cucumber
2   tablespoons chopped red onion
1   tablespoon chopped cilantro
1   teaspoon finely chopped seeded fresh chili pepper
    Salt

4   (10-inch) flour tortillas
4   ounces shredded jack cheese

1. Heat the oil in a nonstick skillet. Add the onion, cover, and cook over medium-low heat, stirring occasionally, until the onion is tender and golden, about 5 minutes. Stir in the garlic and sauté, uncovered, for 1 minute. Add the beans and stir to coat. Cook, stirring, until heated through, about 3 minutes. Add a dash of hot pepper sauce and set aside.

2. Combine the tomatoes, cucumber, red onion, cilantro, chili, and a pinch of salt in a small bowl. Set aside.

3. Heat the oven to 350°F. Wrap the tortillas in foil and place in the oven until heated through, about 5 minutes.

4. Place a spoonful of beans down the center of each tortilla. Add a spoonful of salsa. Wrap the tortilla around filling and place in shallow baking dish. Sprinkle with cheese. Cover with foil and bake for 10 minutes. Serve warm.

Vegetarian Chili with Chipotle Chilies

1	tablespoon olive oil
1	cup chopped carrot
1	cup chopped red bell pepper
1	cup chopped green bell pepper
1	cup chopped onion
2	garlic cloves, finely chopped
1½	teaspoons chili powder
1	teaspoon ground cumin
3	cups chopped cored ripe tomatoes or 1 can (28 ounces) plum tomatoes, with juice
1	cup tomato juice, or as needed
2	tablespoons chopped canned chipotle chilies, or to taste
1	can (16 ounces) red kidney beans, rinsed and drained
1	can (16 ounces) cannellini, rinsed and drained
1	can (16 ounces) black beans, rinsed and drained
	Salt to taste
1	cup finely shredded iceberg lettuce
1	cup nonfat yogurt

This easy recipe, based on three colors of canned beans, is a big batch, but leftovers make a delicious quick meal. Chipotle chilies are dried smoked jalapeños. They are available canned.

Makes 8 servings

1. Heat the oil in a large heavy saucepan over medium-low heat. Add the carrot, red and green pepper, onion, and garlic. Cook, stirring, until the vegetables are golden, about 10 minutes.

2. Stir in the chili powder and cumin and cook, stirring, for 2 minutes to toast the spices. Add the tomatoes, tomato juice, chipotle chilies, and all the beans. Bring to a boil and cook, uncovered, over medium-low heat, stirring occasionally, until flavors are blended, about 45 minutes. Taste and correct seasonings.

3. Ladle into large bowls and top each with some shredded lettuce and a spoonful of yogurt.

Chick Peas in Chunky Tomato Sauce over Couscous

Chick peas are often included in Moroccan meat and vegetable tagines, or stews, served over couscous. Here in the United States, couscous is most readily available in a quick-cooking form, which is partially precooked. Couscous is an excellent protein, and adapts readily to all sorts of sauces and preparations.

Makes 4 servings

4	teaspoons olive oil
1½	cups chopped onion
½	cup chopped carrot
½	cup chopped celery
1	tablespoon finely chopped garlic
1	tablespoon water
1	can (19 ounces) chick peas, rinsed and drained
¼	teaspoon dried oregano
¼	teaspoon dried thyme
¼	teaspoon crushed red pepper, or more to taste
1	can (28 ounces) Italian-style plum tomatoes, with juices
¼	cup finely chopped flat-leaf parsley
	Salt and freshly ground black pepper
2	cups boiling water, or more, as needed
1	package (10 ounces) couscous (1¾ cups)
1	teaspoon finely chopped garlic
1	tablespoon freshly grated parmesan cheese (optional)

1. Heat 1 teaspoon of the olive oil in a large nonstick skillet over medium heat. Add the onion, carrot, celery, 1 tablespoon garlic, 1 teaspoon olive oil, and 1 tablespoon water. Heat, stirring, until mixture is heated through. Cover, reduce the heat to low, and cook, stirring often, until the onion is golden and the vegetables are tender, about 15 minutes.

2. Add the chick peas, oregano, thyme, and red pepper and cook, stirring, over medium-low heat until heated through. Add the tomatoes and stir, crushing them with a spoon. Cook, stirring, until the mixture boils. Simmer, uncovered, over low heat, until the tomato sauce is thickened and the flavors are blended, about 20 minutes.

3. Add the parsley and salt and pepper to taste. Add more dried red pepper, if desired.

4. Pour the boiling water into a shallow bowl. Slowly stir in the couscous and ½ teaspoon salt. Cover with a plate and let stand until the water is absorbed, about 10 minutes. If couscous seems dry add more boiling water.

5. Meanwhile, combine the remaining 2 teaspoons oil and the chopped garlic in a small skillet over low heat and heat, stirring, just until the garlic begins to sizzle. Remove from the heat. When the couscous is ready, drizzle the garlic oil over the couscous and fluff with a fork. To serve, spoon the couscous into a shallow bowl or deep platter. Ladle the tomato and chick pea mixture over the top. Serve with grated cheese, if desired.

Puerto Rican–style Rice and Beans

Adapted from a friend's authentic recipe. Pink beans are a staple of Puerto Rican cooking, although the cooking of that island extends far beyond such basic fare. For a good introduction, have a look at Yvonne Ortiz's book A Taste of Puerto Rico. *In this meatless version of what Ms. Ortiz calls "our daily bread," the beans form their own rich, aromatic sauce as they cook.*

Makes 6 servings

Beans

1	pound dried red kidney beans
1½	tablespoons olive oil
2	cups chopped onion
1	tablespoon minced garlic
4	cups Chicken Broth (page 42) or unsalted canned broth, fat skimmed, or 2 cups each broth and water
1	bay leaf
1	piece 2-inch cinnamon stick
	Salt
	Hot pepper sauce

Rice

2	cups long-grain rice
2	teaspoons olive oil
½	cup chopped onion
¼	cup finely chopped carrot
¼	cup finely chopped celery
1	garlic clove, minced
½	cup red onion, cut into ¼-inch dice
½	cup green bell pepper, cut into ¼-inch dice

1. Soak the beans as described on page 204.

2. Heat the oil in a heavy saucepan or Dutch oven. Sauté the onions over low heat, stirring frequently, covered, until the onions are caramelized to a rich golden brown, about 15 minutes. Stir in the garlic and sauté, uncovered, about 3 minutes longer.

3. Add the beans and the broth. Simmer, covered, for 2 hours, adding more water if needed to keep the beans moist. Add the bay leaf and cinnamon and continue to simmer until the beans are very tender, about 1 hour longer. Add salt and hot pepper sauce to taste.

4. Cook the rice as described on page 218 until it is tender and the liquid is absorbed. While the rice is cooking, heat the oil in a large, heavy skillet, preferably nonstick, and add the onion, carrot, and celery. Sauté over medium-low heat, stirring, until tender but not brown, 8 to 10 minutes. Stir in the garlic and sauté 2 minutes longer. Add the red onion and pepper and continue to sauté until pepper is just crisp-tender, about 3 minutes. Remove from heat. Set aside about 2 tablespoons of this vegetable mixture for garnish. Stir the rest of the vegetable mixture into the cooked rice with a fork or chopstick, fluffing the rice as you combine the ingredients.

5. Bring the rice and the beans to the table in 2 large serving bowls. To serve, place a spoonful of rice in a shallow soup bowl, then spread the rice to the edges. Place a ladleful of beans in the center of the rice, top with the reserved vegetables, and serve.

Baked Lentils, Mushrooms, and Rice Pilaf

This is a simple pilaf, with the lentils partially precooked and the whole thing finished in the oven. Oven heat works well with this kind of simmered pilaf; the flavors combine and meld nicely, and the rice comes out fluffy. You might want to top this all-brown dish with a bright stir-fry of broccoli, carrots, and red peppers.

Makes 4 servings

l	cup brown lentils, rinsed and drained
	Salt
l	tablespoon olive oil
l	package (10 ounces) small white button mushrooms, wiped and quartered
½	cup chopped onion
l	garlic clove, finely chopped
l	cup long-grain white rice
2½	cups Chicken Broth (page 42) or reduced-sodium canned broth, fat skimmed
l	bay leaf

1. Cook the lentils in boiling salted water to cover for 10 minutes. Drain well.

2. Preheat the oven to 350°F.

3. Meanwhile, heat the olive oil in an ovenproof Dutch oven or wide saucepan over medium heat. Stir in the mushrooms, onion, and garlic until blended. Cook, covered, stirring occasionally, until the vegetables are tender, about 10 minutes. Uncover and cook over high heat until the liquid evaporates and the onions are golden, about 3 minutes.

4. Stir in the rice and lentils until blended. Add the broth and bay leaf and bring to a boil. Cover and place in the oven. Cook until the liquid is absorbed, about 25 minutes. Let stand 10 minutes. Remove the bay leaf and correct the seasonings before serving.

Barley and Wild Rice Pilaf

4   teaspoons olive oil
1   cup chopped onion
1   garlic clove, finely chopped
1   cup barley
½   cup wild rice
4   cups water
2   teaspoons salt
1   red bell pepper, stemmed, seeded, and diced (¼ inch)
1   cup thinly sliced mushrooms
1   garlic clove, thinly cut crosswise
4   cups (packed) trimmed and shredded spinach leaves
    (about 10 ounces)
    Freshly ground black pepper

Rice can be combined with any other grains, such as corn and barley. It is a harmonious blend of earthy flavors, and the barley and wild rice take the same amount of time to cook.

Makes 4 servings

1. Heat 2 teaspoons of the oil in a wide 4- to 6-quart saucepan over medium heat. Add the onion and cook, stirring, until the onion is golden, about 8 minutes. Stir in the chopped garlic and cook for 1 minute longer. Stir in the barley and wild rice until coated.

2. Add the water and salt and bring to a boil. Stir thoroughly. Cover and cook over low heat until the liquid is absorbed and the grains are tender, 50 to 60 minutes. Let stand, off heat and covered.

3. When the grains are almost ready, heat the remaining 2 teaspoons of olive oil in a large skillet over medium-low heat. Add the red pepper and cook, stirring, until the edges begin to brown, about 5 minutes. Add the mushrooms and sliced garlic and cook, stirring, until golden, about 3 minutes. Stir in the spinach and heat, stirring, just until wilted.

4. Add the spinach mixture to the grains. Stir just until blended. Correct the seasonings and serve.

Brown Rice Pilaf with Spinach, Parmesan, and White Beans

Beans are so much a mainstay of the cooking of Tuscany that Tuscans are known as mangia-fagioli, *or bean eaters. And spinach is so popular that dishes with spinach are known in French as* à la florentine, *after the capital of Tuscany, Florence. This is a wonderful combination of flavors.*

Makes 4 servings

1	cup dried cannellini beans (page 204) or 2 cans (19 ounces each) canned cannellini, rinsed and drained
1	small onion, halved
1	leafy rib celery
1	clove garlic, bruised

Brown Rice Pilaf

1	tablespoon olive oil
1	cup diced (¼ inch) onion
1	garlic clove, minced
1½	cups long-grain brown rice (such as American-grown brown basmati)
3¾	cups Chicken Broth (page 42) or reduced-sodium canned broth, fat skimmed, or as needed
	Salt (optional)
4	cups (packed) trimmed and torn spinach leaves (about 1¼ pounds)
¼	cup freshly grated Parmigiano-Reggiano cheese
2	tablespoons pine nuts, lightly toasted in a dry skillet
1	tablespoon slivered sun-dried tomato packed in olive oil, rinsed and patted dry

1. Drain the soaked beans and cook in plenty of water with the onion, celery, and garlic until the beans are tender, about 1½ hours. Drain well. *(The beans can be cooked up to 2 days ahead.)*

2. Heat the oil over low heat in a large heavy saucepan. Add the diced onion and minced garlic and sauté, stirring often, until golden, about 10 minutes. Stir in the rice and reduce the heat to medium-low. Sauté, stirring constantly, until the grains turn opaque, about 3 minutes.

3. Stir in the broth and salt, if desired, and bring to a simmer.

Cook, tightly covered, until rice is tender, about 45 minutes. Add the beans, spinach, and grated cheese, folding together just until blended. The mixture should be creamy; stir in a little more warm broth if needed. Cover and cook over medium-low heat until the spinach is just wilted but still bright green, about 3 minutes.

4. Serve at once, sprinkled with pine nuts and the sun-dried tomato.

guide to complementary proteins

While animal products provide complete protein on their own, vegetable-derived proteins are incomplete. That means that on its own, a nonmeat food does not provide sufficient amounts of the nine essential amino acids needed for the body's growth. But when it is combined with another incomplete protein, the body treats the two as a complete protein.

To get maximum nutritional benefits, combine proteins by linking foods from groups listed below. You don't have to eat the complementary proteins at the same meal to benefit.

- **LEGUMES** Beans, peas, lentils, peanuts, bean sprouts, tofu
- **SEEDS and NUTS** Sesame, pumpkin, sunflower seeds; all nuts; alfalfa sprouts, tahini
- **GRAINS** Pasta, bread, wheat, rice, oats
- **DAIRY PRODUCTS and EGGS** Lowfat milk, yogurt, cheese; eggs (limit the number of yolks)

New Vegetable Paella

One fall, several of Spain's leading chefs traveled to California's Sonoma Valley, where they prepared their specialties. One of the most interesting improvisations, on a very traditional theme, was the vegetable paella devised by Gil Martinez Soto, chef at the Restaurante Virrey Palafox in El Burgo de Osma, near Madrid.

Valencia or medium-grain rice works best in this sort of dish, because it absorbs flavors well and because its high starch content helps give the finished dish an almost creamy texture.

Makes 6 servings

2   tablespoons olive oil
1   red bell pepper, halved, stemmed, seeded, and cut into ¼-inch dice (about 1 cup)
1   cup ¼-inch dice sweet onion
2   large artichokes with stems, outer leaves completely trimmed, center leaves and fuzzy choke discarded, hearts cut into ½-inch cubes (or substitute defrosted frozen artichoke hearts)
1   garlic clove, minced
     Salt and freshly ground black pepper
8   saffron threads
½   cup boiling water
1½   cups medium-grain American white rice, Spanish Valencia rice, or Italian Arborio rice
3   cups Chicken Broth (page 42) or reduced-sodium canned chicken broth, fat skimmed
2   cups trimmed and torn escarole or swiss chard
1   can (19 ounces) cannellini beans, rinsed and drained
½   cup cored, seeded, and diced ripe tomatoes or drained, chopped, canned tomatoes
1   teaspoon salt
¾   teaspoon paprika
½   cup fresh or frozen small green peas

1. Heat the olive oil over medium heat in a large sauté pan with a tight-fitting lid, or a wide saucepan or paella pan. Add the red pepper and onion and sauté, stirring, until the onion is golden, about 8 minutes. Add the artichoke and garlic and sauté 5 minutes longer. Sprinkle with salt and pepper.

2. Meanwhile, place the saffron in a cup or bowl, add the boiling water, and let stand for 10 minutes.

3. Add the rice to the sauté pan and stir over low heat, coating the rice with oil. Add the broth, escarole, beans, and tomatoes and bring to a boil. Stir in the salt, paprika, and the saffron and water.

4. Cover and cook over medium-low heat for 15 minutes. Add the peas and continue to cook until the broth is absorbed and the rice is tender, about 5 minutes longer. Let stand, uncovered, for 5 minutes before serving.

what is a carbohydrate?

One of the three macronutrients (along with protein and fat), which are food nutrients needed in large amounts. Nearly all derived from plants, carbohydrates are our principal source of energy—"Life's best fuel," according to Robert Barnett in *The American Health Food Book.* Carbohydrates are constructed of connected multiple units of sugars.

◆ **SIMPLE CARBOHYDRATES** sugars: Glucose and fructose in their pure forms. We usually identify sugars by their sources—cane sugar, molasses, honey, maple syrup. Sugars are also contained naturally in fresh fruits, vegetables, and dairy products. Sugars are added to many processed foods, including spaghetti sauce, soups, and fruit juice drinks.

◆ **COMPLEX CARBOHYDRATES** starches: rice and other grains, wheat products like bread and pasta, and such vegetables as potatoes and beans.

Fresh Corn Risotto

Despite the aura of mystery—or difficulty—that surrounds the making of risotto, it is really an easy dish to prepare. The trick is not to cheat. Risotto is such a simple, straightforward dish that any shortcuts or poor quality ingredients will be obvious and the dish won't have risotto's creamy consistency.

This risotto combines fresh corn with the rice, but you can change the vegetables with the seasons or what the market has to offer. Sliced fresh asparagus, cubes of acorn or butternut squash, diced carrot, even frozen peas all work.

Makes 4 servings

1 tablespoon extra virgin olive oil
⅓ cup finely chopped onion
1½ cups medium-grain Italian or American rice
⅓ cup dry white wine (optional)
5 to 6 cups reduced-sodium canned chicken broth, fat skimmed, simmering
1 cup fresh corn kernels or other vegetable
Salt
2 tablespoons freshly grated Parmigiano-Reggiano cheese, plus more for serving, if desired
1 tablespoon butter (optional)
1 tablespoon basil leaves

1. In a saucepan over medium heat, simmer the broth. In a wide, shallow, heavy saucepan place the oil and onion and cook, stirring, over low heat until the onion is tender but not browned, about 5 minutes. Add the rice and stir until grains are coated and begin to turn from translucent to opaque, about 2 minutes. Add the wine, if using, and cook, stirring, until evaporated.

2. Add ½ cup broth to the rice. Cook, stirring, over medium to medium-low heat until almost all of the broth is absorbed. Keep adding the broth ½ cup at a time, stirring constantly, and adjusting heat so that the broth maintains a steady but low simmer. The mixture will slowly become creamy. Taste the rice occasionally to check its tenderness. When the rice is almost ready (15 to 20 minutes), add the corn and cook, stirring, until tender, 3 to 5 minutes longer. Add salt to taste. Just before serving, stir in the cheese and butter, if desired, and basil. Serve at once.

3. Spoon into shallow bowls and pass additional cheese on the side, if desired.

Baked Stuffed Poblano Chilies with Salsa

4   unblemished, evenly sized poblano chilies, roasted
    (page 10)

⅔ cup prepared salsa, store-bought, or see
    pages 16–19

1   cup cooked long-grain white rice

¼ cup lowfat creamed cottage cheese

¼ cup plus 2 tablespoons shredded jack cheese,
    preferably reduced fat

2   tablespoons finely chopped red onion

1   tablespoon pine nuts or 2 tablespoons chopped
    walnuts, toasted in a hot skillet

1. Slit each chili down its length and remove the clump of seeds, leaving the stem intact, if possible. Don't worry if the chilies tear; you can patch them later. Set aside.

2. Preheat the oven to 350°F.

3. Place half of the salsa in a small baking dish just large enough to hold the chilies. Combine the rice, cottage cheese, ¼ cup jack cheese, onion, and pine nuts in a bowl. Divide evenly among the chilies. Carefully wrap each chili around the filling and transfer to the baking dish. Spoon the remaining salsa on top and sprinkle with the remaining 2 tablespoons cheese. Bake until the cheese has melted and sauce is bubbly, about 25 minutes. Serve hot.

This is a lighter, quicker version of the chiles en nogada *in* Like Water for Chocolate, *Laura Esquivel's wondrous novel-with-recipes.*

In the story, food becomes the principal outlet for forbidden love, magically capable of inflaming passions in those who eat it. Appropriately, the film climaxes in chilies, in the form of chiles en nogada—*fresh poblanos roasted over a flame and peeled, then stuffed with a mixture of meat, fruits, freshly shelled walnuts and almonds, coated with a rich nut sauce and strewn with pomegranate seeds.*

Makes 2 servings

getting to know tofu

Tofu, or bean curd, is made from coagulated soy milk. When you buy tofu, rinse it when you get home. Place it in a container of fresh cool water, and store in the refrigerator, changing the water daily.

These are the basic types of tofu you'll find in the supermarket, Asian groceries, and health food stores:

SOFT TOFU

SILKEN OR KINUGOSHI A Japanese style of tofu, the softest of all, with delicate texture that makes it ideal for soups and sauces. Silken tofu doesn't absorb flavors as well as firm tofu, and falls apart if stir-fried unless first weighted and drained.

CHINESE Firmer than silken tofu, but still smooth and creamy. Good in soups and simmered dishes.

REGULAR TOFU

REGULAR CHINESE OR JAPANESE This tofu is pressed longer than soft tofu to remove more water. A versatile product, it can be used in the same ways as soft tofu, but also holds up well in stir-fries and casseroles.

FIRM TOFU

FIRM AND EXTRA-FIRM When still more water is drained away, tofu develops a pronounced skin on its surface and a grainier interior; it has a higher concentration of nutrients. A good choice for stir-frying.

OTHER FORMS OF TOFU

SMOKED TOFU Has a browned surface and soy sauce seasoning.

TEMPEH (FERMENTED TOFU) Soybeans are cooked, then inoculated with a mold culture that binds the mixture. The result is a firm, dense texture that can be sliced or formed into patties. Tempeh, which originated in Indonesia, is earthy in flavor. Some say tempeh is to tofu as blue cheese is to cheese.

MISO A fermented seasoning paste made from a combination of soybeans and a grain such as rice or barley. Miso is high in sodium; it should be used in moderation.

Three-Alarm Tofu and Mushroom Stir-fry

Tofu (soybean curd) is an excellent and inexpensive source of protein, iron, and sometimes calcium. You shouldn't make the mistake, however, of thinking that because it's a meatless food, it is low in fat. Tofu is, actually, moderate to moderately high in fat, though still considerably lower than beef or other red meats. This is a basic tofu preparation and a good illustration of how tofu absorbs and carries the flavors it is cooked with.

Makes 4 servings

¼   cup Chicken Broth (page 42) or reduced-sodium canned broth, fat skimmed

1   tablespoon low-sodium soy sauce

1   tablespoon honey

1   teaspoon oriental sesame oil

1   teaspoon cornstarch

½   teaspoon crushed red pepper

4   tablespoons mild vegetable oil

½   pound tofu, preferably soft, drained, cubed (½ inch), and patted dry

10   ounces white button mushrooms, wiped clean and cut into ½-inch pieces

7   ounces shiitake mushrooms, stems discarded, caps cut into ½-inch dice

1   tablespoon minced fresh ginger

1   tablespoon minced garlic

1   tablespoon minced jalapeño or serrano chili

½   cup diced red bell pepper

½   cup thinly sliced green scallion tops
    Salt (optional)
    Freshly ground black pepper

1. Combine the broth, soy sauce, honey, sesame oil, cornstarch, and red pepper in a small bowl. Stir until the cornstarch has dissolved. Set aside.

2. Heat 2 tablespoons of the oil in a large skillet or wok over high heat. Add the tofu and stir-fry, adjusting the heat to maintain a lively sizzle, until the cubes are golden on all sides, about 5 minutes. With a slotted spoon, transfer the tofu to a plate and set aside.

3. Add the remaining oil to the skillet and heat over medium-high heat. Gradually add the button mushrooms and the shiitakes and stir-fry, adjusting the heat to between medium-high and high, to maintain a steady sizzle. Stir-fry until the mushrooms begin to brown, about 5 minutes. Sprinkle with the ginger, garlic, and chili and stir-fry 1 minute longer. Add the reserved tofu, the red bell pepper, and the scallion tops and stir-fry 1 minute longer. Add salt, if desired, and a grinding of black pepper.

4. Stir up the broth mixture and over high heat stir it in. Stir-fry just until liquid thickens and glazes the mushrooms and tofu, about 30 seconds. Serve at once.

Baked Polenta with Wild Mushroom and Tomato Sauce

Polenta, Italy's version of cornmeal mush, has become chic. Friends who were brought up eating polenta and pasta in Italian-American families look on this sudden popularity with hilarity: "Polenta and macaroni— my grandmother made them because they were cheap and filling. I swore that when I grew up, I'd never eat polenta again!"

In this recipe, the polenta and mushroom sauce can each be made completely in advance, then quickly combined at serving time. Use the mushroom liquid in the sauce to bring out the mushrooms' earthy flavor.

Makes 4 servings

Polenta

Olive oil, for baking dish

6 tablespoons freshly grated parmesan cheese

1 cup yellow cornmeal

1 cup lowfat (1%) milk

3 cups cold water or 1½ cups each chicken broth, fat skimmed, and water

Salt

Mushroom and Tomato Sauce

½ cup dried porcini or other dried mushrooms (1 ounce)

1 cup hot water

1 tablespoon olive oil

2 garlic cloves, peeled

1 medium onion, halved and thinly sliced

Salt and freshly ground black pepper

½ teaspoon dried oregano

3 tablespoons chopped parsley

2 cups sliced white button mushrooms

Freshly grated nutmeg

1 can (about 1 pound) whole tomatoes, drained, juice reserved

Freshly grated parmesan cheese, for passing at table (optional)

1. Lightly brush an 8-inch square baking dish with oil and sprinkle with 1 tablespoon of the grated parmesan. Set aside.

2. Stirring constantly, gradually add the cornmeal to the cold milk in a mixing bowl. Bring the water and salt to taste to a boil in a wide heavy saucepan. Gradually stir in the cornmeal mixture. With a whisk or large wooden spoon (and wearing an oven mitt to protect your hand from spattering), cook the polenta

over medium-low heat, stirring constantly, until it is stiff enough to stand away from the sides of the pan, about 15 minutes. Stir in 4 tablespoons of the grated parmesan. Scrape the polenta into the baking dish and sprinkle the surface with the remaining grated parmesan.

3. Preheat the oven to 400°F.

4. Bake the polenta until the edges begin to brown, about 30 minutes. Meanwhile, soak the dried mushrooms in hot water for 15 to 20 minutes. Heat the olive oil in a large heavy skillet, preferably nonstick, over medium heat. Add the garlic and cook, stirring now and then, until lightly golden. Discard garlic. Add the onion and sprinkle with salt, pepper, oregano, and 1 tablespoon of the parsley. Cook, stirring occasionally, until onion is translucent, 5 to 8 minutes.

5. Drain the mushrooms, reserving the soaking liquid. Rinse mushrooms to remove grit, then slice or chop. Strain soaking liquid through a coffee filter or strainer lined with a paper towel. Set aside liquid.

6. Raise heat under the skillet to medium-high. Add dried and fresh mushrooms. Sprinkle lightly with salt, pepper, and nutmeg. Sauté the mushrooms, tossing and adding a little more oil if needed, until they begin to wilt, about 4 minutes. Add reserved soaking liquid, the tomatoes, and about half of their juice. Bring to a boil, breaking up the tomatoes and stirring to combine. Lower the heat and simmer, uncovered, until juices have reduced slightly. Add more tomato liquid if the sauce seems dry. Add the remaining parsley and correct the seasonings.

7. Spoon or cut the polenta onto serving plates, top with the sauce and serve immediately. Top with grated parmesan, if you like, and pass a pepper mill at the table.

Crusty Kale and Potato Skillet

Makes 4 servings

½ pound small-leaf kale or collard greens

Salt

2 teaspoons olive or vegetable oil

2 tablespoons finely chopped onion

1 garlic clove, crushed

¾ teaspoon salt, or to taste

2 pounds russet (baking) potatoes, peeled and sliced ⅛ inch thick

¼ teaspoon coarsely ground black pepper

1. Bring a large pot of water to a boil. Strip the leaves from the thick stems of the kale and discard stems. Tear or cut the leaves into 2-inch pieces. You should have about 4 cups.

2. Salt the water, add the kale, and blanch it until tender, 8 to 10 minutes. Drain well. Coarsely chop the kale and set aside.

3. Heat the oil in a 12-inch nonstick skillet or a well-seasoned cast-iron skillet, sauté onion over medium-low heat for about 2 minutes. Stir in the garlic and sauté 30 seconds. Add this mixture to the greens, season with ¼ teaspoon of the salt, and set aside.

4. Arrange half the potato slices in concentric circles in the bottom of the skillet, overlapping them slightly. Sprinkle with ¼ teaspoon of the salt and half of the pepper. Spoon the greens mixture over the potatoes, spreading it evenly. Arrange the remaining potato slices on top, in slightly overlapping concentric circles. Sprinkle with remaining salt and pepper. Select a heavy lid that fits inside edges of pan and lay it on top of the potatoes, weighting them down.

5. Cook, covered, for 35 to 40 minutes, pressing down on the potatoes occasionally, and shaking the pan from time to time to prevent sticking. The potatoes should be crusty and browned on the bottom, tender in the center.

6. Carefully loosen the potatoes with a flexible spatula. Invert a serving plate over the skillet, and invert the skillet onto the plate. Serve hot.

Variation: For a nonmeatless dish, sauté the crumbled meat of 1 link Italian-style pork or turkey sausage in Step 3, discard the fat, then add the onion and continue as described.

how much protein do we need?

Less than we think. After World War II, it was assumed that the ideal diet contained large amounts of protein and moderate amounts of carbohydrates, which were mistakenly considered to cause weight gain without much nutritional benefit.

The average adult male needs about 63 grams (2¼ ounces) of protein per day; most men currently eat almost double that. The average adult female needs about 50 grams (under 2 ounces). Needs vary according to age, weight, activity level, and other factors. Children need more protein because they are growing, as do pregnant or nursing mothers.

Most of us eat too much protein. If you eat a variety of foods, you shouldn't have a problem with too little. "Maintain protein at moderate levels," advises the National Research Council in its publication *Diet and Health: Implications for Reducing Chronic Disease Risk.*

Fish and

Shell

THE FISH PICTURE HAS CHANGED dramatically in the last two decades or so. For many people fish was ritualistic on Friday nights. For Marie's family that sometimes meant spaghetti with homemade clam sauce or fish ovenbaked in tomatoes. In Richard's family fish was rarely served, although he always asked for it broiled "with crumbs on top," after eating it that way at a friend's house when he was about six years old.

Fresh fish was relatively rare then. Today the picture is very different. Improved air freight and the efficient handling of fresh products from around the world, flash-freezing methods that provide fish fresher than any but just-caught, and the emergence of profitable fish farms have made an impressive array of fresh fish available in our markets each day.

fish

This abundance of fresh product has virtually changed the way we eat. Many supermarkets have separate fish markets with fresh swordfish, salmon, cod, and mako shark artistically displayed on ice, next to an assortment of fillets of flounder, sole, and other flat fish, plus catfish, orange roughy, and many more. All this plus shrimp, farm-raised mussels and possibly clams, oysters (often shucked and in their brine), scallops, and a lobster tank with reasonably priced fresh lobster.

According to the National Fisheries Institute, there are as many as 250 fish species commercially available across the nation. This array of fish is overwhelming, especially to a nation of meat eaters raised on a diet of red meat rather than seafood. Americans consume about 15 pounds of seafood per capita, almost twice as much as a decade ago. But, curiously, statistics show that at least half of all the fish consumed in this country is eaten while dining out at restaurants. Many people we know tell us that they eat fish out more often than they cook it at home. Why? They say the reason is that they are confused about which fish to buy and especially what to do with it once they get it home. In fact, fish is one of the simplest foods to cook well, if you remember two words: *Don't overcook.*

Whether the fish is eaten at home or in a restaurant, increased consumption is due to consumer awareness of the health benefits of eating fish. Lean fish is almost as protein-rich as red meat, yet has only a fraction of the fat and slightly less cholesterol. All seafood, even shellfish, is very low in saturated fatty acids.

Previously it was thought that shellfish was too high in cholesterol for frequent consumption. But current sophisticated testing methods show that many types of shellfish, especially crab, scallops, mussels, clams, and lobster, are actually slightly lower in cholesterol than chicken or beef. Although shrimp and crayfish have about twice as much cholesterol as meat, they contain much less fat than meat, and the fat is mostly unsaturated with the added benefit of heart-healthy Omega-3 fatty acids.

Health benefits aside, we think seafood is nature's gift to the busy cook. It is easy to prepare—it needs no chopping or peeling; it cooks quickly; and it is adaptable to a variety of preparations. It is an easily digestible source of protein; it is relatively low in fat—and when it does contain fat, often it is the "good" kind. In general it is a very healthful food. All you have to know is what to do with it.

buying fresh fish

Perfectly fresh fish has a brinelike aroma—just like the seashore. The store where you buy it should have the same aroma. Do not buy fish at a store that smells "fishy."

Fish should be displayed on ice, but not sitting in melted ice or water. When buying fish, make your selection and ask to look at it. While looking, take a sniff. If the smell is off, tell the salesperson you have changed your mind. If the fish smells clean and fresh, examine its appearance. The fish should look moist with firm flesh, not mushy or falling apart.

It is difficult to say how much to buy because appetites vary. Start out by buying six to eight ounces per serving. Serve smaller portions (six ounces) of rich fish like salmon and swordfish. Serve larger portions (eight ounces) of lean fish—sole, snapper, cod. Experience and your own appetite are the best guides.

As soon as you get home, remove the fish from its store wrapping. Pat dry with a damp paper towel. Do not rinse under running water. Place on a plate and cover with plastic wrap. Store in the coldest part of the refrigerator. Use within 48 hours of purchasing; home refrigerators are not cold enough to keep fish longer than that.

basic fish
cookery

PERFECTLY COOKED FISH

Many variables—variety, thickness, intensity of heat source—determine when fish is fully cooked. Perfectly cooked fish is moist and juicy (and it retains more of its valuable nutrients). Overcooked fish is dry and flavorless. It is better to err on the side of undercooking; you can always pop slightly undercooked fish back on the heat.

Regardless of fish variety, the so-called Canadian Method is a basic rule: If the fish is baked in a preheated hot oven (400°F to 450°F), calculate 10 minutes cooking time per inch of thickness of the fish (measure it at its thickest point). But that's only a general guideline. In actual practice, we always check the fish early, to prevent overcooking.

For years, "experts" have written "cook fish until it flakes easily with a fork." *Wrong.* Fish cooked until it flakes is overcooked. For perfect, moist results, cook the fish (any type) just until the center is opaque, no longer translucent. Use the point of a knife to make a small cut into the thickest part of the fish and take a peek. Raw fish is translucent; cooked fish is opaque, or milky looking. In the following recipes we say to cook the fish until it turns from translucent to opaque and then give the suggested cooking time. Remember that the residual heat inside the fish will continue to cook it as it stands off the heat. If you think the fish looks cooked, remove it from the heat.

Another way to tell if fish is done is to lightly press the surface with your fingertip. The fish will be firm when it is just cooked; if overcooked, it will be hard and rubbery.

Shrimp and scallops turn opaque when they are done. Clams and mussels open when they are fully cooked. Discard any that refuse to open after being cooked adequately.

BROILED OR GRILLED FISH

STEAKS (TUNA, SWORDFISH, SHARK, SALMON, HALIBUT, COD) These firm-fleshed fish, cut ½ to ¾ inches thick, are excellent when broiled or grilled. The thick cut means they brown without overcooking, and are easy to turn without breaking up. Brush or spray the broiler pan or grill rack lightly with vegetable oil before heating. (Disposable ridged foil pans are very convenient for broiling.) Steaks cook in about 4 to 5 minutes per side.

FILLETS (FLOUNDER, ORANGE ROUGHY, CATFISH, GROUPER, SALMON, SEA BASS, SEA TROUT, TURBOT, WEAKFISH, SOLE) These require an especially gentle touch because often the flesh is more tender and the thinness makes them more fragile. Brush or spray the broiler pan lightly with a film of vegetable oil. Broil skin side down and do not try to turn over. Because most home broilers are not hot enough to brown the fillet without overcooking it, it's a good idea to drizzle the fillet with olive oil and sprinkle it with finely chopped fresh herbs, or lightly brush the fillet with a thin film of olive oil. Broil just until fish turns from translucent to opaque, about 4 to 5 minutes.

WHOLE SMALL FISH (1 to 1½ pounds) will cook through in the time it takes to brown the fish. To oven broil fish, position the rack so the fish is about 4 inches from the heat source. Place fish on a baking sheet and add a little wine or broth to keep the fish moist on the bottom. Tuck a lemon slice or fresh herb sprig (parsley, dill, thyme, or basil) in the cavity. Broil for 10 to 15 minutes, depending on the intensity of the heat and the thickness of the fish. Do not turn the fish over.

SHELLFISH (SHRIMP AND SCALLOPS) Best when skewered and basted with a marinade.

BAKED FISH

STEAKS Baking fish at a high oven temperature (400°F to 450°F) for 10 minutes per inch of thickness is a foolproof method for juicy flavorful fish—especially fish steaks. Swordfish, salmon, cod, halibut, and tilefish are all good choices.

FILLETS Thicker cuts of fillets—cod, salmon, red snapper, flounder—are good choices for baking. To ensure even cooking, fold the thin end of the fillet under the thicker portion.

POACHED FISH

Fish simmered in a liquid—water, fish stock, or clam juice—produces tender seafood plus a flavorful broth.

STEAKS AND FILLETS Simmer ½ cup dry white wine, ½ cup water, 1 garlic clove, a leafy celery top, an onion slice, bay leaf, and ½ teaspoon salt for 10 minutes. Add the fish, cover, and cook over low heat for 5 to 10 minutes, depending on the thickness of the fish.

WHOLE FISH Follow directions for steaks and fillets, but increase cooking time to about 10 minutes per inch of thickness.

SHELLFISH, FISH SOUP, OR CHOWDER Cook thick pieces of fish and shellfish slowly in the broth, just until cooked through.

STEAMED FISH

To steam fish use a collapsible steaming rack or a Chinese-style bamboo steamer set in a deep skillet over ½-inch boiling water.

STEAKS AND FILLETS Use a serving platter that will fit in the steaming rack or bamboo steamer. Rub fillets with grated ginger, crushed garlic, salt and freshly ground black pepper, a little soy sauce or fresh lemon juice. Cover and steam over simmering water for 5 to 8 minutes. Garnish with thinly sliced scallions, chopped fresh herbs, or diced, seeded tomatoes.

WHOLE FISH Bass, trout, or porgies are small enough to fit on a steamer. Season as suggested above. Cover and steam for 10 minutes, or until fish is opaque in center of thickest portion when tested with the tip of the knife.

Cod en Papillote with Tomatoes, Dill, and Orange

2 teaspoons olive oil

4 thick cod or other fish fillets, such as halibut, salmon, or haddock, about 1 inch thick (4 to 5 ounces each)

Salt and freshly ground black pepper

¼ cup fresh dill, coarsely chopped, or another fresh herb

2 ripe plum tomatoes, cored, seeded, and cut into strips

2 strips orange zest, cut into fine shreds

1. Heat the oven to 450°F.

2. Arrange a large sheet of heavy-duty aluminum foil on a baking sheet, with a long side facing you. Drizzle 1¹/₂ teaspoons of the oil over the long half of the foil closest to you. Place the fish on the oil-covered part of the foil, and turn each piece over to coat it with oil. Sprinkle the fish with salt and pepper.

3. Scatter most of the dill over the fish, dividing it evenly. Sprinkle with the orange zest strips, the tomato strips, and the remaining dill. Drizzle with a little more olive oil. Fold the long edge of aluminum foil over the fish, enclosing the fillets. Fold up the sides tightly and double-fold the long end near you to seal the package well.

4. Bake the fish for 15 minutes (11 or 12 minutes if the fillets are only ³/₄ inch thick). Immediately cut through the foil and transfer each portion to a serving plate with a large spatula. Spoon juices over and serve hot.

Cooking en papillote is a quick way to have a healthy dinner ready in minutes. Because you seal the fish and seasonings tightly in a foil package, all of their juices and flavor are trapped inside. We've made it even easier by forming one large package with four servings, rather than sealing four individual ones.

S e r v e s   4

Swordfish Steaks in Tomato, Fennel, and Citrus Sauce

This dish is based on a recipe from chef Michel Richard, which we both enjoyed at his Citrus Restaurant in Los Angeles. Broiling the fish right in the sauce keeps the flesh moist. Another oily, rich fish such as bluefish would also work well in this recipe.

Makes 4 servings

1	tablespoon extra virgin olive oil
½	cup chopped onion
1	small fennel bulb, well trimmed with feathery tops reserved, bulb quartered and thinly sliced crosswise (about ¾ pound)
1	garlic clove, crushed
1	can (14½ ounces) Italian plum tomatoes, with juice
3	strips lemon zest (about 2 × ½ inch), cut into ¼-inch dice
1	strip orange zest (about 2 × ½ inch), cut into very thin slivers
½	teaspoon fennel seeds
	Salt and freshly ground black pepper
4	swordfish steaks, about ½ inch thick (6 to 8 ounces each)
4	very thin lemon slices
	Fennel sprigs, for garnish

1. Heat the olive oil in a stovetop-to-oven skillet or baking dish large enough to hold swordfish in a single layer. Add onion and fennel and sauté over medium-low heat, stirring, until tender, about 10 minutes. Do not brown. Stir in the garlic and sauté 1 minute longer. Stir in the tomatoes, lemon and orange zest, and fennel seeds. Bring to a boil, stirring, over low heat. Simmer, uncovered, until sauce has reduced slightly, about 15 minutes. Season to taste with salt and pepper.

2. Set the broiler rack so that the top of the fish will be about 2 inches from the heat source. Heat the broiler.

3. Place the swordfish steaks in the baking dish, pushing the sauce aside with a spatula. Broil until the tops of the swordfish steaks are lightly browned and the inside is opaque, 3 to 5 minutes.

4. To serve, place a swordfish steak in the center of a dinner plate. Spoon some of the sauce around each steak, dividing sauce evenly. Garnish with lemon and a fennel sprig.

Grilled Tuna with Warm Balsamic Vinaigrette

4   tuna steaks, about ½ inch thick (6 or 7 ounces each)

3   tablespoons balsamic vinegar

2   garlic cloves, bruised
     Freshly ground black pepper

Vinaigrette

1½   cups reduced-sodium canned chicken broth, fat skimmed

¼   cup balsamic vinegar

4   medium shallots, minced

1   garlic clove, minced

1   teaspoon chopped fresh thyme leaves, stripped from stems,
     or pinch dried thyme

1   small ripe tomato, peeled, seeded, and diced

1   small package (3.5 ounces) enoki mushrooms (optional)
     Coarsely cracked black and white peppercorns

1   tablespoon minced parsley
     Thyme sprigs, for garnish

The full richness of tuna stands up to the flavor of balsamic vinegar in this recipe from chef Esther Carpenter, who devised this dish when she was at the Four Seasons Hotel in Newport Beach, California. She suggests serving the tuna with a mixture of baby vegetables (zucchini, summer squash, carrots, and eggplant) grilled with olive oil, shallots, and fresh thyme.

Makes 4 servings

1. Arrange the tuna steaks in a single layer in a shallow non-aluminum dish. Add the vinegar, thyme, and garlic. Add a sprinkling of black pepper and turn the fish over to coat. Cover and marinate at least 1 hour or overnight.

2. Boil the broth in a small heavy saucepan until reduced to ³/₄ cup. Add vinegar, shallots, garlic, and chopped thyme and return to a boil. Stir in the tomato and optional enoki mushrooms and season with black pepper. Set aside.

3. Heat a grill or broiler. Arrange rack about 4 inches from the heat source.

4. Coat both sides of the tuna with a thin layer of cracked peppercorns. Grill the tuna until the outside is seared, but inside is still pink, 5 minutes for the first side, 4 minutes for the second.

5. Reheat vinaigrette if necessary. Add parsley. Transfer tuna to plates and spoon vinaigrette over. Garnish with thyme.

Grilled Grouper with Red and Golden Tomato Relish

This recipe is from Robbin Hass, chef at the Colony Bistro in Miami's South Beach. Chef Hass prepares this dish with Florida black grouper, but any firm-fleshed whitefish fillet can be substituted. In recent years, salsas and relishes have replaced the butter-based sauces that used to be standard with fish.

Makes 4 servings

Salsa

1	teaspoon whole cumin seed
1	teaspoon whole coriander seed
½	cup peeled, seeded, and diced (¼ inch) ripe red tomato
½	cup peeled, seeded, and diced (¼ inch) ripe yellow tomato
2	tablespoons finely diced red onion
1	tablespoon fresh lime juice
1	scallion, thinly sliced
1	teaspoon honey
1	teaspoon minced cilantro
⅛	teaspoon minced habanero, jalapeño, or other hot chili pepper, or more to taste

2	teaspoons olive oil
4	skinless grouper fillets, or tilefish, sea bass, or other firm-fleshed whitefish (about 6 ounces each)
	Coarsely ground black pepper
	Cilantro sprigs or flat-leaf parsley

1. Heat the cumin and coriander seeds in a small dry skillet over medium-low heat until fragrant, about 30 seconds. Grind in a mortar or spice mill. Combine the spices, tomatoes, onion, lime juice, scallion, honey, cilantro, and chili pepper in a bowl. Stir to blend. Let stand at room temperature about 1 hour.

2. Heat a grill or broiler. Brush the grill or the broiler pan with olive oil. Lightly brush the fish fillets with olive oil and sprinkle with pepper. Grill or broil until the center turns opaque, about 5 to 8 minutes. Do not turn the fish.

3. To serve, divide the salsa among 4 large dinner plates and spread in a thin layer. Place a portion of fish in the center of each plate. Garnish with sprigs of cilantro.

Fish Steaks Glazed with Ginger, Soy, and Lime

4   fish steaks (tuna, mako shark, swordfish, halibut,
      or salmon), 1 inch thick (about 6 ounces each)
3   tablespoons fresh lime juice
2   tablespoons low-sodium soy sauce
2   garlic cloves, crushed
1   teaspoon grated ginger
1   teaspoon toasted sesame oil
2   slices fresh hot chili pepper, or 1 small pinch
      crushed red pepper (optional)

This quick glaze is per-fect for grilling outdoors as well as for broiling indoors.

Makes 4 servings

1. Arrange the fish steaks in a shallow ceramic or glass dish. Whisk together the lime juice, soy sauce, garlic, ginger, sesame oil, and chili pepper, if using, in a small bowl. Pour marinade over the fish and turn the fish to coat both sides with marinade. Cover with plastic wrap and let stand about 30 minutes at room temperature or 1 hour in the refrigerator, turning fish over once or twice and spooning marinade over the fish.

2. Heat the grill or broiler with the rack about 4 inches from the heat source. Transfer the fish to a broiler pan spooning a little of marinade over the fish. Grill or broil, basting once or twice with marinade, until first side is nicely glazed and golden, about 5 minutes. Turn fish carefully with a wide spatula and spoon remaining marinade on top. Grill or broil second side, basting at least once with marinade left in the dish, just until fish is glazed but still pink inside, about 4 minutes. Do not overcook. Transfer fish to heated serving plates or a platter.

Baked Halibut with Golden Onions and Orange

For this dish, onions are caramelized in a hot oven with paper-thin strips of orange zest. Fresh or dried thyme provides a nice flavor accent.

Makes 4 servings

Marinade

2   tablespoons fresh orange juice

1   teaspoon grated orange zest

1   garlic clove, crushed

1   teaspoon fresh thyme leaves or ¼ teaspoon dried thyme

2   halibut steaks, or cod, salmon, or swordfish steaks,
     1 inch thick (about 1¼ pounds)
     Freshly ground black pepper

Onions

1   tablespoon extra virgin olive oil

1   large sweet onion, quartered, cut into ¼-inch-thick wedges

4   strips (3 × ½-inch) orange zest, cut into long slivers

1   teaspoon fresh thyme leaves or ¼ teaspoon dried thyme

½   teaspoon salt, or more to taste
     Freshly ground black pepper
     Fresh thyme, for garnish (optional)

1. Combine the orange juice, grated zest, garlic, and thyme in a shallow dish. Add the fish and turn to coat, spreading the marinade over the surface. Sprinkle with pepper and let stand until ready to bake.

2. Heat the oven to 425°F.

3. Combine the oil, onion, slivered zest, and thyme in a 13 × 9-inch baking dish and stir to blend. Bake until the onions begin to brown, 20 minutes, stirring once after 10 minutes. Remove from the oven and add salt and a grinding of black pepper. Push the onions to the side of the dish and place the fish steaks in the center. Top with any marinade left in the dish. Spoon some of the onions over the fish. Bake until the center of the fish has turned from translucent to opaque, about

10 minutes. Remove from oven. Let stand 5 minutes before serving.

4. To serve, spoon the onion mixture onto a serving platter. Carefully remove the skin and center bone from the fish. Transfer the fish to the platter. Top each portion with a spoonful of onion and a small sprig of thyme, if using.

quicker marinades for fish fillets and steaks

These marinades are very simple to make. Although we call them marinades, they can be added to the fish as little as 10 minutes before serving or as long as 1 or 2 hours ahead. All are for 4 portions of fish.

ORANGE-BASIL MARINADE

Chop together ¼ cup (packed) basil leaves, 1 strip (about 2 × ½ inch) orange zest, and 1 garlic clove until fine. Combine with ¼ cup fresh orange juice. Add salt and pepper to taste. Spoon over fish and let stand until ready to cook.

LEMON AND BLACK PEPPER MARINADE

Sprinkle 2 teaspoons freshly grated lemon zest on the fish. Add a generous grinding of black pepper and 1 teaspoon extra virgin olive oil to each portion. Spread evenly over the surface of the fish. Let stand until ready to cook.

SOY, SESAME, AND GINGER MARINADE

Combine 2 tablespoons low-sodium soy sauce, 2 teaspoons oriental sesame oil, and 1 tablespoon grated fresh ginger. Stir to blend. Spoon onto fish steaks and spread evenly. Let stand until ready to cook.

Oven-steamed Salmon on a Bed of Aromatic Vegetables

A delectable one-dish meal. The pink salmon looks particularly pretty in this dish, but any firm-fleshed fish steak (such as halibut, shark, or even tilefish) would be good prepared this way.

Makes 4 servings

4   salmon steaks, about ¾ inch thick (6 to 8 ounces each)
3   tablespoons fresh lemon juice
1   pound small new potatoes, scrubbed and quartered
2   medium leeks, white portions with a little green, trimmed, washed well, and chopped into ¼-inch pieces
1   medium-size sweet onion, cut into ¼-inch dice
4   medium carrots, sliced diagonally about ¼ inch thick
4   medium shallots, cut into ½-inch pieces
2   tablespoons extra virgin olive oil
     Salt and freshly ground black pepper
1   small zucchini, sliced diagonally about ¼ inch thick
¼   cup chopped dill

1. Heat the oven to 425°F.

2. Blot the salmon steaks dry with a paper towel. Place on a platter and sprinkle with 1 tablespoon of the lemon juice.

3. Combine the potatoes, leeks, onion, carrots, and shallots in a large heavy baking dish. Drizzle with the olive oil and stir to blend. Sprinkle with salt and pepper. Bake the vegetables until edges begin to brown, about 30 minutes, stirring at least twice. Remove the pan from the oven, stir the zucchini into the vegetable mixture, and bake 10 minutes longer.

4. Remove the pan from the oven and sprinkle vegetables with the remaining 2 tablespoons lemon juice and 2 tablespoons of the dill, turning the vegetables gently with a spatula to blend. Tuck the salmon steaks into the vegetable mixture, moving the vegetables aside with a spatula. Spoon some of the vegetables on top of the salmon. Return baking dish to the oven and bake, uncovered, until the salmon is cooked through but still moist, 10 to 12 minutes. Sprinkle with the remaining 2 tablespoons chopped dill and serve hot.

Swordfish Baked with Sweet Peppers and Vinegar

1   tablespoon olive oil
3   cups thin (¼ inch) lengthwise slices red bell pepper
    (2 or 3 peppers)
1   garlic clove, thinly sliced
1   tablespoon chopped fresh oregano leaves or
    ½ teaspoon dried oregano
2   tablespoons red wine vinegar
    Salt and freshly ground black pepper
4   swordfish steaks, or mako shark, salmon, or halibut
    steaks, ¾ inch thick (about 6 ounces each)

1. Heat the oven to 400°F.

2. Heat the oil in a large nonstick skillet, add the peppers, and sauté, stirring, over medium-high heat, for about 5 minutes. Add the garlic and 1 teaspoon of the fresh oregano or a pinch of the dried. Cover and cook over medium-low heat until peppers are almost tender, about 5 minutes.

3. Add the vinegar and cook, uncovered, until vinegar boils down, about 3 minutes. Transfer mixture to a 13 × 9-inch baking dish. Season with a pinch of salt and a grinding of black pepper. Set aside.

4. Wipe out the skillet. Heat skillet over high heat until hot enough to evaporate a drop of water immediately upon contact. Add the swordfish, sear 1 minute, turn, and sear the other side for 1 minute. Sprinkle with a pinch of salt, a grinding of black pepper, and the remaining oregano.

5. Push the peppers in the baking dish aside and arrange the swordfish in a single layer. Spoon the peppers over the swordfish. Bake swordfish until opaque in the center, 5 to 8 minutes. To serve, spoon the peppers onto a serving platter. Top with the swordfish, spooning pan juices over the fish.

Here peppers are lightly cooked in a skillet and the swordfish seared to give it color and a crust. Then the ingredients are transferred to a baking dish and finished off in a hot oven. The fish is moist and tender and the entire dish rich in flavor, yet light.

Makes 4 servings

Seared Peppered Fish Steaks
with Crispy Slaw and Soy Vinaigrette

This East-meets-West recipe is from Allen Wong, a Japan-born chef with a Chinese-Hawaiian father and a Japanese mother. Chef Wong is now at the Mauna Lani Hotel on the big island of Hawaii. This is a good basic method by which you can cook several types of fish steaks: ahi tuna, sword-fish, or halibut. Wonton wrappers are sold in many supermarkets in the specialty produce sec-tion. When fried, they add a nice crisp touch. If they are not available, simply omit them.

Makes 4 servings

Crispy Slaw

1 cup finely shredded Napa cabbage
½ cup matchstick-size strips snow peas
½ cup matchstick-size strips carrot

4 tuna, swordfish, or halibut steaks, ½ inch thick (about 6 ounces each)
2 teaspoons coarsely ground black pepper
2 tablespoons plus 1 teaspoon peanut oil
2 tablespoons matchstick-size strips fresh ginger
2 wonton wrappers, cut into matchstick-size strips
Soy Vinaigrette (recipe follows)
12 thin tomato wedges
Radish sprouts or watercress, for garnish

1. Combine the cabbage, snow peas, and carrot and toss to blend. Sprinkle both sides of the fish with the pepper. Cut each fish steak into 3 or 4 evenly sized pieces. Cover vegetables and fish separately and refrigerate for 1 to 4 hours.

2. Heat 2 tablespoons of the oil in a small skillet over medium heat, add the ginger, and fry until golden, under 30 seconds. Remove with a slotted spoon and transfer to a paper towel to drain. Add the wonton strips and fry until crisp and golden, stirring constantly, about 1 minute. Remove with a slotted spoon and transfer to a paper towel. Discard the oil.

3. Heat remaining 1 teaspoon oil in a heavy nonstick skillet over high heat until very hot. Add tuna and cook until browned and juicy and pale pink in the center, about 3 minutes. Other fish should be cooked through, about 2½ minutes per side. Transfer the fish to 4 dinner plates.

4. Toss half the vinaigrette with the crispy slaw and divide among the 4 plates. Sprinkle the ginger and wonton strips over the slaw. Spoon the remaining vinaigrette over the fish, dividing evenly. Garnish each plate with tomato wedges and radish sprouts.

Soy Vinaigrette

2	tablespoons low-sodium soy sauce
1	tablespoon flavorless vegetable oil, such as canola
1	tablespoon rice wine vinegar
1	tablespoon mirin (sweet rice cooking wine)
1	tablespoon fresh lime juice
1½	teaspoons sugar
1	teaspoon grated ginger
1	teaspoon oriental sesame oil
1	small garlic clove, crushed

Combine all ingredients in a small bowl. Cover and refrigerate until ready to use. *(Can be prepared up to 2 days ahead.)*

Oven-fried Fish Fillets with Sweet Potato Slices and Gremolata

Fish fillets dipped in egg white, dusted with some dried bread crumbs, and baked in a very hot oven are a good alternative to fried fish. Here they are served with sweet potatoes and a mixture of finely chopped parsley, lemon zest, and garlic.

Makes 4 servings

4 medium sweet potatoes, peeled and cut into ¼-inch slices (about 2¼ pounds)
2 tablespoons olive oil
¼ cup all-purpose flour
Salt and freshly ground black pepper
1 egg white
1 cup fine dried bread crumbs, or more as needed
1 tablespoon grated parmesan cheese (optional)
4 fish fillets, such as turbot, orange roughy, or sole (about 6 ounces each), cut into equal pieces
1 recipe gremolata (page 7)

1. Heat the oven to 400°F. Place the sweet potato slices in a bowl, add 1 tablespoon of olive oil, and toss to coat. Spread in a single layer on a nonstick baking sheet. Bake until browned, about 15 minutes. Turn potatoes over and bake until tender, about 10 minutes.

2. Spread the flour on a sheet of wax paper and season with a little salt and pepper. Place the egg white in a shallow bowl and whisk just until foamy. Combine the bread crumbs and cheese, if using, on a separate sheet of wax paper. Brush a second nonstick baking sheet with the remaining 1 tablespoon olive oil.

3. Coat the fish with flour and shake off the excess. Dip in the egg white to coat evenly. Then dredge in the bread crumbs until coated. Place on the baking sheet.

4. Remove the potatoes from the oven and leave on the baking sheet. Place the baking sheet with the fish on the lowest rack. Raise oven temperature to 450°F. Bake for 6 minutes. Using a wide spatula, carefully turn the fish. Bake until golden, about 6 minutes more. Reheat the potatoes on the top oven rack during the last 3 minutes of cooking.

5. To serve, place the potatoes and fish on a large platter and sprinkle with gremolata. Serve at once.

Seafood and Vegetable Sauté with Chardonnay Glaze

3   or 4 scallions

1½   teaspoons olive oil

2   large garlic cloves, minced

½   to ¾ pound shrimp, peeled with tails left on and deveined
     Salt and freshly ground black pepper

½   pound sea scallops, cut into pieces if large,
     or use more shrimp

3   slender carrots, cut into thin julienne strips

⅔   cup Chardonnay wine

3   ripe plum tomatoes, cored, halved, seeded, and
     cut into ¼-inch dice

2   tablespoons chopped mixed herbs, such as parsley and
     chives, parsley, chives, and tarragon, or just parsley
     Juice of ½ lemon

This simple dish can be prepared with a combination of shrimp and scallops or with shrimp alone. The carrots, tomato, and herbs add color. Serve the dish with an aromatic rice like basmati.

Makes 4 servings

1. Cut the scallion whites into 1¹/₂- to 2-inch lengths. Halve the whites lengthwise, then cut into very fine julienne. Slice scallion greens ¹/₈-inch wide on a sharp diagonal. Set aside.

2. Heat the oil in a large nonstick skillet over medium-high heat. Add the garlic and let it sizzle for a few seconds. Add the shrimp in 1 layer. Season lightly with salt and pepper. Let the shrimp cook, without tossing, for 1 minute. Add the scallops and toss. Add the carrots and scallion whites and greens and toss to combine ingredients. Pour in the wine. Cover the skillet and lower the heat slightly.

3. Cook, stirring, for 4 minutes. Uncover, stir in tomatoes, and cook until seafood is opaque, 1 minute longer. With a slotted spoon, lift out seafood and place on 4 warm dinner plates.

4. Raise the heat and reduce the juices to a thin glaze, about 3 minutes. Swirl in the herbs and lemon juice, cook 2 or 3 seconds longer, and pour the glaze over the seafood. Serve immediately.

Poached Snapper with Tomato and Herb Broth

Serve the fish in shallow soup bowls in the broth, which is delicately flavored with ginger, orange, and thyme. This makes a light main course for four. For a first course, use only two fillets, cutting each one in half.

Makes 4 servings

1	cup dry white wine
1	cup water
1	thick slice onion
1	garlic clove, bruised
1	slice (¼ inch) ginger
1	bay leaf
1	fresh thyme sprig or pinch of dried thyme
1	strip (2 × ½ inch) orange zest
4	red snapper, sea bass, or sea trout fillets (about 6 ounces each)
⅓	cup drained, seeded, and diced canned tomatoes
	Salt and freshly ground black pepper
1	tablespoon minced chives
1	teaspoon thyme leaves, stripped from stems, for garnish (optional)

1. Combine the wine, water, onion, garlic, ginger, bay leaf, thyme, and orange zest in a large skillet and bring to a boil. Boil, uncovered, over medium-high heat for 5 minutes. Lower the heat slightly and slip the fish fillets into the broth. Cover and cook over medium heat until the fish is opaque through to the center, 5 to 7 minutes. Transfer the fish to a plate, cover with foil, and set aside.

2. Strain the poaching liquid through a sieve and pour back into the skillet. Reserve the orange zest but discard the remaining solids. Bring broth to a boil. Boil, uncovered, until reduced to 1¼ cups, about 5 minutes. Meanwhile, cut the reserved orange zest into julienne strips and set aside.

3. Add the tomatoes and orange strips to the broth. Taste and add salt and pepper if needed. Place the fish fillets in shallow soup bowls. Spoon the broth over the fish, distributing the tomato and orange zest evenly. Garnish with chives and fresh thyme leaves, if using, and serve.

handling clams and mussels

Buy only clams that are tightly closed. Mussels sometimes open slightly, but when tapped they should close up tightly.

Do not refrigerate clams or mussels in a plastic bag. As soon as you get them home from the store rinse with very cold water, drain well, and arrange in a shallow pan or platter. Cover lightly with a dampened cloth or paper towel. Store in the coldest part of the refrigerator and use within 48 hours.

Scrub clams and mussels with a stiff brush and rinse several times in clean cold tap water. Do not let them sit in cold water. The beard, the strawlike thing protruding from the mussel, should be grasped between the fingers and pulled off.

Spicy Seafood Stew

This lively, peppery shellfish stew is inspired by the Italian specialty, zuppa di pesce fra diavolo. We use shrimp, mussels, and clams, but you can make it with any combination of seafood.

Makes 4 servings

1	tablespoon olive oil
2	garlic cloves, finely chopped
½	teaspoon crushed red pepper, or more to taste
1	can (28 ounces) Italian-style plum tomatoes, with juice, chopped
½	cup dry white wine
1	bay leaf
	Salt and freshly ground black pepper
8	large shrimp, peeled and deveined
12	littleneck clams, scrubbed and rinsed
12	mussels, scrubbed, debearded, and washed
4	thick slices Italian or French bread, toasted
2	tablespoons finely chopped flat-leaf parsley, for garnish

1. Heat the oil in a large wide saucepan or deep skillet over low heat. Add the garlic and red pepper and cook, stirring, until aromatic, about 3 minutes. Do not brown the garlic.

2. Stir in the tomatoes with their juice, the wine, and bay leaf. Simmer, uncovered, stirring to break up tomatoes, about 5 minutes. Add salt and pepper to taste.

3. Add the shrimp and stir for 2 minutes over medium heat. Add the clams and mussels in an even layer and spoon sauce over the shellfish. Cover tightly and cook over high heat until all the mussels and clams have opened, 3 to 5 minutes. Discard any unopened shellfish. Correct seasonings.

4. Place a slice of bread in each of 4 shallow soup bowls. Top with the shrimp, clams, and mussels. Discard the bay leaf and spoon the sauce over the shellfish. Sprinkle with parsley and serve.

Lima Beans with Clams

1   tablespoon extra virgin olive oil
1   large sweet onion, quartered and cut crosswise
    into ¼-inch slices
1   bay leaf
1   bag (20 ounces) frozen baby lima beans, thawed
¼   cup finely chopped parsley
2   garlic cloves, minced
    Salt and freshly ground black pepper
24 small clams, littlenecks or manillas, scrubbed and rinsed
½   cup diced seeded tomato

1. Heat the oil in a large deep skillet or wide saucepan with a tight-fitting lid. Add the onion and bay leaf and sauté, stirring, over medium-low heat until onion is golden, about 10 minutes.
2. Add the lima beans, parsley, and garlic and cook, stirring, over medium-low heat for 5 minutes. Season with salt and freshly ground pepper to taste.
3. Arrange the clams on top of the limas. Raise heat to medium-high, cover, and cook until the clams open, about 8 minutes. Discard any unopened clams
4. Transfer the clams to a side dish. Spoon the beans and the clam juices into a deep platter or shallow serving bowl. Remove half of the clams from the shells and stir into the lima beans. Sprinkle with tomato. Arrange the remaining clams in their shells on top of the limas and serve at once.

Lima beans and clams? This unusual, yet deliciously memorable, combination of ingredients is adapted from a recipe by Angel Garcia, the chef at Lúculo restaurant in Madrid. Mussels can be substituted for the clams, or you can use a combination of the two.

Makes 4 servings

Poul

try

WE EAT A LOT OF CHICKEN, and with good reason: It is one of the most versatile meats around. Chicken is economical, easy to prepare, and cooks quickly. You can roast it, crumb and bake it, poach it, casserole it, sauté or braise it. With its clean, neutral flavor, chicken adapts well to just about any flavor scheme. And chicken has markedly less fat and fewer calories than red meat, yet provides similar amounts of protein.

But there's an "if." Chicken, like all poultry, is only low in fat and cholesterol when you remove the skin— as succulent and crispy as that skin might be. In fact, removing chicken skin lowers the bird's fat by as much as *50 percent*. In a recent test, it was found that you get the reduced fat benefits even if you cook the chicken with its skin on (which helps keep it moist), then remove it before serving.

With poultry, the way it's cooked makes all the difference. Stay away from frying. Instead, try quick, light sautés, using a teaspoon of olive oil instead of butter and a nonstick skillet—one of the most beneficial tools ever to hit the healthy kitchen.

Many traditionally rich chicken dishes such as curry and Chicken Paprikás can be lightened not only by cutting the fat in the sauces but by preparing them with breast meat instead of a cut-up whole bird. But the leanness of chicken breasts, their great lowfat selling point, can also be their undoing. Because they are so lean, chicken breasts dry out quickly. Strips of chicken breast can cook in under a minute. Always cook chicken breasts just until done, no longer.

Chicken breasts cook up plump and moist when poached or steamed. One of our favorite methods is to steam boneless chicken breasts in plastic wrap, a technique that traps every last drop of moisture. It was pioneered by chef Seppi Renggli, who worked at the Four Seasons restaurant in New York City for years and now oversees the restaurants at Rockefeller Center.

We've also included recipes using Cornish hens, each of which serves one or two, and one for pheasant, which is naturally lean, full of flavor, and no trickier to cook than chicken. Because game birds are so lean, it's particularly important to avoid overcooking them.

Once upon a time, turkey was a big bird usually cooked once a year, on Thanksgiving Day. Times have changed. Today, one can buy just about any part of the turkey, and only that part: whole or half breasts (on the bone or boneless, with skin or without), thin cutlets, thicker fillets, tenderloins, thighs (on the bone or boneless), drumsticks, wings, wing "drumettes," ground turkey, turkey sausage, you name it. As a result, the rise in turkey consumption is nothing short of spectacular: In 1960, the average American ate about six pounds of turkey each year. By 1992, that figure had tripled to over eighteen pounds, and it's still rising fast.

The reason? It's as much the growing awareness of healthy eating as convenience. While comparably high in protein to red meat, lean cuts of turkey have only a fraction of the fat of any other meat.

Turkey is adaptable. Because so many different cuts are now readily available, you can substitute turkey for red meats in many favorite dishes, making them healthier without sacrificing flavor. Boneless turkey breast cutlets, for example, lend themselves to quick sautés. Turkey thighs are especially versatile, since they can be braised, roasted, or grilled, and still remain moist and succulent. In old-fashioned stew recipes, they cut the cooking time in half. And nothing beats ground turkey, which has 7 to 11 percent fat, compared to up to 30 percent in ground beef chuck. You can use ground turkey in virtually any ground beef recipe; you'll wind up with good flavor and considerably less fat and cholesterol. With lively seasonings, turkey makes a tasty meat loaf, chili, spaghetti sauce, burger, or taco filling.

handling and cooking poultry safely

Because of possible bacterial contamination, particularly with salmonella, careful handling in the kitchen is very important whenever you cook any sort of poultry. Bacteria are killed in cooking, so you should always cook chicken thoroughly. The meat should reach an internal temperature of 180°F (160°F for boneless poultry), at which point the juices run clear, with no trace of pink.

Bacteria on raw poultry can come into contact with other surfaces, where they can thrive. If you cut chicken on a board, and then use that same board to cut other ingredients that will not be cooked—tomatoes for a salad, for example—then you may have transferred salmonella bacteria to these raw foods and possibly contaminated your hands; any and all kitchen utensils that come in contact with raw poultry—especially knives and cutting boards—must be washed thoroughly with soap and very hot water immediately after use. Every couple of weeks, clean your cutting board with a solution of ¼ cup chlorine bleach with 2 quarts very hot water.

Steamed Chicken Breasts with Vegetable Stew Provençale

Steaming chicken or fish in plastic wrap keeps in every last drop of natural moisture, and lets you cook without any additional fat. Because you don't have the advantage of browning, however, which caramelizes and adds flavor and color when you sauté, grill, or roast, steamed foods need some flavor boosters. Seasoning food well with salt and pepper, fresh herbs, citrus zest, and the like is the secret to successful steaming. Or, you can do as we do here, and poach the chicken, then serve it with a flavorful vegetable stew.

Makes 6 servings

6   boneless and skinless chicken breast halves (about 5 ounces each), well trimmed
    Salt and freshly ground black pepper
2   tablespoons chopped fresh basil
1   tablespoon chopped parsley
1   garlic clove, sliced thin
1   recipe Vegetable Stew Provençale (page 198)
    Rosemary or thyme sprigs, for garnish
    Basil sprigs, for garnish

1. Half-fill a skillet with water and bring to a boil. Spread 4 sheets of plastic wrap on a work surface. Place 1 chicken breast half on each piece. Sprinkle with salt, pepper, basil, parsley, and 1 or 2 slices garlic. Wrap tightly.

2. Slip the chicken breasts into the water, lower the heat, cover, and simmer over low heat until done, 8 to 10 minutes. Timing can vary with thickness; do not overcook. The breasts are done when they are firm but not rubbery when pressed in the center with a fingertip. With tongs, transfer the chicken breasts to a plate. Carefully unwrap the plastic, saving the juices.

3. Warm the vegetable stew in a saucepan. Stir the reserved chicken juices into the stew. Place a chicken breast on each of 4 warm serving plates. Spoon the stew over and around each breast. Garnish with herb sprigs and serve hot or at room temperature.

Chicken Paprikás

4   teaspoons vegetable oil
4   boneless and skinless chicken breast halves, cut crosswise
     into ½-inch strips (about 1¼ pounds)
     Salt and freshly ground black pepper
1   large red bell pepper, halved lengthwise, trimmed and
     cut into thin crosswise slices
½   medium onion, halved and thinly sliced
1   garlic clove, minced
     Pinch dried marjoram (optional)
1   teaspoon flour
2   teaspoons Hungarian paprika, preferably medium-hot
½   cup reduced-sodium canned chicken broth, fat skimmed
½   cup nonfat or lowfat yogurt

1. Heat 2 teaspoons of the oil in a large nonstick skillet over medium heat. Add chicken strips, a few at a time. Sauté, stirring, until lightly browned, about 2 minutes per side. Sprinkle with salt and pepper. Remove the chicken strips and set aside.
2. Add the remaining 2 teaspoons oil to skillet. Stir in the red pepper and onion. Cook, stirring, over medium-low heat until the onion is limp and lightly browned, about 10 minutes. Add the garlic and marjoram, if using, and cook 1 minute longer. Sprinkle with flour, stir in the paprika, and cook for a few moments. Stir in the broth, cover and simmer for 10 minutes. Cool briefly.
3. Transfer the broth and half of the vegetables to a blender or food processor. Add the yogurt and puree until smooth. Return to the skillet. Stir in the chicken and any juices. Reheat, stirring, over low heat. Sprinkle with herbs and serve.

After two visits to Hungary, Richard is a great fan of traditional Hungarian cooking, generously seasoned with what restaurateur George Lang, the author of The Cuisine of Hungary, *calls the holy trinity of paprika, onions, and lard.*

When cutting down on fat, you have to coax every bit of flavor from this dish. Use real Hungarian paprika. Substitute vegetable oil for lard and lowfat yogurt for sour cream. When using yogurt for sauces, heat the sauce without boiling, or the yogurt will curdle and separate. Stabilize it with a spoonful of flour or cornstarch.

Makes 4 servings

Oven Barbecued Chicken Breasts

There is nothing more mouth-watering than the smoky aroma of chicken slathered with barbecue sauce. This is our lighter barbecued and crumb-coated fried chicken. It's crisp, flavorful, and good, with a little crunchy topping.

M a k e s 4 s e r v i n g s

Barbecue Sauce

⅓ cup ketchup

l tablespoon chili sauce

l tablespoon (packed) dark brown sugar

l tablespoon cider vinegar

l garlic clove, crushed

Freshly ground black pepper

4 large boneless and skinless chicken breast halves (about 6 ounces each)

Crumb Topping

l tablespoon olive oil

l garlic clove, crushed

½ cup fine soft bread crumbs

½ teaspoon fresh thyme leaves or pinch of dried thyme

Salt and freshly ground black pepper

1. Combine the ketchup, chili sauce, brown sugar, vinegar, and garlic in a small saucepan. Bring to a boil over medium-low heat. Cook, uncovered, stirring frequently, until thickened, about 5 minutes. Remove from heat. Add a grinding of black pepper.

2. Heat the oven to 400°F. Place a sheet of heavy-duty aluminum foil on a baking sheet and crimp the edges up slightly so the juices won't drip over.

3. Coat the undersides of the chicken breasts lightly with the barbecue sauce. Place the breasts, sauce side down, on the foil-lined baking sheet. Coat the tops of the chicken breasts with the remaining barbecue sauce, dividing it evenly.

4. Meanwhile, heat the olive oil in a medium skillet. Add the garlic and sauté over medium heat for 1 minute. Add the crumbs, thyme, a pinch of salt and a grinding of black pepper. Sauté the crumbs, stirring frequently, until lightly toasted, about 5 minutes. Spoon the crumbs evenly on top of the chicken breasts.

5. Bake the chicken for 15 minutes. Let stand until slightly cooled. Cut each breast crosswise into ½-inch slices.

"Un-Fried" Fried Chicken

This is an adaptation of a very high fat recipe. The original was unbelievable—skinned pieces of chicken were thickly slathered with sour cream, then baked in a thick coating of bread crumbs, all anointed with rivers of melted butter. (It's delicious.) This version uses a lighter coating of crumbs, a drizzle of olive oil instead of butter, and thickened yogurt in place of sour cream. Believe it or not, it's just as tasty. Since the chicken is just as good at room temperature as hot, it's great for a picnic.

Makes 6 servings

1 pint nonfat yogurt, or as needed
2 chickens, each cut into 8 serving pieces, skin and fat removed (3 to 3¼ pounds each)
  Salt and freshly ground black pepper
2 cups soft fresh bread crumbs, part or all whole wheat if desired, or more as needed
¼ teaspoon paprika
¼ teaspoon cayenne
3 tablespoons olive oil, or as needed

1. Place a wide strainer lined with a double thickness of dampened cheesecloth over a bowl or in the sink. Spoon the yogurt into the strainer and let drain, turning yogurt over with a spoon once or twice, until it thickens to the consistency of thick sour cream, at least 30 minutes. Transfer the thickened yogurt to a measuring cup or small bowl. Discard the liquid.

2. To remove the skin from the chicken pieces, grab the skin with a kitchen towel and pull firmly, cutting as needed. Season the chicken pieces with salt and pepper.

3. Place bread crumbs in a pie plate or on a piece of wax paper. Season with salt, paprika, and cayenne. Line up the chicken pieces, yogurt, and bread crumbs assembly line style. Lightly oil a nonstick baking sheet, or line a baking sheet with aluminum foil and lightly oil the foil with olive oil or spray with nonstick cooking spray.

4. With a rubber spatula, thickly coat all surfaces of each piece of chicken with yogurt. Place the coated chicken pieces in the bread crumbs and pat the surface with crumbs to coat. Lift the chicken from the crumbs, letting excess crumbs drop off, and place the breaded chicken on the baking sheet. Refrigerate the breaded chicken on baking sheet for at least 30 minutes, uncovered, to help the coating adhere.

5. Place the rack in the upper third of the oven. Heat the oven to 400°F.

6. Drizzle breaded chicken pieces lightly with olive oil and bake, without turning, until nicely golden brown, 60 to 70 minutes. Serve hot or at room temperature.

Chicken and Vegetable Curry

Here is a traditional stew-with-gravy dish, with the fat, but not the flavor, drastically reduced. We've thickened the gravy by pureeing some of its cooking vegetables, then lightened it with a little yogurt. Actually, this is not an authentically Indian dish. It's loosely based on a dish that Bert Greene used to cook at The Store in Amagansett, America's first gourmet take-out shop. It's a great dish for a crowd. Set out condiments, such as pappadams, toasted almonds, and/or mango or other chutney, to dress it up and serve it with rice.

Makes 4 servings

1   can (13½ ounces) reduced-sodium chicken broth, fat skimmed

½   cup cold water

4   boneless and skinless chicken breast halves, well trimmed (about 1½ pounds)

1   tablespoon vegetable oil

2   onions, thinly sliced

2   carrots, sliced on a sharp diagonal

1   rib celery, strings peeled, sliced on a sharp diagonal

1   medium red bell pepper, cut into short slivers

2   garlic cloves, sliced thin

2   teaspoons minced fresh hot chili pepper or canned jalapeño (optional)

1½   teaspoons grated ginger

1½   to 2 tablespoons curry powder, or more to taste

1   Granny Smith apple, peeled, cored, and diced

½   cup plain lowfat or nonfat yogurt, or more as needed

¼   cup dried currants or raisins

1   teaspoon grated orange zest

     Salt

     Cayenne

1. Bring the broth and water to a boil in a large skillet. Slip in the chicken. Cover and simmer just until firm, about 8 minutes. Timing can vary; do not overcook. Remove the chicken from the broth, uncover, and cool slightly. Set aside the broth.
2. Heat the oil in a large nonstick skillet over medium-high heat. Add the onions, carrots, celery, and bell pepper and cook, tossing, until crisp-tender, about 4 minutes. Add the garlic, chili, ginger, and curry powder and toss until fragrant, about 2 minutes. Add the reserved broth from the chicken and the

apple and bring to a boil. Lower the heat and simmer, covered, until the vegetables are tender, about 15 minutes. Cut the chicken crosswise into $\frac{1}{2}$-inch strips.

3. With a slotted spoon, transfer 1 cup of the vegetables to a food processor or blender with a little of the broth. Puree until smooth and stir back into the broth. If you'd like the sauce a little thicker, puree more of the solids. Stir in the chicken, yogurt, currants, and orange zest until blended. Heat through, but do not allow to boil or the yogurt will curdle and separate. Add salt, cayenne, and/or more yogurt to taste. Cover and cook very gently for 5 minutes. Serve hot.

Cornish Hens Braised in the Style of Osso Buco

The flavorings of osso buco, the Milanese dish of veal shanks braised in tomatoes, wine, broth, vegetables, and herbs, are used to cook Cornish hens. Prepared this way, half a Cornish hen will be enough for each person, along with polenta, potatoes, rice, or a small pasta. Moisten everything with the aromatic braising liquid.

Makes 4 servings

2 Cornish hens, split in half, well trimmed with wing tips and tails discarded, rinsed and patted dry (about 1¾ pounds each)
   Salt and freshly ground black pepper
1 small onion, quartered
1 small carrot, thinly sliced
1 small rib celery, thinly sliced
1 clove garlic, bruised
1 cup dry white wine
1 can (14½ ounces) Italian-style plum tomatoes, with juice, coarsely chopped
½ cup reduced-sodium canned chicken broth, fat skimmed
1 bay leaf
1 recipe Orange Gremolata (page 34)

1. Select a large wide Dutch oven or other stovetop-to-oven pot, preferably nonstick. Season the hens with salt and pepper. Brown the hens on both sides over medium heat, about 5 minutes per side. Transfer the hens to a platter and wipe the fat from the pot with paper towels.

2. Heat the oven to 350°F.

3. Add the onion, carrot, celery, and garlic to the pan. Cover and cook the vegetables over medium-low heat until tender, stirring once or twice, about 10 minutes. Add the wine and bring to a boil. Boil the wine over high heat until reduced by half, about 5 minutes. Stir in the tomatoes, broth, and bay leaf.

4. Return the hens to the pan, spooning the tomatoes and vegetables over them. Cover and cook in the oven for 25 minutes, or until the hens are tender when you poke a thigh with a knife blade or fork. Transfer hens to a deep platter and set aside, loosely covered with foil to keep warm. Blot any fat from the cooking liquid with a folded paper towel and correct the seasonings.

5. Sprinkle the hens with gremolata and serve at once.

Debra Ponzek's Coq au Riesling

This recipe is from the chef of Montrachet in New York City, a gifted woman whose food is at once light and earthy. It is a free, lightened adaptation of the delicious Alsatian dish, which is traditionally enriched with egg yolks and cream. Note how Debra has eliminated the egg yolks and cream entirely, using reduced stock as the liquid, and flavoring it with just a touch of bacon, aromatic vegetables, and a generous sprinkling of fresh tarragon.

Makes 4 servings

2   or 3 Cornish hens, each cut in 6 serving pieces
    (legs, thighs, 2 breast halves)
    Salt and freshly ground black pepper
2   tablespoons coarsely chopped shallots
2   fresh thyme sprigs, or ¼ teaspoon dried thyme
1   cup Riesling wine, Alsatian or American
1   slice thick-cut bacon, preferably lightly smoked
1   tablespoon olive oil
8   white pearl onions
2   carrots, peeled, trimmed, and cut into ½-inch cubes
    or chunks
3   turnips, peeled, trimmed, and cut into ½-inch cubes
    or chunks
4   large white mushrooms, quartered
⅔   cup defatted chicken broth, preferably unsalted
1   tablespoon minced tarragon leaves, plus 4 tarragon sprigs,
    for garnish

1. Season the hen pieces with salt and pepper. Layer them in a bowl with the shallots and thyme; add the wine. Marinate, covered, in the refrigerator overnight, or for at least 2 hours.

2. Remove the hen pieces from the marinade; strain and reserve the marinade. Pat the hen pieces dry. Brown the bacon in a large (12-inch) skillet, preferably nonstick; drain bacon on a paper towel-lined plate. Discard the fat; wipe out the skillet. Cut the bacon in ¼-inch pieces and set aside.

3. Add the olive oil to the skillet; heat over medium heat. Add the hen pieces, skin side down, and cook until browned on both sides, about 5 to 7 minutes per side.

4. Meanwhile, bring a saucepan half filled with water to a boil. Add the onions; boil for 5 minutes. Add the carrots and turnips; cook 5 minutes longer. Drain the vegetables.

5. Scatter the vegetables, mushrooms, and reserved bacon around the hen pieces in the skillet. Cook, over medium heat, stirring gently, until the vegetables are lightly browned, 3 or 4 minutes. Cover and cook over medium-low heat for 10 minutes, or until the hens are just cooked through.

6. Using tongs, arrange the hen pieces on a warmed serving platter; remove the vegetables with a slotted spoon and arrange them around the hen pieces. Cover with foil to keep warm.

7. Add the reserved strained marinade and the chicken broth to the skillet; bring to a boil. Boil over high heat until the liquids are slightly thickened and reduced to about ³/₄ cup. Taste and correct seasonings. Stir in the tarragon; then spoon the juices over the hen pieces and vegetables. Garnish with tarragon sprigs and serve hot.

Roast Pheasant with Apples

This recipe is adapted from one of Kay O'Flynn's, the chef and proprietor of an Irish country hotel called Rathsallagh House. In Ireland, pheasants are hunted in the wild. In American markets, most game we buy is farm-raised; it is milder in flavor and more tender than wild game.

Makes 4 servings

1	pheasant (about 3 to 3½ pounds)
	Salt and freshly ground black pepper
2	tablespoons unsalted butter
1	cup chopped onion
1½	cups chopped cored unpeeled apple
4	juniper berries, crushed or coarsely chopped, if soft
1	thyme sprig
¾	cup dry red wine
¾	cup reduced-sodium canned beef or chicken broth, fat skimmed
	Thyme sprigs, for garnish

1. Rinse the pheasant thoroughly and pat dry. Pull off any pin feathers and discard any clumps of fat. Sprinkle the bird inside and out with salt and pepper.

2. Melt 1 tablespoon of the butter in a large skillet and add the onion and apple. Cook, stirring, over medium-low heat, until apple is very tender and onion is golden, about 8 minutes. Stir in the juniper berries and salt and pepper to taste. Cool mixture completely.

3. Spoon the mixture into the cavity and neck section of the pheasant, add the sprig of thyme, and close the cavities with wooden or metal skewers.

4. Melt the remaining butter in the same skillet, add the pheasant, and cook over low heat, turning, until it is lightly browned on all sides, about 10 minutes.

5. Heat the oven to 375°F.

6. Place the pheasant on its side in a roasting pan and roast for 15 minutes. Turn pheasant over, baste with pan juices, and roast 15 minutes longer, basting once. Turn pheasant breast side up, baste with pan juices, and roast, basting occasionally, until the juices run clear when the thickest part of the thigh is pierced with the tip of a knife, about 20 to 30 minutes longer. Transfer the pheasant to a carving board and cover with foil to keep warm.

7. Spoon off the fat from the roasting pan; place the pan with the juices over medium heat. Add wine and broth; boil until reduced to ¾ cup, about 8 minutes. Season to taste with salt and pepper. Carve the legs off the pheasant and cut the breast meat into thick slices. Spoon the stuffing on a platter and arrange the pheasant on top. Drizzle with the sauce, garnish with thyme sprigs, and serve.

turkey vs. other meats —

3 ounces cooked meat, fat trimmed	Protein g	Calories	Fat g	Cholesterol mg

Figures for poultry are "as sold," usually with skin. Fat and cholesterol will be even lower once the skin is removed.

TURKEY

	Protein g	Calories	Fat g	Cholesterol mg
Whole	25	129	3	64
Breast	26	119	1	55
Thigh	23	142	5	66
Ground	20	152	8	100
Ground (breast only)	28	124	trace	64

CHICKEN

	Protein g	Calories	Fat g	Cholesterol mg
Whole	23	135	4	76
Breast	24	116	2	72
Ground (white meat; 10% fat)	24	204	12	148

CORNISH HEN

	Protein g	Calories	Fat g	Cholesterol mg
White meat (with skin)	20	72	8	100
Dark meat (with skin)	16	108	12	120

BEEF

	Protein g	Calories	Fat g	Cholesterol mg
Rib roast	23	201	11	69
Sirloin steak	26	165	6	76
Ground (83% lean)	22	217	14	71

a look at the figures

VEAL

Loin chop   22   149   6   90

PORK

Loin chop   26   172   7   70

Spareribs   25   338   26   103

LAMB

Leg   24   162   7   76

Loin chop   25   183   8   80

Turkey en Escabeche

Cooking en escabeche is an old tradition of lightly pickling in vinegar and spices, often used for fat-rich fish. Here, Gil Martinez Soto, chef at Restaurante Virrey Palafox in El Burgo de Osma, near Madrid, uses the technique for lowfat turkey breast, garnished with colorful vegetables.

This is a terrific dish for a buffet, since it's prepared in advance and can stand at room temperature.

Makes 6 servings

½ boneless turkey breast, pop-up timer removed if necessary (about 1½ pounds)
2 cups red onions, cut into thin lengthwise slices
1 cup reduced-sodium canned chicken broth, fat skimmed
⅓ cup white wine vinegar, or more to taste
2 tablespoons olive oil
6 black peppercorns
4 allspice berries
2 bay leaves
1 rosemary sprig
1 thyme sprig
½ teaspoon salt
1 red bell pepper, seeds and stem removed, cut into thin lengthwise slices

1. Place the turkey breast in a deep skillet or wide shallow saucepan and add 1 cup of the onions, the broth, vinegar, olive oil, peppercorns, allspice berries, bay leaves, rosemary, thyme, and salt. Bring to a simmer over low heat. Cover and cook, turning after 20 minutes, until the turkey is cooked through, about 40 minutes in all.

2. Transfer the turkey, onions, spices, and herbs to a deep platter and scatter with the strips of red pepper and the remaining uncooked onion. Pour the hot liquid over the top. Let stand at room temperature until cooled. Cover with plastic wrap and refrigerate until chilled.

3. To serve, lift the turkey from the marinade and remove and discard the skin. Cut the turkey into thin crosswise slices. Arrange the slices on a platter, overlapping them slightly, and top with the onions and peppers. Drizzle some of the sauce over the meat and serve.

Sautéed Turkey Cutlets with Orange Sauce

2   tablespoons all-purpose flour
    Salt and freshly ground black pepper
1   pound turkey cutlets
1   tablespoon mild vegetable oil
⅓   cup sliced scallion, white part only
1   garlic clove, thinly sliced
¾   cup orange juice, preferably freshly squeezed
1   tablespoon low-sodium soy sauce
1   teaspoon oriental sesame oil
1   tablespoon finely sliced green scallion tops
2   cups cooked rice

1. Put the flour on a sheet of wax paper and combine with the salt and pepper. Lightly dredge the turkey cutlets in the flour, shaking off any excess.

2. Heat the oil in a large nonstick skillet over medium-high heat. When it's hot enough to sizzle a pinch of flour, add the cutlets, a few at a time, and cook until lightly browned, about 2 minutes per side. Transfer to a plate and continue to cook the remaining cutlets.

3. Add the whites of the scallions and the garlic to the skillet and cook, stirring, for 3 minutes. Add the orange juice and soy sauce and bring to a boil. Boil, stirring with a wooden spoon to scrape up any flavorful browned bits, until the juices thicken slightly, about 5 minutes. Stir in the sesame oil.

4. Return the turkey and any juices to the skillet, stirring gently to blend. Simmer, uncovered, for 5 minutes. Transfer the turkey to warm dinner plates, spoon or pour the sauce over, and sprinkle with the sliced scallion tops. Serve with rice.

This recipe is a basic method for a quick turkey sauté. You could deglaze the pan with white wine, Marsala, broth, or even water instead of orange juice. Or sauté a few mushrooms after browning the meat, then add a little wine, reduce, add some chopped herbs, and drizzle the concentrated juices over the turkey. Take care not to overcook the turkey cutlets.

Makes 4 servings

Turkey Cutlets with Arugula and Tomato Salad

Made with veal, this dish has been enjoying a vogue at American Italian restaurants from coast to coast. It's actually an old home-cooked Italian dish called orrechio d'elefante, *or elephant's ear. It's usually made with a veal cutlet or chop that has been breaded and fried in olive oil. We substitute a turkey cutlet and ovenfry it in a very hot oven. For the breading, we use egg whites instead of whole eggs to cut down on cholesterol.*

Makes 4 servings

Salad

1 large bunch (about 7 ounces) arugula, stems trimmed and coarsely cut up, or 3 cups mixed salad greens
4 ripe plum tomatoes, cored and cut into ½-inch dice
½ small red onion, cut into slivers
Salt and freshly ground black pepper
10 or 12 basil leaves, torn

Turkey

3 tablespoons extra virgin olive oil
¼ cup all-purpose flour
1 cup fine dried bread crumbs
Salt and freshly ground black pepper
2 large egg whites plus 1 tablespoon water
1 pound turkey cutlets

1 tablespoon red wine vinegar, or more to taste

1. Wash the arugula thoroughly in warm and then cold water and dry with paper towels or spin dry in a salad spinner. Refrigerate until ready to serve. Combine the tomatoes, onion, and salt and pepper to taste in a bowl and set aside at room temperature.

2. Heat the oven to 450°F. Brush a large nonstick baking sheet with 1½ tablespoons of the olive oil.

3. Place the flour and bread crumbs on separate sheets of wax paper and stir salt and pepper into the flour. Whisk the egg whites and water in a shallow soup bowl.

4. Coat the cutlets, one at a time, first with flour, then with egg wash, and finally with bread crumbs, shaking off excess. If time allows, refrigerate cutlets 20 minutes before cooking.

Arrange on the baking sheet. Bake until the turkey is browned and crisp, 4 to 5 minutes per side.

5. When the cutlets are ready, place one in the center of each dinner plate. Add the arugula to the bowl with the tomato mixture, drizzle with the remaining 1½ tablespoons olive oil and the vinegar, and toss. Spoon the salad on top of the cutlets, dividing it evenly. Serve hot.

Spring Turkey Ragout
with Lemon and Tarragon

Boneless turkey thighs, which are moist and suc-culent, can stand in for beef and other meats in stews and braised dishes. The dark meat is higher in fat than the breast meat (hence its juiciness), but by combining the dark meat with plenty of vegetables, you can make a healthier stew with plenty of turkey flavor. Serve it with barley, noodles, rice, or another carbohydrate side dish.

Makes 4 servings

2 boneless turkey thighs, skin and fat trimmed, cut into 1-inch cubes

2 tablespoons all-purpose flour
Salt and freshly ground black pepper

2 tablespoons olive oil

2 scallions, white and green parts sliced separately

½ cup dry white wine

1 cup low-sodium canned chicken broth, fat skimmed

1 cup carrots cut into 1½-inch lengths, available in 16-ounce bags

1 cup cubed (1 inch) scrubbed new potatoes

1 tablespoon chopped fresh tarragon or 1 teaspoon dried tarragon

1 cup cubed (1 inch) scrubbed zucchini

1 cup cubed (1 inch) scrubbed yellow crookneck squash or yellow squash

1 teaspoon grated lemon zest

1. Put the turkey thighs, flour, ¼ teaspoon salt, and a grinding of black pepper in a bag and shake to coat the turkey. Heat the oil in a large deep skillet, preferably nonstick, over medium heat. Add the turkey, shaking off any excess flour, and cook, turning with tongs, until it has browned evenly, about 6 minutes. Transfer the turkey to a plate. Add the sliced white part of the scallion to the pan and cook, stirring, for 2 minutes.

2. Add the wine and boil, stirring the pan with a wooden spoon or spatula to scrape up any browned bits, until the wine is reduced to a thick, syrupy glaze. Return the turkey and any juices to the skillet. Add the broth, carrots, potatoes, half of the fresh tarragon or all of the dried, a pinch of salt, and a grinding of pepper. Cover and simmer over medium heat until the turkey and carrots are tender, about 20 minutes.

3. Add the zucchini, yellow squash, sliced scallion tops, lemon zest, and the remaining fresh tarragon, if using. Cover and cook just until the squash is crisp-tender, about 5 minutes. Taste, add additional salt and pepper, if desired, and serve.

Spring Turkey Ragout with Artichokes Cut off the stems of 2 large artichokes. Peel the stems, cut into thin slices, and set aside. Pull off all the outside leaves and discard. Remove the prickly center leaves and scoop out the choke with a teaspoon. Cut each heart into 8 wedges. Combine the heart, the reserved sliced stems, and 1 tablespoon lemon juice in a small bowl. Add to the stew with the carrots and potatoes in Step 2.

Turkey Burgers with Dried Tomato Ketchup

These unusual cheese-stuffed burgers are low in fat and cholesterol but have plenty of flavor. Adding a little water to the ground turkey helps keep the burgers light. If you don't want to bother making the homemade ketchup—though it's quick—spread the burgers with a little Dijon mustard, then top with lettuce, tomato, and pickle slices.

Makes 4 servings

Dried Tomato Ketchup

1 tablespoon vegetable or olive oil
½ cup finely chopped onion
1 garlic clove, finely chopped
1 can (14½ ounces) tomatoes, pureed in blender or food processor
2 tablespoons sundried tomato bits, cut up with scissors
1 tablespoon dark brown sugar
1 tablespoon cider vinegar, or more to taste
 Salt
 Dash hot pepper sauce

Burgers

1 pound ground turkey
1 tablespoon cold water
1 tablespoon grated onion
1 tablespoon finely chopped parsley
2 tablespoons crumbled goat cheese

 Sliced dill pickles, for serving
 Toasted hard rolls, for serving

1. For the ketchup, heat the oil in a large skillet over medium-low heat. Add the onion and garlic and cook, stirring, until the onion is golden and very tender, about 10 minutes. Add the pureed canned tomatoes, sundried tomatoes, brown sugar, and vinegar. Bring to a simmer over medium heat. Cook, stirring and adjusting heat as necessary, until the ketchup has thickened, about 20 minutes. Add salt, hot pepper sauce, and additional vinegar to taste. (Makes about 1 cup.)

2. Place the ground turkey in a bowl and add the water, onion, and parsley and stir gently, without mashing, to combine.

Divide the meat into 4 equal portions and divide each portion in half. Shape the turkey into 8 flat patties about 3 inches in diameter. Crumble the goat cheese into the center of 4 of the patties. Top with the remaining patties and pinch the edges together to seal.

3. Heat a large skillet, preferably nonstick, over medium-high heat until hot enough to evaporate a drop of water upon contact. Add the burgers and cook, uncovered, until browned, about 3 minutes. Turn and cook just until the burgers are cooked through, 3 to 5 minutes longer. Do not overcook, or the meat will be dry.

4. Top each burger with a spoonful of ketchup and a few pickle slices. Serve on toasted rolls.

Turkey Burgers with Ginger, Garlic, and Soy Combine $1\frac{1}{4}$ pounds ground turkey with 3 tablespoons cold water, 1 teaspoon grated fresh ginger, and 1 crushed garlic clove. Form into burgers and drizzle each with 1 teaspoon low-sodium soy sauce. Grill or sauté as directed above.

Diner-style Turkey Meat Loaf

For this meat loaf, we've gone in several directions: used ground turkey instead of the usual beef-veal-pork blend, omitted egg yolks, and packed the meat mixture with plenty of vegetables. To replace ketchup, we've mashed up some canned tomatoes and added a touch of vinegar and brown sugar to give ketchup's edge without its hefty calorie count. Leftovers are great when served pâté-style, with mustard and dill pickles.

Makes 6 servings

1½	teaspoons olive oil
1	onion, chopped
1	carrot, chopped
1	rib celery, strings peeled and chopped
1	scallion, halved lengthwise, and thinly sliced
3	mushrooms, coarsely chopped
	Salt and freshly ground black pepper
1	teaspoon fresh thyme leaves or pinch dried thyme
2	garlic cloves, minced
2	tablespoons chopped parsley
⅔	cup canned tomatoes, with a little puree or juice
1	tablespoon balsamic or red wine vinegar
1	tablespoon dark brown sugar
	Few drops hot pepper sauce
1	egg white, lightly beaten
½	cup fresh bread crumbs
1½	pounds ground turkey
2	tablespoons Dijon mustard, or more as needed, for glaze

1. Heat 1 teaspoon of the olive oil in a large nonstick skillet over medium-high heat. Add the onion, carrot, celery, scallion, and mushrooms and sprinkle with salt, pepper, thyme, and garlic. Sauté, tossing occasionally, until the vegetables begin to soften, about 6 minutes. Transfer the vegetable mixture to a plate, add parsley, and set aside to cool slightly.

2. Heat the oven to 375°F.

3. Place the tomatoes, vinegar, brown sugar, and hot pepper sauce in a large bowl. Mash the mixture with a fork, breaking up the tomatoes until coarsely pureed. Stir in the egg white and bread crumbs. Add the ground turkey and sprinkle with salt and pepper. Combine the mixture with your fingers, without squeezing or compacting the ground meat. Add the vegetable mixture and mix lightly just until combined.

4. Transfer the mixture to a nonstick 8 × 4-inch loaf pan (if the pan isn't nonstick, oil it lightly). Tap the pan on a work surface a couple of times to eliminate air bubbles. With moist fingertips, smooth the surface of the loaf, mounding the mixture slightly along the center of its length. Lightly brush the surface of the loaf with mustard.

5. Bake until the meat loaf is lightly golden and a skewer inserted in the center of the loaf feels hot, about 55 minutes. Spoon off any congealed fat. Let the loaf stand for 5 to 10 minutes. Cut into thick slices and serve.

Turkey Sausage and Peppers

By using turkey sausage in an old Italian-style recipe for pork sausage and peppers, we've slashed the fat and cholesterol. The flavor of this dish improves when it's made in advance.

Makes 6 servings

2 pounds Italian-style turkey sausage links
2 teaspoons olive oil
2 medium onions, coarsely chopped
3 red peppers, cored, seeded, and cut into long slivers, 1 inch wide at thickest point
2 green peppers, cored, seeded, and cut into long slivers, 1 inch wide at thickest point
5 garlic cloves, minced
⅓ cup dry white wine
2 cans (14½ or 16 ounces each) Italian-style plum tomatoes, with juice, or tomatoes in puree
 Salt
½ cup finely shredded fresh basil leaves or ¾ teaspoon dried basil and 3 tablespoons fresh parsley
 Freshly ground black pepper

1. Prick the sausages with the tip of a sharp knife. Place in a large nonstick skillet in a single layer. Add ¼ inch cold water and cook over medium heat, turning the sausages once, until the water evaporates, 6 to 8 minutes. Raise heat slightly and cook, turning sausages with tongs, until they are browned on all sides, about 5 minutes longer. Add a little of the olive oil if the pan is dry. Transfer the sausages to a plate and wipe any fat from pan.

2. Add the oil and the onions and raise the heat slightly. Sauté, tossing, until onion begins to wilt, about 6 minutes. Stir in the peppers and garlic and cook 2 minutes. Cover and steam until the peppers begin to soften, about 5 minutes.

3. Add the wine, scraping up any browned bits in the pan, and boil for 2 or 3 minutes. Add the tomatoes and salt to taste. Cook, stirring and breaking up the tomatoes, until the sauce begins to thicken, 8 to 10 minutes. Stir in 3 tablespoons of the fresh basil or the dried basil. Lower the heat and tuck in the sausages, spooning the juices over them. Simmer, partially covered, until the sauce has thickened slightly, 20 to 30 minutes. Add water if sauce is too thick or uncover the pan if it is too thin.

4. Add pepper to taste and the remaining fresh basil or the parsley, correct seasonings. Serve with mashed potatoes or rice.

Turkey and Black Bean Chili

This dish—though made with ground turkey with plenty of black beans and vegetables—has the kick of real chili, especially if you can get your hands on chili powder that is pure ground chilies, nothing else. (Most commercial brands are blends that include other seasonings like cinnamon, cumin, garlic powder, and salt.) Make the chili a day in advance; the flavors will improve overnight. Serve the chili with any or all of the toppings suggested.

Makes 8 servings

1 tablespoon olive oil

1 cup chopped onions

1 cup diced (¼ inch) red bell pepper

1 cup diced (¼ inch) green bell pepper

½ cup diced (¼ inch) carrot

1 garlic clove, finely chopped

1 tablespoon chili powder, or more to taste

2 teaspoons ground cumin

1 pound ground turkey

2 cans (16 ounces each) black beans, drained and rinsed, or 3¾ cups cooked dried black beans (1½ cups dried)

3 cups reduced-sodium canned chicken broth, fat skimmed

1 tablespoon tomato paste

Salt and freshly ground black pepper

Toppings

Chopped cilantro

Diced tomato

Chopped fresh green chili peppers

Lowfat yogurt

1. Heat the oil in a large wide saucepan over medium-low heat. Add the onions, peppers, carrot, and garlic and cook, stirring, until the vegetables are very tender and the onions are golden, about 8 minutes. Sprinkle with the chili powder and cumin and stir to blend, letting the spices toast for a minute or so.

2. Add the turkey and cook, stirring and breaking up the meat, until the turkey loses its pink color, about 5 minutes. Add the beans, broth, and tomato paste. Bring to a simmer over medium heat. Reduce the heat and simmer, uncovered, stirring occasionally, until the liquid has reduced and the chili has thickened, about 1 hour. Correct the seasonings and serve with bowls of toppings.

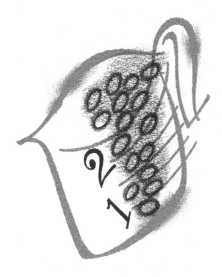

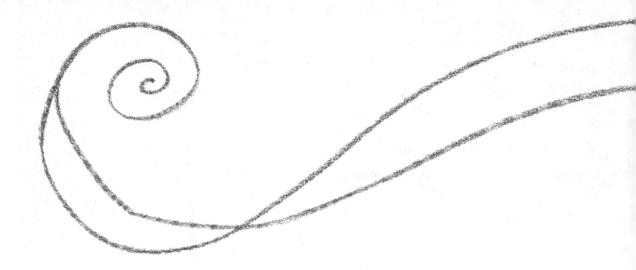

WE DON'T EAT RED MEAT on a daily basis, but every once in a while we do feel like indulging in a juicy hamburger or savoring a grilled garlic and rosemary–marinated leg of lamb. In fact, we probably appreciate the taste of meat a lot more now that we eat it less frequently.

A decade ago both of us, like many others, consumed a lot of red meat. This shift away from red meat was both conscious and unconscious. For one thing we've balanced our menus better by eating more of a variety of foods rather than following the old meat, potato, and vegetable meal blueprint. When you  eat more pasta, rice, and other grains, as well as plenty of fresh vegetables, you find yourself just naturally eating less meat or smaller portions of it.

eats

Now when we cook red meat, we try to select lean cuts and serve smaller portions or use just a small amount to lend flavor to a larger plateful of vegetables, rice, or other grains. Beef round and lamb and pork loin, especially pork tenderloin, are much lower in fat than sirloin, shoulder, or rib cuts. But with these leaner cuts, you need to take more care in cooking than with cuts with lots of fat, which keeps meat succulent and juicy. The simple secret to cooking lean cuts of meat is to cook them just until done, no longer. Otherwise, they will dry out and become tough.

Some types of game offer a healthy alternative for meat lovers. Though still in limited supply for most consumers, game meats and birds are gradually becoming more widely available.

meat: the facts about fat and cholesterol

All figures are for a 3-ounce cooked serving. All figures are approximate, as meats can vary.

Meat	Calories	Fat g	Cholesterol mg
BEEF			
Sirloin steak	232	15	77
Top round	196	8	94
Lean ground	217	14	71
VEAL			
Cutlet, from round	150	5	112
LAMB			
Loin chop	184	10	81
Leg	175	8	79
PORK			
Center loin	196	9	79
Tenderloin	141	4	78
CHICKEN			
Breast, no skin	142	3	71
Leg, with skin	198	11	79
TURKEY			
Breast, no skin	115	3	33

Flank Steak in Zinfandel Marinade with Sautéed Shiitakes

Makes 4

servings

1   cup full-flavored California Zinfandel wine

6   juniper berries

6   garlic cloves, halved

1   piece orange zest (2 × ½ inch)

1   thyme sprig

1   thick slice onion

1   bay leaf

1   piece flank steak, well trimmed (about 1¼ pounds)
    Salt and freshly ground black pepper

1   tablespoon olive oil

6   ounces shiitake mushrooms, stems removed

1   tablespoon finely chopped parsley
    Thyme sprigs, for garnish

1. Combine the wine, juniper, garlic, orange zest, thyme, onion, and bay leaf in a shallow dish. Add the beef, turning to coat with marinade. Cover and refrigerate overnight, turning at least once.

2. Remove beef from the marinade, reserving marinade, and pat beef dry. Sprinkle with salt and pepper. Strain the marinade and set aside the wine and solids separately. Dry the pieces of garlic and chop fine. Place 1 teaspoon of the olive oil in a large heavy nonstick skillet and add the chopped garlic. Cover and cook over very low heat, stirring once or twice, until the garlic is tender, about 5 minutes. Scrape the garlic from the skillet and add to the strained wine. Set aside.

3. Brush the remaining oil over the shiitake caps. Add the mushrooms to the skillet and sauté over medium heat, stirring and turning, until tender, about 10 minutes. Transfer to a serving platter and sprinkle with salt, pepper, and parsley. Cover with foil and place in a low oven to keep warm.

4. Turn the heat under the skillet to high. Add the steak and cook, uncovered, over medium to high heat, adjusting heat to prevent smoking and turning once, until done, 5 to 6 minutes per side for rare. Set meat aside on cutting board to rest.

5. Add the wine with the garlic to the skillet and bring to a boil, stirring and scraping pan until the wine is reduced by half and thickened slightly, about 5 minutes.

6. Meanwhile, slice the beef thin on a diagonal and arrange on the platter with the mushrooms. Drain any juices on the platter, both mushroom and meat, and pour back into the skillet with the reducing sauce.

7. Strain the reduced sauce over the meat. Garnish with thyme sprigs and serve at once.

Fillet of Beef Stroganoff over Poppy Seed Noodles

This really is fast. We've reinterpreted stroganoff using lowfat yogurt instead of the traditional sour cream. You know you're getting top-quality beef and plenty of meaty mushrooms, which satisfy appetites with minimal calories. Adding a bit of flour to the yogurt lets you heat it without curdling.

Makes 4 servings

4　ounces snow peas, soaked briefly in ice water, trimmed

3　teaspoons olive oil

1　pound fillet of beef in 1 piece, trimmed well and cut across the grain into thin (⅛ to ¼ inch) slices

2　cups thinly sliced mushrooms (about ½ pound)

½　cup slivered onion

½　garlic clove, crushed or finely chopped

½　cup Beef Broth, homemade (page 43), or reduced-sodium canned broth, fat skimmed

1　tablespoon tomato paste

1　teaspoon cornstarch

¼　cup lowfat yogurt, at room temperature

1　teaspoon all-purpose flour

　　Salt and freshly ground black pepper

1　tablespoon finely chopped parsley

　　Poppy Seed Noodles (recipe follows)

1. Steam the snow peas until crisp-tender, about 3 minutes. Rinse under cold water to stop cooking and set aside.

2. Brush a large heavy nonstick skillet with 1 teaspoon of the olive oil and heat over medium-high heat. Add half the pieces of beef and brown quickly on both sides. Transfer to a plate. Brown remaining beef slices and transfer to the plate. Set aside.

3. Add the remaining 2 teaspoons of oil to the hot skillet and stir in the mushrooms and onion. Sauté over medium-high heat, tossing, just until edges begin to brown. Stir in the garlic. Cover and cook over low heat until mushrooms have released some of their liquid and vegetables are tender, about 5 minutes.

4. Meanwhile stir together the broth, tomato paste, and corn-starch in a small bowl until smooth. Stir into the mushroom mixture and add juices from the beef. Heat over medium heat, stirring, until broth boils and mixture thickens slightly.

5. Stir the yogurt and flour in a cup until smooth. Add the beef to the mushroom mixture. Add salt and pepper to taste and the yogurt mixture; heat through. Remove skillet from heat and stir until blended. Arrange the hot noodles on dinner plates, spoon the stroganoff over, and serve immediately.

Poppy Seed Noodles

8   ounces fresh fettuccine or dried wide egg noodles

1   teaspoon poppy seeds

Makes 4 servings

1. Cook noodles in plenty of boiling salted water until al dente. Ladle out about 2 tablespoons of the cooking water before draining. Drain noodles.

2. Combine the reserved noodle cooking water and the poppy seeds in the saucepan. Add the hot noodles and toss. Serve at once.

Stir-fried Beef with Broccoli and Red Peppers

This is a great way to incorporate a small amount of beef into a mostly vegetable and grain dinner. Serve on a bed of cooked rice, prefer-ably short grain brown.

Makes 4 servings

2 tablespoons chicken broth or water

1 tablespoon dry sherry

1 tablespoon low-sodium soy sauce

1 tablespoon honey

2 teaspoons cornstarch

2 teaspoons finely chopped ginger

2 teaspoons finely chopped garlic

¾ pound boneless sirloin, about ¾ inch thick, fat trimmed and cut into thin (¼ inch) slices

3 teaspoons vegetable oil

2 cups trimmed broccoli florets

½ cup thin slices carrot

½ red bell pepper, cut into ¼-inch strips

1 small yellow squash, halved lengthwise and cut into ¼-inch slices

½ cup thin diagonally sliced scallions, white and green parts

¼ teaspoon crushed red pepper, or more to taste

1. Combine the broth, sherry, soy sauce, honey, cornstarch, 1 teaspoon of the ginger, and 1 teaspoon of the garlic in a pie plate or other shallow dish. Stir with a fork to blend. Add the steak slices and turn to coat.

2. Heat a large nonstick skillet over high heat until a drop of water evaporates upon contact. Add 2 teaspoons of the oil and the broccoli, carrot, red bell pepper, and squash. Stir-fry, adjusting the heat to maintain a steady sizzle, until the vegeta-bles are almost tender, about 5 minutes. Add the scallions and remaining ginger and garlic and stir-fry for 1 minute. Transfer to a side dish.

3. Add the remaining 1 teaspoon oil to the hot skillet and gradually add the slices of beef. Sprinkle with the crushed red pepper. Stir-fry the beef until browned on both sides, about 3 minutes.

4. Add the vegetables to the skillet. Stir-fry just to heat through, about 1 minute. Serve at once.

Southwestern-style Meat Loaf

This is more a meat and vegetable loaf than a meat loaf. It is adapted from a recipe from our friend Anne Riives, who used two pounds ground pork and beef in hers. In this recipe we use less meat, part of it ground turkey, which is lower in fat. The mixture has cornmeal and corn kernels plus lots of spices.

Makes 8 servings

¼ cup cornmeal

½ cup tomato juice, vegetable juice, or cold water

1 large red onion, chopped (about 1½ cups)

2 large garlic cloves, minced

1 tablespoon olive or vegetable oil

1 cup fresh, frozen, or canned and drained corn kernels

¼ cup (packed) chopped cilantro

1½ teaspoons chili powder

1 teaspoon ground cumin (see Note)

1 pound ground turkey

½ pound ground pork shoulder or beef chuck

1 egg white

2 hot red and green pickled cherry peppers, drained, seeded, and chopped

2 pickled jalapeño peppers, drained, seeded, and chopped

½ teaspoon salt

1. Stir the cornmeal and tomato juice together in a large bowl until smooth. Set aside.

2. Cook the onion and garlic in olive oil in a nonstick skillet over medium-high heat until lightly golden, 8 to 10 minutes. Process the corn kernels in a food processor until finely chopped. Transfer the corn to the skillet, add the cilantro, chili powder, and cumin and cook, stirring, 2 minutes. Add to the cornmeal mixture.

3. Heat the oven to 375°F.

4. Add the meats, egg white, chopped cherry and jalapeño peppers, and salt to the cornmeal and onion mixture. Blend with a spoon or fingertips, using a light touch to avoid compacting, until thoroughly blended. Spoon mixture into a 9 × 5-inch loaf pan. Tap the pan on a work surface to eliminate air bubbles. With fingertips moistened in cold water, smooth the surface of the meat.

5. Cover the loaf with foil and bake for 30 minutes. Remove the foil and raise the heat to 400°F. Continue to bake until loaf is golden brown and cooked through, about 45 minutes longer.

6. Remove from the oven; let meat loaf stand about 20 minutes before serving. Cut into thick slices and serve. The meat loaf may also be served cold.

Note: For maximum flavor, toast any amount of whole cumin seeds in a dry skillet, stirring, until fragrant, about 3 minutes. Grind and measure before using. Store any unused ground cumin in a tightly covered jar.

Osso Buco with Lemon Zest

This lightened adaptation of a classic northern Italian dish is from former chef Bruce Lim and executive chef Jean-Marie Lacroix at the Fountain Restaurant in the Four Seasons Hotel in Philadelphia. The technique of slowly simmering meat with chopped vegetables, then using the pureed vegetables to give body to the sauce is a very effective way to thicken the gravy, adding flavor without fat.

Makes 6 servings

Vegetable oil or nonstick cooking spray

1   meaty veal shank, split by the butcher into 6 even pieces, about ⅝ inch thick (about 2¼ pounds)

¼   cup dry white wine

½   cup diced (¼ inch) zucchini

½   cup diced (¼ inch) red onion

½   cup diced (¼ inch) carrot

½   cup diced (¼ inch) celery

1   small garlic clove, minced

Salt and freshly ground black pepper

1   cup Chicken Broth, homemade (page 42), or reduced-sodium canned broth, fat skimmed

1   tablespoon tomato paste

1   strip (2 × ½ inch) lemon zest

¼   cup (packed) flat-leaf parsley leaves, with thin stems

Steamed Vegetables (recipe follows)

1. Select a heavy Dutch oven, preferably nonstick. Brush pan with a light film of vegetable oil or spray with nonstick cooking spray. Brown the pieces of veal over medium heat until golden on both sides, about 5 minutes per side.

2. Heat the oven to 350°F.

3. Stack the veal on 1 side of the pan, add the wine, and bring to a boil. Add the zucchini, red onion, carrot, celery, and garlic. Cook over medium-low heat, stirring the vegetables, until liquid has reduced, about 5 minutes. Arrange veal in a single layer in pan and sprinkle with salt and pepper.

4. Whisk together the chicken broth and tomato paste in a small bowl until smooth. Pour over and around the veal, cover, and bake until the veal is tender, about 40 minutes.

5. Transfer veal to 6 warm serving plates and cover loosely with foil. Leave vegetables and juices in pan. Puree the vegetables and juices in a food mill or food processor. Return juices to the Dutch oven over medium heat and boil briefly, until slightly reduced. Finely chop the lemon zest and parsley together. Stir and add half of the lemon-parsley mixture to the juices. Correct seasonings. Spoon sauce evenly over each piece of veal; arrange steamed vegetables on the platter. Sprinkle meat and vegetables with the remaining lemon-parsley mixture. Serve immediately.

Steamed Vegetables

6   thick carrots, diagonally sliced

6   small new potatoes, scrubbed and halved

6   thick zucchini, diagonally sliced

6   thick yellow squash, diagonally sliced

Place a steaming basket over 1 inch of boiling water. Add the carrots and potatoes in a single layer. Cover and cook until tender, about 5 minutes. Add the zucchini and yellow squash. Cover and cook until crisp-tender, but still brightly colored, about 2 minutes.

Makes 6

servings

Yogurt-Marinated Spice-Grilled Lamb

This recipe is from Gary Danko, friend and talented chef at the Ritz-Carlton Hotel in San Francisco, who likes to serve this lamb medium-rare, along with an herb chutney. With it, he slices cucumbers very thin and quickly pickles them in salt and lime juice. This is a terrific dish for a crowd. For best flavor begin marinating the meat two to three days before serving. Make the chutney about 4 hours before serving.

Makes 10 to 12 servings

Yogurt and Spice Marinade

1	cup lowfat yogurt
½	cup fresh lime juice
1½	teaspoons ground coriander
1	teaspoon ground ginger
½	teaspoon cayenne
½	teaspoon ground cinnamon
½	teaspoon ground cardamom
¼	teaspoon ground cloves
¼	teaspoon freshly ground black pepper
½	teaspoon salt

½ leg of lamb, boned and butterflied by the butcher (about 3½ pounds)
Fresh Herb Chutney (recipe follows)

1. Combine the yogurt with all other marinade ingredients in a large glass pie plate or other shallow dish and stir to blend. Add the lamb and turn to coat with marinade. Cover with plastic wrap and marinate, refrigerated, for 2 or 3 days, turning meat over at least once a day.

2. Heat a grill or broiler.

3. Lift lamb from marinade, letting excess marinade drip off. Meat should be coated with a light film of marinade. Grill or broil the meat until done, 8 to 10 minutes per side for medium rare. Timing varies depending on heat of grill and thickness of meat.

4. Let the meat rest for about 5 minutes, then slice on the bias and serve with the lamb juices drizzled over. Pass the chutney separately.

Fresh Herb Chutney

¼   cup chopped cilantro

¼   cup chopped mint

¼   cup chopped tarragon

¼   cup chopped chives

1   garlic clove, minced

2   teaspoons grated fresh ginger

1   teaspoon fresh lime juice

½   teaspoon salt

1   tablespoon olive oil

Combine the chutney ingredients in a small bowl and stir to blend. Cover and refrigerate. Remove from refrigerator about ¹/₂ hour before serving.

Honey-Roasted Pork Tenderloins

The tenderloin is the thin strip of meat that lies underneath the loin. It is among the leanest and tenderest of all meat cuts. This is a quick, flavorful dish; take care not to overcook the pork.

Makes 8 servings

2   pork tenderloins, well trimmed (8 to 10 ounces each)
2   garlic cloves, crushed
2   teaspoons grated orange zest
2   teaspoons fresh thyme leaves, stripped from stems, or ½ teaspoon dried thyme
½   teaspoon freshly ground black pepper
⅓   cup orange juice
2   tablespoons rice wine vinegar
2   tablespoons honey

1. Place the pork tenderloins on a shallow platter. Combine the garlic, orange zest, thyme, and black pepper in a small bowl and work into a paste with a fork. Rub the paste into the surfaces of the pork tenderloins. Stir the orange juice and vinegar together and pour over the pork. Cover and refrigerate for 2 hours, turning the pork occasionally.

2. Heat the oven to 425°F. Select a heavy baking pan, preferably cast iron, or a heavy ovenproof skillet and brush the pan with a thin film of vegetable oil. Place pan in the oven until hot, about 4 minutes.

3. Remove the pan from the oven and place the tenderloins in it, spacing them slightly apart. Drizzle 1 tablespoon of the honey over the pork and roast for 10 minutes. Turn the loins over, spoon any juices over the meat, and drizzle with the remaining tablespoon of honey. Roast 10 to 15 minutes, basting once or twice with the juices.

4. Let the meat stand for 5 minutes. Carve into ¼-inch slices and serve hot. This is also good cold, in a sandwich or salad.

Choucroute Garnie

1 strip bacon

1 teaspoon vegetable oil

½ large sweet onion, cut into ¼-inch vertical slices

1 garlic clove, minced

1½ pounds sauerkraut, rinsed thoroughly in cold water and drained well

4 medium all-purpose potatoes, peeled and chopped (¼ inch)

1 medium apple, quartered, peeled, cored, and chopped (¼ inch)

1 cup apple cider

4 juniper berries, bruised

2 whole cloves

½ bay leaf

¼ teaspoon dried thyme

½ pork tenderloin (about 6 ounces)

1 piece fully cooked smoked turkey breast, at room temperature (about 12 ounces)

Finely chopped parsley

1. Cook the bacon in a heavy Dutch oven or other stovetop-to-oven pan, until crisp. Drain on a paper towel. Crumble bacon and set aside. Wipe the bacon fat from the pan with paper towels.

2. Heat the vegetable oil in the pan. Add the onion and sauté, stirring, just to coat with oil. Cover and cook over very low heat, stirring occasionally, until onion is wilted and golden, about 10 minutes. Stir in the garlic and sauté for 1 minute.

3. Heat the oven to 350°F.

4. Add the sauerkraut, potatoes, apple, apple cider, juniper berries, cloves, bay leaf, and thyme to the pan. Bring to a boil,

The classic recipe for this sauerkraut extravaganza uses lots of sausage, bacon, and other fatty cuts of meat. We have cut the bacon down to one slice to keep the fat at a minimum but still retain the smoky flavor. For the meats we use a piece of lean pork tenderloin and smoked turkey. Some ethnic butchers sell excellent sauerkraut in bulk, right from the barrel. If you can't get that, use sauerkraut that comes vacuum packed in plastic bags.

Makes 4 servings

cover, and simmer until the potatoes are tender, about 10 minutes. Push the sauerkraut mixture to the sides and place the pork in the center. Spoon some of the sauerkraut over the top. Sprinkle the bacon on top.

5. Cover and bake for 15 minutes. Add the turkey breast and cover it with sauerkraut. Cover and bake until the pork is done and the turkey is heated through, about 15 minutes longer.

6. To serve, spoon the sauerkraut mixture onto a large platter. Transfer the pork and turkey to a cutting board and slice ¼ inch thick. Arrange the pork, overlapping the slices, down one side of the sauerkraut; arrange the smoked turkey down the other side. Sprinkle with the parsley and serve hot.

Stir-fried Orange Pork with Vegetables and Peanuts

8   ounces lean boneless pork loin or a tenderloin, cut
    into thin strips (1 to 1½ × ¼ × ¼ inch)

1   teaspoon low-sodium soy sauce

½   teaspoon grated orange zest

1   garlic clove, crushed

½   pound green beans, trimmed and cut on the diagonal
    into 1-inch lengths

2   medium carrots, cut into strips (1 × ¼ × ¼ inch)

Orange Sauce

¼   cup freshly squeezed orange juice

1   tablespoon honey

1   tablespoon rice wine vinegar

2   teaspoons low-sodium soy sauce

1   teaspoon cornstarch

¼   teaspoon crushed red pepper

1   tablespoon vegetable oil

6   strips (2 × ½ inch) orange zest, cut into ⅛-inch
    julienne strips

1   tablespoon minced fresh ginger

1   teaspoon minced garlic

1   cup diagonally sliced (about ½ inch) scallions

1   small red bell pepper, quartered, trimmed, and cut
    crosswise into ¼-inch pieces

1   small yellow squash, halved lengthwise and sliced
    ⅛ inch thick

2   tablespoons finely chopped unsalted dry-roasted peanuts
    Steamed rice or cooked udon (whole wheat)
    noodles, if desired

Well-trimmed pork loin, and especially pork tenderloin, are among the leanest cuts of pork. The tenderloin is also one of the most tender cuts of meat; it remains juicy if you cook it until it is just done, no longer. You can find it, often two to a package, in the meat section of the supermarket.

Makes 4 servings

1. Stir the pork, soy sauce, grated orange zest, and crushed garlic in a small bowl. Cover and refrigerate for about 30 minutes.

2. Steam the green beans and carrots on a rack over 1 inch of simmering water, tightly covered, until crisp-tender, about 3 minutes. Rinse under cold water and set aside at room temperature.

3. Stir together the orange juice, honey, vinegar, soy sauce, and cornstarch in a small bowl. Stir in the hot pepper and set aside.

4. Just before serving, heat a large heavy nonstick skillet over high heat until hot enough to evaporate a drop of water upon contact. Add the oil, tilting the pan to coat. Add the orange zest and stir-fry until zest is fragrant and edges begin to brown, about 30 seconds. With a slotted spoon, transfer half of orange zest to a plate and set aside. Immediately add the ginger and garlic and stir-fry 30 seconds. Add the scallions, pepper, green beans, and carrots and stir-fry 2 minutes. Add the yellow squash and stir-fry 30 seconds. Scrape the contents of the pan into a serving dish and set aside, uncovered.

5. Reheat the pan over high heat until hot enough that a piece of the pork sizzles and browns instantly. Add the pork, a few pieces at a time, to prevent the pan from cooling down, and stir-fry, using a chopstick to keep pieces separated, until pork is browned on all sides, about 2 minutes.

6. Add the reserved vegetables to the sizzling pork all at once and stir to blend. Stir the orange juice mixture to blend. Pour juice mixture over the contents of the pan and stir-fry over high heat until mixture is coated and glazed.

7. Spoon the mixture into the serving dish, sprinkle with reserved orange zest and chopped peanuts, and serve with steamed rice or udon noodles, if desired.

Sautéed Venison Medallions
with Lentils

1   cup dried lentils

2½   teaspoons vegetable oil

2   tablespoons finely chopped shallots

2   tablespoons finely chopped carrot

2   teaspoons minced garlic

2   teaspoons minced ginger

¼   cup Chicken Broth, homemade (page 42), or
     reduced-sodium canned broth, fat skimmed

1   tablespoon low-sodium soy sauce

1   pound boneless venison loin, cut into 8 medallions
     about ⅓-inch thick

1   tablespoon ground coriander

¼   teaspoon salt

¼   teaspoon freshly ground black pepper
     Fresh cilantro or parsley leaves, for garnish

This full-flavored recipe is adapted from one of Philippe Boulot's, now at the Heathman Hotel in Portland, Oregon. The combination of lentils and meat is a perfect example of how to combine meat and legumes in a single dish.

Makes 4 servings

1. Cook the lentils in boiling water until tender, about 15 minutes. (Do not overcook.) Drain. Heat 2 teaspoons of the vegetable oil in a large nonstick skillet over low heat. Add chopped shallots, carrot, garlic, and ginger and cook, stirring, until tender, about 5 minutes. Add the lentils, broth, and soy sauce and heat through. Keep warm over low heat.

2. Pat venison dry, if necessary, with paper towels. Combine the coriander, salt, and pepper in a small bowl. Sprinkle lightly over both sides of the venison medallions.

3. Heat a large nonstick skillet over medium-high heat. Brush the skillet with the remaining ½ teaspoon vegetable oil. Add half the venison and quickly cook 1 to 1½ minutes per side for medium-rare. Shake the pan to prevent sticking. Do not overcook or the venison will be dry. Transfer to a platter, repeat with the remaining medallions, and transfer to the platter. Add the lentils to the same skillet and stir to scrape up any browned bits, until the lentils are heated through. Add any juices from the platter of venison medallions.

4. Divide the lentils among 4 warmed serving plates. Place 2 medallions on each plate. Garnish with cilantro or parsley.

Grilled Rabbit with Ancho Chili Sauce

1   rabbit, cut into 8 pieces (2¾ to 3 pounds)

Marinade

2   tablespoons dry white wine

2   tablespoons olive oil

1   tablespoon ground coriander

1½   teaspoons ground cinnamon

½   teaspoon crushed red pepper

¼   teaspoon salt

Ancho Chili Sauce

3   dried ancho chilies

2   teaspoons peanut oil

1   cup finely chopped onions

2   teaspoons fennel seed

1   tablespoon minced garlic

1½   teaspoons minced seeded serrano chili or
     other fresh hot chili

1   cup Chicken Broth, homemade (page 42),
     or reduced-sodium canned broth, fat skimmed

⅓   cup dry red wine

1   cup chopped tomato

1   teaspoon cinnamon

⅓   cup lowfat milk

1   teaspoon honey, or more to taste

2   teaspoons fresh lime juice, or more to taste

2   tablespoons chopped cilantro
     Salt and freshly ground black pepper

White Corn Relish

2   cups fresh white corn kernels, cut from cobs

¼   cup diced red bell pepper

¼   cup chopped red onion

¼   cup (loosely packed) chopped basil or cilantro leaves

An exuberant treatment for rabbit, this recipe is from John Ash, restaurateur, cookbook author, and chef at Fetzer Vineyards. The simple overnight marination and grilling technique can be used for chicken, also cut into eight pieces. The ancho chili sauce and corn relish add color and deep, lively flavor. Ash uses cream in the chili sauce; we've substituted milk to reduce fat.

Makes 4 servings

½   teaspoon minced seeded serrano chili or
     other fresh hot chili, or more to taste
2   tablespoons rice wine vinegar
2   tablespoons olive oil
2   teaspoons fresh lime or lemon juice
I   teaspoon honey
     Salt and freshly ground black pepper
     Lime wedges, for garnish
     Cilantro sprigs, for garnish

1. Wash the rabbit pieces and pat dry. Combine the wine, olive oil, coriander, cinnamon, red pepper, and salt in a bowl. Add the rabbit, including the kidneys, liver, and heart, and turn the pieces to coat, rubbing the marinade into the rabbit. Cover and refrigerate overnight.

2. Cover the chilies with hot water and soak until softened, about 30 minutes. Drain, discarding stems and seeds. Set aside.

3. Heat the oil in a saucepan over medium heat and sauté the onions for 2 or 3 minutes, until softened. Add the fennel seed, garlic, and serrano chili and sauté for 3 minutes longer. Add the broth, wine, tomato, cinnamon and reserved ancho chilies and simmer, uncovered, for 15 to 20 minutes. Add the milk and heat through. Transfer the mixture to a food processor and puree until smooth. Add honey and lime juice, taste, and add more if desired. Strain if desired. Stir in cilantro and correct seasoning with salt and pepper. You should have about 1⅔ cups. Set aside.

4. About 1 hour before serving, prepare the salsa. Combine the corn, red pepper, red onion, basil, chili, vinegar, oil, lime juice, and honey in a bowl and stir to blend. Add salt and pepper to taste. You should have about 2 cups. Cover and refrigerate until ready to serve.

5. Just before serving, heat a grill or broiler until hot. Lift the rabbit legs from the marinade and place on the fire. Grill or broil for 5 minutes. Turn the legs over and add the loin pieces. Grill or broil the pieces, turning them once or twice more, until golden brown and cooked through, about 15 to 20 minutes longer. The timing can vary based on the heat of the fire. Do not overcook, or the rabbit will be tough. Grill the kidneys, liver, and heart for the last 5 minutes.

6. To serve, rewarm the sauce, if necessary. Spoon sauce on each of 4 serving plates. Spoon the salsa in the center; then place 2 pieces of rabbit on each plate. Garnish the plates with lime wedges and sprigs of cilantro and serve.

Br

a n

eads

GOOD BREAD IS ONE OF THE CORNERSTONES of a healthy diet. The recipes in this chapter are quick and easy, maybe because we are both fortunate enough to have a huge variety of quality breads available close by.

Because muffins and quick breads are so easy to make, they are among the most popular baked goods for home cooks. We've added all sorts of flavorful, nutrient-dense ingredients to lower-fat muffin batters. We use a variety of grains, including cornmeal, bran, and wheat germ, and fold in naturally sweet dried fruits such as figs and dates. A good-quality nonstick muffin pan is an excellent investment; it really does work. We usually spray with a light coating of nonstick cooking spray, just as insurance.

d muffins

Biscuits and muffins are among the baked goods that work best when adapted to lower-fat versions. Fat not only adds flavor, it adds tenderness as well. When you leave out the fat, it is important to compensate for the omission. Be sure to handle biscuit doughs with an extra light touch. Always true, this is even more important when you are trimming fat.

We found it is possible to omit an egg yolk and substitute lowfat dairy products (yogurt, buttermilk, skim milk) and still have an acceptable texture. We've kept amounts of sugar low, instead adding naturally sweet dried fruits, or mashed or chopped fresh fruits. To lower saturated fat levels further, we often use vegetable oil instead of butter, with maple syrup, molasses, or brown sugar adding an interesting flavor element.

Buttermilk Biscuits

1½ cups unbleached all-purpose flour,
 or more as needed
2 teaspoons sugar
2 teaspoons baking powder
½ teaspoon baking soda
½ teaspoon salt
⅔ cup buttermilk
¼ cup vegetable oil

1. Heat the oven to 425°F. Spray a nonstick baking sheet with nonstick cooking spray.

2. Combine the flour, sugar, baking powder, baking soda, and salt in a large bowl and stir to blend.

3. Stir the buttermilk and oil together in a small bowl. Add to the flour mixture, stirring with a fork just until the mixture clears the sides of the bowl. It will be very lumpy. Do not overmix.

4. Sprinkle work surface with flour. Turn out the biscuit dough. With well-floured hands, pat the dough into a circle about 6 or 7 inches in diameter and ½ inch thick. Use a 2¾-inch biscuit cutter or glass to cut out biscuits, gathering up the scraps. Transfer to the baking sheet.

5. Bake until golden on top and bottom, 10 to 12 minutes. These are best eaten warm.

Marie first learned to make real Southern biscuits from her friend Sarah Gaede, who insisted on White Lily self-rising flour and gobs of lard. Sarah taught Marie to use a light hand when mixing the dough and to "de-gunk your fingers." These biscuits are not quite the same, but when we follow Sarah's advice, they are light as a feather.

**Makes
six 2¾-inch
biscuits**

Parmesan Cornbread

Like traditional Southern cornbread, this batter is baked in a hot cast-iron skillet. Parmesan cheese adds a new dimension. This is good any time of day—breakfast, brunch, or dinner.

Makes 4 servings

I	tablespoon vegetable oil
I½	teaspoons unsalted butter
I½	cups cornmeal, preferably stoneground
½	cup unbleached all-purpose flour
2	teaspoons baking powder
I	teaspoon baking soda
I	teaspoon salt
I	tablespoon sugar
⅛	teaspoon cayenne
I	cup lowfat yogurt
½	cup cold water
I	large egg
2	tablespoons grated parmesan cheese

1. Place the oil and butter in a 9-inch cast-iron skillet or cake pan and place in the oven. Heat the oven to 425°F.

2. Meanwhile, sift the dry ingredients into a bowl. Beat together the yogurt, water, egg, and the oil and butter from the pan. Make a well in the dry ingredients and pour in the liquid, stir just until blended, and pour into hot pan. Sprinkle with cheese.

3. Bake until lightly golden, 20 to 25 minutes. Serve warm, cut in wedges.

Cornmeal Spoonbread with Fresh Greens

1	pound collard greens, swiss chard, kale, or mustard greens
½	cup chopped onion
1	tablespoon olive oil
1	tablespoon minced garlic
	Salt and freshly ground black pepper
1	cup yellow cornmeal
1½	cups cold water
1	cup lowfat milk
1	large egg yolk
½	cup shredded jack cheese
½	cup corn kernels
	Dash hot pepper sauce
3	large egg whites

Soft and puffy like a soufflé, spoonbread is one of the family of traditional hot Southern cornmeal breads. Stirring the cornmeal with cold liquid before adding it to boiling liquid helps prevent lumps.

Makes 6 servings

1. Prepare the greens as described on pages 174–175. Chop the cooked greens fine and set aside.

2. Combine the onion and oil in a nonstick skillet and cook over medium heat until golden, about 10 minutes. Add the garlic and cook, stirring, for 1 minute. Add the greens and stir to blend. Season to taste with salt and pepper. Set aside.

3. Stir together the cornmeal and cold water in a bowl. Scald the milk in a medium saucepan. Gradually stir in the cornmeal mixture, stirring until smooth. Cook, stirring, over medium heat until the cornmeal boils and thickens, about 5 minutes. Transfer to a large bowl and stir to cool slightly.

4. Stir some of the warm cornmeal mixture into the yolk in a small bowl, then stir the yolk mixture back into the cornmeal. Add the greens and onion mixture, the cheese, corn kernels, and hot pepper sauce.

continued

5. Heat the oven to 375°F. Spray a 3-quart soufflé dish or other deep casserole with nonstick cooking spray.

6. Whisk the egg whites in a large clean bowl until soft peaks form. Gently fold the whites into the cornmeal mixture until blended. Spoon into the prepared dish and bake until top is slightly puffed and browned, 35 to 40 minutes. Serve immediately as a main dish or as a side dish with poultry or fish.

Maple-sweetened Oat Bran and Fig Muffins

2 cups oat bran

2 teaspoons baking powder

2 teaspoons grated orange zest

1 teaspoon ground cinnamon

½ teaspoon salt

¾ cup diced moist dried figs

½ cup pure maple syrup

½ cup nonfat yogurt

¼ cup vegetable oil

1 large egg

We particularly like the way the flavors of maple and fig combine with the oat bran in these muffins. Dried figs and oat bran are both excellent sources of fiber.

Makes 6 muffins

1. Heat the oven to 400°F. Use 2½-inch nonstick muffin pans and spray with nonstick cooking spray, or use paper muffin cup liners.

2. Stir together the oat bran, baking powder, orange zest, cinnamon, and salt in a large bowl until blended. Add the figs and toss to coat.

3. Measure the maple syrup in a 2-cup measuring cup, add the yogurt, oil, and egg, and stir until blended. Pour the liquid ingredients over the dry ingredients and gently fold with a rubber spatula just until the dry ingredients are moistened. Do not overmix. Spoon into prepared muffin cups, filling them almost full.

4. Bake until golden, 16 to 20 minutes. Cool briefly in the pan, then transfer the muffins to a wire rack to continue cooling. Serve warm or at room temperature.

Carrot Muffins

Belgian-born Michel Stroot is chef at The Golden Door, the luxurious spa north of San Diego. He was successfully coaxing the natural flavor from foods and making them delicious without adding fat long before it became a trend.

M a k e s   1 2

m u f f i n s

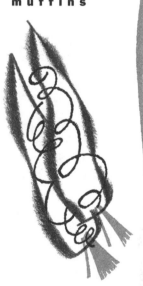

½	cup raisins or dried currants
1½	cups whole wheat flour
1	cup bran cereal (All-bran or 100% Bran)
⅓	cup sesame seeds
2	teaspoons ground cinnamon
1	teaspoon ground allspice
½	teaspoon ground cloves
1	teaspoon baking powder
1	teaspoon baking soda
1½	cups finely shredded or grated raw carrots
⅔	cup nonfat yogurt
½	cup mashed banana
½	cup fresh orange juice
¼	cup honey
2	tablespoons vegetable oil
1	tablespoon grated lemon zest

1. Heat oven to 350°F. Use nonstick muffin pans and spray with nonstick cooking spray, or use paper muffin cup liners.

2. Place the raisins in a bowl and add boiling water to cover. Let stand until plump, about 15 minutes. Drain and pat dry.

3. Combine the flour, bran, sesame seeds, cinnamon, allspice, cloves, baking powder, and baking soda in a large bowl and stir to blend. Make a well in the center. Blend the raisins, carrots, yogurt, banana, orange juice, honey, vegetable oil, and lemon zest in a separate bowl. Pour into the well in the dry ingredients. Fold gently, but thoroughly, until all the ingredients are evenly moistened. Do not overmix. Spoon batter into muffin cups, filling them almost to the top.

4. Bake until the batter begins to pull away from the sides of the cups, about 25 minutes. Cool slightly in pans. Transfer to a wire rack. Serve warm or at room temperature.

Toasted Cornmeal-Apple Muffin Wedges

1⅓   cups unbleached all-purpose flour

⅔   cup cornmeal, preferably stoneground

⅓   cup firmly packed light brown sugar

1   tablespoon baking powder

1   teaspoon baking soda

¼   teaspoon salt

½   cup nonfat or lowfat yogurt

¼   cup plus 2 tablespoons skim milk, or as needed

2   large eggs

1   large egg white

3   tablespoons unsalted butter, melted, or
     3 tablespoons vegetable oil

2   apples or pears, peeled, quartered, cored, and
     cut crosswise into chunks

½   teaspoon ground ginger

½   teaspoon ground cinnamon

½   teaspoon ground allspice

½   cup dried currants or raisins
     Pure maple syrup, warmed with a large pinch
     of ground cinnamon

Yogurt and lowfat or skim milk add lightness and moisture to this quick muffin/bread. The wedges can be baked ahead and toasted the next day for breakfast or brunch.

Makes 6 servings

1. Heat the oven to 375°F. Spray a 9-inch round cake pan with nonstick cooking spray. Set aside.

2. Place the flour, cornmeal, brown sugar, baking powder, baking soda, and salt in a large bowl and whisk to combine. Measure the yogurt and milk in a glass measure, add the eggs and egg white, and whisk to combine. Stir in the melted butter and set aside.

3. Toss the apples with ginger, cinnamon, and allspice, and add the raisins. Toss with the dry ingredients. Make a well in the center and pour in the liquids. With a large rubber spatula, mix until moistened but still lumpy. Do not overmix. Scrape into the pan and spread to the edges.

4. Bake until golden and a toothpick inserted in the center comes out clean, 40 to 45 minutes. Cool briefly in the pan, then on a rack.

5. With a serrated knife, cut the muffin bread into 6 large wedges. Split each horizontally. Toast the cut sides. Serve hot, drizzled with warm maple syrup.

Cranberry Cornmeal Muffins

1¼   cups unbleached all-purpose flour
½   cup cornmeal, preferably stoneground
¼   cup whole wheat flour
⅓   cup sugar
1   tablespoon baking powder
1   teaspoon baking soda
½   teaspoon ground cinnamon
     Salt
1   cup cranberries, fresh or frozen but not thawed, sorted
¼   cup golden raisins
1¼   cups buttermilk or yogurt thinned with lowfat milk
¼   cup vegetable oil
1   large egg
1   large egg white

The tartness of the cranberries in these muffins is balanced by the intense sweetness of the golden raisins. We like these muffins for breakfast or as an accompaniment to a soup and salad for lunch or dinner.

Makes 12 muffins

1. Heat the oven to 425°F. Use 2½-inch nonstick muffin pans and spray with nonstick cooking spray, or use paper muffin cup liners.

2. Combine the all-purpose flour, cornmeal, whole wheat flour, sugar, baking powder, baking soda, cinnamon, and a pinch of salt in a large bowl and stir well until thoroughly blended. Add the cranberries and raisins and stir to coat.

3. Measure the buttermilk into a 2-cup measuring cup, add the vegetable oil, whole egg, and egg white, and stir with a fork until thoroughly blended. Add the liquid mixture to the dry mixture, all at once, and gently fold with a rubber spatula just until the dry ingredients are nearly incorporated. The batter will be lumpy. Do not beat or overmix, or muffins will be tough. Spoon into the muffin pan, dividing batter evenly. Bake until the tops are golden and edges are browned, 15 to 20 minutes. Cool in the pan for a minute or two, loosen sides with a small spatula, lift from the pan, and serve warm.

Dess

erts

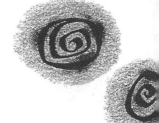

SETTING OUT TO DEVISE a healthy brownie, Marie tried substituting prune puree for some of the fat. She baked a panful, cut it into squares, and, fairly satisfied with the results, set them out on a plate in her kitchen. Soon afterward, her husband, John, came in, picked one up, and ate it. "This isn't bad," he said. "What is it?"

Marie decided that if he couldn't even tell it was a brownie, there was no sense trying to fiddle around, although we do offer a recipe for a lower-fat brownie (page 404).

Desserts pose what is probably the biggest challenge when you're trying to eat lighter. How can you still have the desserts you crave—cakes, ice cream, chocolate—if you're cutting back on fat, sugar, cholesterol, and calories?

In a way, we feel that this dilemma, the contradiction between eating healthy and the rich desserts so many people love, cannot and, perhaps, should not be resolved.

Look at the figures: Americans are eating less animal fat in the interests of good health, and yet, in the last couple of years, consumption of the so-called superpremium category of ice cream has gone up dramatically. And consumption of chocolate has also risen steadily. As one industry spokesperson put it, "People clearly have shown that they have a strong preference to treat themselves."

After experimenting over the years, we've come up with a broad collection of desserts that are low in fat and sugar but still high in flavor. The way we've gone about it is to find the things that work best in healthier versions. We don't have a lowfat crème brûlée recipe, because it's the cream and egg yolks that give that dessert its characteristic (and wonderful) texture. Lowfat fruit desserts, on the other hand, work especially well, because even their full-fat versions rely on the flavor of the fruits themselves. We've lightened them by using a minimum of sugar and adding such no-fat flavor enhancers as fresh ginger, spices, and wine syrups, to come up with a broad range of refreshing—but not austere—fruit desserts for every season.

We both love the soothing comforts of puddings, mousses, and soufflés. But how to keep them creamy without cream? Sometimes, yogurt can stand in for whipped cream, as in Guenter Seeger's masterfully simple mango mousse, which is lightened with nonfat yogurt and beaten egg whites. This mousse, by the way, is a basic formula, and can be used for any pureed soft fruit.

For an Italian-style baked ricotta pudding, we use part-skim ricotta cheese and only one egg yolk, to come up with a pudding that's suave enough to satisfy even the most ardent pudding lover. Some of our soufflés are made with nothing but a concentrated fruit puree lightened with beaten egg whites—no yolks, no cooked roux-thickened sauce base.

Frozen desserts offer infinite possibilities. By relying on intensely flavored fruits and coffee, you can have knockout desserts that are almost calorie free. And there is nothing more refreshing.

Finally, a quick dessert sauce can be just the thing when you want to end a meal with something special but don't have the time. Our dessert sauces can be made in advance, in minutes, and then served over fresh berries or fruit, sorbet, or a slice of angel food cake.

Fall Fruit Compote with Molasses Yogurt

A simple, old-fashioned dessert, made with a combination of fresh and dried fruits. Using a dessert wine gives intensely concentrated fruit flavor. Likely choices include Chateau St. Jean's late-harvest Riesling or Gewürztraminer, Muscat de Beaumes-de-Venise, or of course, Sauternes, the prototype for them all. With our Buttermilk Biscuits (page 341), this makes a terrific shortcake.

Makes 6 servings

3	cups unsweetened apple juice or cider
1	slice (about ¼ inch) ginger
2	firm-ripe Comice or Anjou pears (about 1 pound)
2	Golden Delicious apples
1	tablespoon fresh lemon juice
⅓	cup dried apricot halves (about 2 ounces)
6	pitted prunes
½	cup lowfat yogurt
1	tablespoon molasses, preferably dark, or honey
2	tablespoons sliced unblanched almonds
	Julienne strips of lemon zest

1. Combine the apple juice and ginger in a large shallow saucepan and bring to a simmer. Meanwhile, peel, quarter, and core the pears and apples, toss with lemon juice, and add to the saucepan. Cover and cook over low heat until pears are just tender, about 10 minutes. Add apricots and prunes, cover, and cook over low heat 5 minutes longer.

2. With a slotted spoon, transfer the fruit to a shallow bowl. Raise the heat and boil the apple juice, uncovered, until it has reduced to 1¾ cups. Cool the liquid slightly, then pour it over the fruit. *(The fruit mixture can be prepared ahead. Cover and refrigerate up to 8 hours. Remove from the refrigerator at least 30 minutes before serving, to return the fruit to room temperature.)*

3. Stir the yogurt and molasses together in a small bowl. Set aside. Toast the almonds in a small dry skillet over low heat until pale golden, about 2 minutes.

4. Drizzle the fruit lightly with a spoonful of the yogurt mixture. Garnish each serving with a few strips of lemon zest and a sprinkling of toasted almonds.

Fall Fruit Shortcake: Prepare the compote as directed above through Step 3. Bake Buttermilk Biscuits (page 341) just before serving. Split the warm biscuits in half with a serrated knife. Place a biscuit bottom on each dessert plate. Spoon some fruit over each biscuit and distribute the remaining fruit, with syrup, around the biscuits. Drizzle the fruit with a spoonful of the yogurt mixture. Replace biscuit tops. Garnish each serving with lemon zest and toasted almonds.

Broiled Caramelized Pears
with Toasted Almonds

This dessert is made in minutes. It's an easy method that can be used with other fruits: in summer, peaches or nectarines; in winter, sliced ripe pineapple.

Makes 4 servings

3 ripe Bartlett, Anjou, or Comice pears, scrubbed, quartered, cored, and thinly sliced
1 tablespoon firmly packed light brown sugar
1 tablespoon sliced unblanched almonds
½ cup lowfat vanilla yogurt

1. Place the broiler rack about 3 inches from source of heat. Heat the broiler.

2. Arrange the pears in a shallow flameproof dish in slightly overlapping rows or concentric circles. Sprinkle with some of the brown sugar.

3. Broil until the sugar has caramelized and the pears begin to brown, 5 or 6 minutes. Sprinkle with the almonds and broil until golden, about 1 minute. Serve warm, topping each serving with a spoonful of vanilla yogurt.

Cool Strawberry-Rhubarb Coupe

6   tablespoons sugar

3   cups thinly sliced hulled strawberries (about 1½ pints)

1   tablespoon fresh lemon or lime juice

¼   cup cornstarch

    Cold water, as needed

1   cup diced (¼ inch), trimmed rhubarb, fresh or frozen thawed

½   teaspoon grated orange zest

    Nonfat yogurt

    Mint sprigs, for garnish (optional)

1. Stir together 2 tablespoons of the sugar, the strawberries, and lemon juice in a bowl. Cover and let stand at room temperature until the sugar dissolves and the mixture is juicy, about 30 minutes.

2. Stir the remaining sugar and the cornstarch in a medium saucepan until blended and free of lumps. Strain the juice from the berries into a 2-cup measure and add enough cold water to measure 1¼ cups. Gradually stir the juice mixture into the cornstarch-sugar mixture until smooth. Add the rhubarb and ½ cup of the strawberries.

3. Stir the mixture over medium-low heat until boiling. Reduce the heat and boil gently, stirring and mashing the berries with the back of a wooden spoon, until the juices are thickened and shiny, about 5 minutes. Remove from heat.

4. Cool the fruit mixture just until lukewarm, about 15 minutes. Fold in the remaining strawberries and the orange zest until blended. Spoon into goblets and cool thoroughly before serving. This dessert is best eaten the day it is prepared and kept at cool room temperature rather than refrigerated.

5. Serve topped with a spoonful of yogurt and a sprig of mint, if desired.

Rhubarb and straw-berries have a natural affinity, the sweet berries cutting through what early Americans called "pie-plant's" astringency. This is a light variation on the classic spring fruit combination.

Tossing strawberries with sugar is a good idea for almost any use. The sugar helps draw out the berries' natural juices, forming a light natural syrup; it also intensifies and heightens their color and flavor.

Makes 4 servings

Granola Topping or Cereal

Granola is one of the great "healthy food myths." While the mixture of grains does offer plenty of protein, vitamins, and fiber, most prepared granola mixtures are loaded with fat and a non-nutritive simple carbohydrate like sugar or honey. You can, however, make a healthy granola.

Makes about 3 cups

2 cups old-fashioned or quick-cooking oats, not instant
1 cup broken walnuts or sliced almonds or a combination
½ cup dark or golden raisins or a combination
⅓ cup honey
1 tablespoon mild vegetable oil
½ teaspoon ground cinnamon

1. Heat the oven to 350°F.

2. Spread the oatmeal, nuts, and raisins in a 13 × 9-inch baking pan.

3. In a small saucepan, combine the honey, oil, and cinnamon. Bring to a boil. Pour over the oats and stir until evenly distributed. Bake 25 to 30 minutes, stirring frequently, until the mixture is golden. Cool mixture in the baking pan. Crumble the granola into small pieces when it is cooled. Store in a jar or plastic bag.

Wine-poached Pineapple Compote
with Candied Ginger

1   cup dry white wine

½   cup cold water

¼   cup sugar

1   tablespoon slivered candied ginger

4   dried apricot halves

4   thick slices (about ¾ inch) peeled, trimmed,
    and cored fresh pineapple

1. Combine the wine, water, and sugar in a wide shallow
saucepan over medium heat. Heat, stirring, until the sugar dissolves and the liquid comes to a boil, about 10 minutes. Add
the ginger and apricots, cover, and simmer over very low heat
for 10 minutes. Do not boil.

2. Arrange the pineapple slices in a single layer in a large shallow heatproof bowl. Pour the hot syrup with the apricots and
ginger over the pineapple. Cover and refrigerate until well
chilled, about 2 hours.

3. Serve in wide shallow bowls, spooning some of the syrup
over each portion.

*No-fat flavorings like
wine and ginger can fla-
vor a fruit dessert memo-
rably without fat. Hot
syrup is poured over ripe
pineapple, so it infuses
without cooking. This is
also good with sliced
peaches, oranges, or a
combination of fruits,
including a few slices of
kiwi for color.*

**Makes 4
servings**

Clementines Poached
in Spiced Riesling Syrup

Make this pretty and refreshing orange dessert with clementines, tangerines, or small navel oranges. It's a good buffet dish served in a large glass bowl. Prepare the dish in advance to give it a chance to chill well.

Flavoring desserts this way with bay leaves and other herbs, rediscovered by pastry chefs, actually dates back centuries. Sliced ripe peaches or nectarines can also be prepared like this.

**M a k e s 8
s e r v i n g s**

1 bottle (750 ml) Riesling or other fruity white wine

1 cup sugar

1 tablespoon long thin julienne strips clementine, tangerine, or orange zest, without pith

1 piece (about 2 inches) cinnamon stick

2 whole cardamom seeds

1 whole clove

1 bay leaf

8 clementines, tangerines, or small navel oranges

1. Combine the wine, sugar, zest, cinnamon, cardamom, clove, and bay leaf in a large wide nonaluminum saucepan. Bring to a boil, stirring until the sugar has dissolved. Reduce the heat and simmer, uncovered, for 20 minutes.

2. Using a very sharp thin knife, cut the peel and pith from the clementines. Leave the fruit whole. Work over a bowl or plate and save any juices. Carefully lower the fruit into the simmering syrup and add any reserved juices. Cook over low heat for 10 minutes, basting often with the syrup. Remove from heat and cool to room temperature.

3. Refrigerate the oranges in their syrup until very cold, preferably overnight, before serving. Serve the oranges in shallow bowls with plenty of syrup, and a knife and fork.

Lighter Strawberry Fool

1½   cups nonfat yogurt
 1   pint ripe strawberries, hulled and coarsely chopped
1½   tablespoons framboise or Grand Marnier (optional)
      Sugar or honey
⅓   cup whipping cream
      Small sprigs mint
      Nonfat yogurt, for garnish

1. Place the yogurt in a colander or strainer lined with cheese-cloth and set over a bowl or in the sink. Let drain at room temperature until the yogurt has reduced to 1 cup, about 1 hour.

2. Toss the strawberries with the framboise or Grand Marnier, if using, in a nonaluminum bowl mashing gently with the back of a spoon, and let stand for 30 minutes.

3. Combine the strawberries with the yogurt and sugar or honey to taste. Whip the cream until stiff, then fold into the berry mixture. Spoon into 4 parfait glasses or dessert dishes. Refrigerate for 1 hour. Top each serving with a dollop of yogurt and a sprig of mint.

A lightened version of the traditional British fool, which is a mash or puree of fruit folded with copious amounts of whipped cream. Berries, goose-berries, or plums are most commonly used in fools. This fool is made with thickened yogurt, enriched with a small amount of whipped cream. The recipe is from Alan Hill, chef at Gleneagles, a spectacular golf resort in the Scottish Highlands, where he puts the considerable local bounty to imaginative use.

Makes 4 servings

Hawaiian Tropical Fruit Sundae

A dazzling spa recipe from Kathleen Daelmans at the Grand Wailea Resort and Spa on the big island of Hawaii. Concocting lowfat desserts is a pleasure when you've got such dazzling fresh fruits available.

**M a k e s   4
s e r v i n g s**

Fruit Sauce

2   very ripe mangoes or papayas, peeled, seeded
and cut into thin wedges or ½-inch cubes
Maple syrup (optional)

Fruits (Select 4 or 5 of the following)

2   cups cubed peeled, trimmed, and cored fresh pineapple

1   cup thin wedges or ½-inch cubes peeled and
seeded fresh papaya

1   or 2 ripe peaches and/or nectarines, pitted and
cut into thin wedges

2   plums, pitted and cut into thin wedges

1   cup ripe strawberries with stems, halved if large

1   cup fresh blueberries

1   cup raspberries and/or blackberries

2   small red bananas, peeled and halved lengthwise,
or 1 cup sliced peeled banana
Fresh mint leaves, for garnish (optional)

1. Puree the mangoes in a blender or food processor until smooth. Press through a sieve. Taste and add maple syrup to sweeten, if using.

2. Select and prepare the fruits. Arrange the fruits on 4 plates, with the bananas at the "tops" and "bottoms" of the plates. Using a teaspoon, drizzle the fruit sauce in thin lines over the surface of the plate and over the fruits. Garnish with mint and serve at once.

Mango Mousse

2   ripe mangoes, peeled and seeded (¾ pound each)
1   envelope unflavored gelatin
    Juice of ½ lemon
1   cup lowfat or nonfat yogurt
¼   teaspoon pure vanilla extract
¼   cup plus 2 tablespoons confectioners' sugar
2   large egg whites, at room temperature
    Mango slices, for garnish
    Ripe berries, such as strawberries, raspberries,
    and/or blueberries, for garnish (optional)
    Lime wedges, for garnish

1. If you are serving the mousse in a bowl, select an attractive serving bowl, preferably a glass one, and set aside. Or oil six ½-cup ramekins and set aside.

2. Puree the mangoes in a food processor or blender and sieve the puree. You should have about 1 cup. Set aside.

3. Soften the gelatin in lemon juice in a small saucepan. Place the pan over very low heat and stir until the gelatin is clear and dissolved. Add it to the mango puree. Add the yogurt and vanilla. Sift the sugar into the puree and whisk until the mixture is smooth. Chill, stirring occasionally, until the mixture starts to thicken but has not yet set.

4. Beat the egg whites until nearly stiff. Fold a little of the egg whites into the mango mixture. Gently fold in the remaining whites. Pour the mousse into the bowl or spoon into ramekins and chill until set, at least 2 hours.

5. To serve, scoop the mousse onto serving plates (or unmold each ramekin, running a knife around the edge, then inverting it onto a plate). Surround the mousse with mango slices and fresh berries, if using, garnish with a lime wedge, and serve.

This is a never-fail dessert, adapted from a recipe by chef Guenter Seeger of the Ritz-Carlton Buckhead in Atlanta. Instead of a cooked custard base, Seeger uses lowfat yogurt, and to lighten it, egg whites instead of whipped cream.

You can substitute an equal amount of any other fruit puree—blackberry, raspberry, soaked dried apricots—for the mango.

Makes 6 servings

Lemon Soufflé with Warm Cider-Lemon Sauce

Citrus desserts are among the most refreshing ways to end a meal. This soufflé is made with just yolks and lemon as the base—no roux means lowering the fat, and no milk means that the lemon flavor comes through more sharply. The cider-lemon sauce is optional; you can serve the soufflé with just a dusting of confectioners' sugar.

Makes 6 servings

3   large eggs, at room temperature
6   tablespoons granulated sugar
3   tablespoons fresh lemon juice
    Grated zest of 1 lemon
2   large egg whites, at room temperature
    Confectioners' sugar, for dusting
½   recipe Warm Cider-Lemon Sauce (page 387) (optional)

1. Coat the inside of a 5- or 6-cup soufflé dish with butter or spray with nonstick cooking spray. Sprinkle evenly with sugar. Refrigerate. Place the bottom oven rack at its lowest position and remove the middle rack. Heat the oven to 425°F.

2. Separate two of the eggs, placing the whites and yolks in 2 separate large mixing bowls. Add the remaining whole egg and 3 tablespoons of the granulated sugar to the egg yolks. Beat or whisk until the eggs are pale in color and airy. Whisk in the lemon juice and zest until blended.

3. Add the 2 egg whites to the whites in the bowl and whisk until foamy. Whisking at slightly higher speed, gradually add the 3 remaining tablespoons of sugar, 1 tablespoon at a time, until soft but glossy peaks form.

4. Carefully fold about ⅓ of the beaten whites into the yolks until thoroughly blended. Add the remaining whites and gently fold until blended.

5. Spoon the batter into the prepared soufflé dish, smooth the top with a spatula, and run your finger around the rim of the dish, so the soufflé will form a high hat as it bakes. Bake until the soufflé is puffed and golden, about 12 minutes. Dust with confectioners' sugar and serve at once. To serve, spoon some warm sauce, if using, on each dessert plate and top with a spoonful of hot soufflé, serving each person a little of the crust and some of the interior of the soufflé.

Prune and Armagnac Soufflé

½ pound moist pitted prunes

½ cup warm water

I strip orange zest

3 tablespoons Armagnac, cognac, or other brandy

3 large egg whites, at room temperature
   Salt

2 tablespoons granulated sugar
   Confectioners' sugar, for dusting

1. Combine the prunes, water, orange zest, and Armagnac in a small saucepan and bring to a simmer. Cover the pan and remove from heat. Let stand 15 minutes to steep. Remove the orange zest and stir the mixture vigorously with a wooden spoon to form a chunky paste. *(The recipe can be prepared in advance to this point.)*

2. Place the bottom oven rack at its lowest position and remove the middle rack. Heat the oven to 400°F. Lightly spray a 2-quart soufflé dish with nonstick cooking spray or brush lightly with vegetable oil. Sprinkle with sugar, shaking out excess.

3. Beat the egg whites with a pinch of salt until soft peaks form. Gradually beat in the granulated sugar, 1 tablespoon at a time, beating about 30 seconds after each addition, until the whites are stiff and shiny.

4. Fold a spoonful of the whites into the prune puree to lighten. Spoon the prune mixture over the whites and gently fold just until the mixture is blended. Pour into the prepared soufflé dish. Smooth the top with a spatula; run your thumb around the mixture about ½ inch from the rim of the dish to form a high hat.

5. Bake until puffed and golden, 12 to 15 minutes. Dust the top lightly with confectioners' sugar and serve at once.

Prunes and Armagnac are traditionally paired in the southwest of France. Instead of starting with a roux-thickened cooked sauce base as would be done there, you begin by lightening a prune puree with beaten egg whites. Except for a small amount of sugar to stabilize the egg whites, this yolkless soufflé is sweetened only by the prunes themselves. Prunes are an excellent choice for flavoring healthy desserts; because they are so concentrated in flavor, a little goes a long way.

Makes 6 servings

Super Chocolate Pudding

You see recipes for chocolate mousse everywhere, but when was the last time you had homemade chocolate pudding? By using cocoa powder instead of melted chocolate, skim or lowfat milk instead of whole milk, and one whole egg instead of several egg yolks, you can cut back radically on the fat. But that thick texture and chocolaty flavor you remember from childhood is still there.

Makes 4 servings

2¼ cups skim or lowfat (1%) milk
½ cup sugar
    Salt
2 tablespoons cornstarch
⅔ cup unsweetened cocoa powder
1 large egg, beaten
1 teaspoon pure vanilla extract

1. Place 2 cups of the milk, ¼ cup of the sugar, and a pinch of salt in a heavy saucepan and bring to a boil. Mix the cornstarch, cocoa, and remaining ¼ cup sugar in a bowl. Whisk in the remaining ¼ cup cold milk until smooth. Whisk hot milk mixture into the bowl and return to the saucepan. Bring to a boil, stirring. Boil 2 minutes, stirring.

2. Whisk 1 cup of the hot mixture into the egg, then whisk back into the hot mixture. Cook, stirring, over medium-low heat, for 2 minutes without boiling. Stir in vanilla. Pour the pudding into sundae dishes and cool. If you want to prevent a skin from forming, place sheets of wax paper directly on the surface of the pudding. Serve chilled.

Lighter Rice Pudding

2   cups cold water

¼   teaspoon salt

1   cup long-grain rice (not parboiled)

3   cups lowfat (1%) milk

½   cup pure maple syrup

1   cinnamon stick

⅓   cup raisins (optional)

2   teaspoons pure vanilla extract

1. Bring the water to a boil in a heavy saucepan, add salt, and stir in the rice with a fork. Simmer over low heat, covered and stirring now and then, until the water has been absorbed, about 15 to 20 minutes. Stir in 2½ cups of the milk, the maple syrup, and cinnamon stick and raisins, if using, and bring the mixture to a boil. Simmer, uncovered, stirring often, until the rice is very tender and the mixture has thickened, about 30 minutes.

2. Remove from the heat. Stir in the vanilla and transfer the pudding to a large bowl, removing the cinnamon stick. Let cool. Chill if you like. Thin the pudding with the remaining ½ cup milk, or as needed for the consistency you like.

When the going gets tough, rice pudding may not solve everything, but it can help console along the way. This pudding is made with lowfat milk and no eggs.

Makes 4 servings

Baked Ricotta Pudding with Strawberry Sauce

Italian budino di ricotta, *with a texture something like cheesecake, is one of a category of desserts called* dolci ai cucchiaio, *or spoon desserts. Included are puddings, mousses, and other soft, custardy sweets. We've used part-skim ricotta cheese, one egg yolk, and a minimum of sugar to make a light and creamy baked pudding. It's nice served with a fresh berry sauce.*

Makes 6 to 8 servings

2	containers (15 ounces each) part-skim ricotta cheese
½	cup plus 1 tablespoon granulated sugar
1	large egg yolk
1	teaspoon pure vanilla extract
¼	teaspoon pure almond extract
¼	teaspoon ground cinnamon
3	tablespoons unbleached all-purpose flour
2	tablespoons finely chopped candied citron or dried currants, if citron is unavailable
½	teaspoon grated lemon zest
2	large egg whites, at room temperature
	Salt
	Strawberry Sauce (recipe follows)

1. Empty the ricotta into a sieve set over a bowl. Cover with plastic wrap and let drain, refrigerated, overnight.

2. Heat the oven to 350°F. Spray a shallow 1¾-quart baking dish with nonstick cooking spray or grease lightly with vegetable oil. Bring a kettle of water to a boil for a water bath and set aside.

3. Using an electric mixer, beat the ricotta, ½ cup sugar, egg yolk, vanilla, almond, and cinnamon until light, about 5 minutes. The mixture will still be a little grainy. Fold in the flour, citron, and lemon zest.

4. Beat the egg whites with a pinch of salt until soft peaks form. Gradually beat in the remaining 1 tablespoon sugar until the whites are stiff and shiny. Gently fold the whites into the ricotta mixture.

5. Pour mixture into the prepared baking dish and place in a larger shallow baking pan. Place on the oven shelf and pour enough boiling or very hot water into the larger baking pan to come halfway up the sides of the baking dish. Bake until the pudding is puffed and golden, about 55 minutes. Carefully remove the pudding dish from the water bath and place on a rack to cool to room temperature. Serve the pudding at room temperature, spooned into bowls and drizzled with strawberry sauce.

Strawberry Sauce

| | pint fresh strawberries, hulled, or I bag (12 ounces) individually flash-frozen strawberries, thawed
½ cup water
3 tablespoons sugar, or more to taste
| tablespoon lemon juice

Puree the strawberries, water, sugar, and lemon juice in a food processor or blender. Press through a sieve to remove seeds. Taste and add more sugar if needed. Refrigerate until ready to serve.

Makes 1²/₃ cups

Crème Caramel

A first-class crème caramel or flan, with a smooth-as-silk custard set off by deep amber caramel, is one of the best desserts imaginable. The classic formula for crème caramel is four egg yolks to two cups of whole milk, sometimes enriched with cream. This version uses lowfat milk and one less yolk, cutting fat and calories by about a third.

Makes 4 servings

Caramel syrup

½ cup sugar
2 tablespoons cold water
1 tablespoon very hot tap water

Custard

1¾ cups lowfat (1%) milk
2 large eggs
1 large egg yolk
⅓ cup sugar
1 teaspoon pure vanilla extract

1. Heat ¹/₂ cup sugar and the cold water in a small heavy skillet over moderate heat. Brush the sugar crystals from the sides of the skillet with a pastry brush dipped in cold water. Be sure that all of the sugar has dissolved before syrup comes to a boil. If there is some sugar left undissolved, remove the pan from the heat for a moment and stir until smooth. Boil the syrup, without stirring, until the syrup becomes golden. Add the hot water; the mixture will sputter. Swirl the pan over low heat until the caramel is smooth. Pour immediately into four 4-ounce custard cups or ramekins, dividing evenly. Set aside.

2. Heat the oven to 325°F. Bring a kettle of water to a boil for a water bath and set aside.

3. Scald the milk in a small saucepan and set aside.

4. Whisk the eggs, egg yolk, and sugar in a bowl until well blended. Gradually whisk in half of the hot milk until thoroughly blended. Then gradually whisk in the remaining milk and the vanilla.

5. Place the caramel-lined custard cups in a large shallow baking pan. Strain the custard mixture into the cups. Set on the center oven rack and add enough hot water to the baking pan to come halfway up the sides of the custard cups. Bake until the custard is set but still slightly wobbly in the center, usually 35 to 45 minutes. Do not overcook. Let cool in the water bath for 1 hour.

6. To serve, carefully loosen the edges of each custard with the tip of a sharp knife blade. Place an individual serving plate on top of each one and invert carefully, letting the caramel syrup drip over and around the custard. *(The custards can also be made ahead and chilled. Remove from the refrigerator about 20 minutes before serving.)*

Strawberry Ice Milk with Chunky Strawberry Sauce

Over the years, Marie has developed a large repertoire of creamy, refreshing frozen desserts. By using skim milk and lots of ripe fruit, she gets the creaminess and flavor intensity of ice cream, with only a fraction of the fat. This ice milk, which adapts to any kind of berry, can be made with or without an ice-cream maker.

Makes 4 servings

3 pints small, juicy ripe strawberries, rinsed and hulled
¼ cup plus 1 tablespoon sugar, or more to taste
1 cup skim milk
1 teaspoon fresh lemon juice

1. Set aside 4 perfect berries for garnish. Cut 2 pints of the berries into halves or quarters. Puree in a food processor with ¼ cup sugar and the milk until very smooth.

2. Freeze the ice milk in an ice-cream maker, following the manufacturer's instructions. Or use the still-freeze method (see Note). Pack into a plastic freezer container and cover tightly. *(This can be prepared 1 day in advance.)*

3. About 1 hour before serving, coarsely chop the remaining berries. Toss together the berries, the remaining 1 tablespoon sugar or more to taste, and the lemon juice in a small bowl. Let the sauce stand at room temperature.

4. If necessary, place the container of ice milk in the refrigerator 20 to 30 minutes before serving to soften it slightly. Spoon some of the sauce onto each of 4 chilled dessert plates. Scoop the ice milk over the sauce, using 2 spoons dipped in cold water to form 3 egg shapes per serving, if you like. Garnish each plate with a reserved strawberry and serve immediately.

Note: To use the still-freeze method, transfer the mixture to a 9-inch square shallow baking pan and place it in the freezer. Freeze until the edges of the mixture are solid and the center is slushy, about 2 hours. Scrape the mixture into a food processor and process until smooth and creamy. Return the puree to the baking pan, freeze again until the edges are solid and center is slushy, and puree again in the food processor.

Very Berry Ice Milk

1 cup rinsed, hulled, and cut-up ripe strawberries

1 cup ripe blueberries, rinsed and sorted

1 cup ripe raspberries, rinsed and patted dry

½ cup sugar

1 cup lowfat (1%) milk or lowfat or nonfat yogurt

1. Toss the berries with the sugar in a large bowl. Let stand, stirring occasionally, until the berries are juicy and the sugar has dissolved, about 20 minutes. Combine the berry mixture with the milk or yogurt in a food processor. Process for a full 3 minutes. The berries should be very well pureed. Press the mixture through a sieve set over a bowl, to strain out any large raspberry seeds.

2. Freeze in an ice-cream maker following the manufacturer's instructions or use the still-freeze method (page 372). Scrape the mixture into a plastic container, cover tightly, and freeze several hours before serving.

3. If the mixture has been frozen overnight, let stand at room temperature until soft enough to scoop, usually about 20 minutes, before serving.

For maximum berry flavor, use only the sweetest, juiciest berries. A combination of berries adds complexity of flavor, and tossing them with sugar and letting them sit briefly help intensify their flavor. You can also make this with blackberries or red currants, increasing the sugar slightly to taste. This dessert works with either milk or yogurt.

Makes about 6 servings

Cranberry Ice Milk
with Raspberry Sauce

Cranberries are one of only three fruits native to North America. (The others are blueberries and Concord grapes.) They make terrific desserts, particularly frozen desserts, since their intense tartness shines through. We've used apple juice as part of the sweetening, to avoid adding too much sugar. The raspberry sauce goes beautifully with the cranberries, both tart and ruby-colored.

M a k e s 4 t o 6
s e r v i n g s

1   bag (12 ounces) fresh or thawed frozen cranberries, rinsed and picked over
2   cups unsweetened apple juice
½   cup sugar
1   cinnamon stick
1   cup lowfat (1%) milk
    Raspberry Sauce (recipe follows)

1. Combine the cranberries, apple juice, sugar, and cinnamon stick in a saucepan. Bring to a boil over low heat, reduce the heat, and simmer, uncovered, until the cranberries pop and the mixture has thickened slightly, about 10 minutes. Cool briefly. Remove and discard the cinnamon stick. Press the mixture through a sieve, let cool, then refrigerate until thoroughly chilled.

2. Stir the milk into the cranberry mixture until blended. Freeze in an ice-cream maker, following the manufacturer's instructions, or use the still-freeze method (page 372). Transfer the ice milk to a plastic container with a tight-fitting lid. Freeze at least 3 hours to allow the flavor to mellow.

3. To serve, spoon some sauce into the bottoms of 4 dessert bowls and top with scoops of ice milk.

Raspberry Sauce

1   bag (12 ounces) individually flash-frozen raspberries
½   cup water
3   tablespoons sugar, or more to taste
1   tablespoon lemon juice

Puree the thawed raspberries, water, sugar, and lemon juice in a food processor or blender. Press through a sieve to eliminate seeds. Taste and add more sugar if needed. Refrigerate until ready to serve.

Makes 1 ⅔ cups

Deep and Glossy Chocolate Sauce

1   cup sugar
1   cup cold water
1   teaspoon lemon juice
¾   unsweetened cocoa powder
1½   tablespoons unsalted butter
1   teaspoon pure vanilla extract

1. Stir the sugar, water, and lemon juice together in a heavy saucepan over medium heat until the sugar has dissolved. Boil the syrup, uncovered, for 1 minute. Remove from heat.
2. Sift the cocoa powder and whisk it into the syrup with the butter until mixture is smooth. Add the vanilla, and cool to lukewarm or room temperature. Store, refrigerated, in a tightly covered jar or container. Rewarm or serve cold.

Our all-time favorite chocolate sauce is made with two kinds of melted chocolate, lots of cream, and sometimes a splash of brandy. This low-fat sauce made with cocoa doesn't stint on chocolate flavor.

Makes about 2 cups

Red Plum Sorbet

Plums have a natural tartness and depth of flavor that make them ideal for a summer sorbet. We've used less sugar than in classic formulas but enough to keep the ice from freezing too hard.

**M a k e s 4
s e r v i n g s**

2 pounds sweet ripe red plums, washed,
   cut up, and pitted
½ cup sugar, or more as needed
¼ cup water, or more as needed
2 to 3 teaspoons fresh lime juice

1. Combine the plums, sugar, and water in a medium saucepan. Cook over low heat, stirring frequently, until the plums soften and the mixture is very juicy, about 10 minutes. If the plums are not juicy enough, stir in additional water as needed as plums cook down to make a medium-thin puree. Cool slightly.

2. Puree the plum mixture in a food processor until very smooth. Add lime juice to taste.

3. Freeze in an ice-cream maker following the manufacturer's instructions or use the still-freeze method (page 372). Scrape the mixture into a plastic container, cover tightly, and freeze several hours before serving.

4. If the mixture has been frozen overnight, let stand at room temperature until soft enough to scoop, usually about 20 minutes, before serving.

Pink Grapefruit and Campari Sorbet

1   cup cold water
⅓   cup sugar
1½ cups freshly squeezed pink or ruby red
    grapefruit juice, with pulp
2   tablespoons Campari
1   tablespoon lemon juice

1. Stir the water and sugar in a small saucepan over low heat until the syrup comes to a boil and the sugar has dissolved. Cover and set aside to cool for about 10 minutes.

2. Stir in the grapefruit juice, Campari, and lemon juice. Pour the liquid into a shallow container and freeze until semifirm, 2 to 3 hours.

3. Scrape the sorbet into a food processor and process until smooth. Return the sorbet to the container and freeze again until semifirm, about 1 hour longer. Process again until smooth. Scrape the sorbet into a plastic container, cover tightly, and freeze for several hours or overnight before serving.

A streamlined adaptation of a recipe from Rudy Sodamin, the Cunard Line's executive chef, and also chef-owner of Café Mozart in Stamford, Connecticut. The bitterness of Campari, the Italian apéritif, is refreshingly astringent when combined with pink grapefruit.

Makes 4 servings

Coffee Granita

A classic Italian dessert, with no fat at all. A granita, or frozen flavored ice water, is fresh tasting with a distinctive granular texture. It's like eating intensely flavored ice. Granitas are easy to make—you simply cut the syrup repeatedly as it freezes until it forms coarse crystals. They melt very quickly, so we suggest serving granita in stemmed glasses which have been frosted in the freezer for at least an hour before serving. There's nothing more refreshing in hot weather. This granita is dessert and after-dinner coffee, all in one.

**M a k e s 4
s e r v i n g s**

3 cups hot freshly brewed strong coffee, preferably espresso
½ to ⅔ cup sugar

1. Sweeten the coffee with sugar to taste while it is still hot. Cool, then chill thoroughly.

2. Pour the coffee into a shallow metal pan such as a pie plate or ice cube trays without dividers. Place in freezer 2 to 3 hours before serving. When the mixture is firm around the edges, usually about 45 minutes, cut it into coarse crystals with 2 knives, blending the firm and liquid portions. Return to the freezer.

3. Repeat cutting and blending 1 or 2 more times. The last time, the mixture should be crystallized throughout. Cut the ice into coarse, even crystals or scrape it with a fork, spoon into wine glasses, and serve.

Warm Orange Caramel Sauce

1   cup sugar
¼ cup cold water
¼ cup hot water
¼ cup orange juice, preferably freshly squeezed,
     or blood orange juice

1. Place the sugar and cold water in a small heavy saucepan over medium heat. Dissolve the sugar, stirring and brushing down any crystals from the sides of the pan with a pastry brush dipped in hot water. Raise the heat and bring the syrup to a boil.

2. Boil, without stirring, until the mixture caramelizes to a medium-dark amber color, usually about 8 minutes. Timing can vary, but do not allow to burn. Gradually add the hot water, stirring until the mixture is smooth. Turn off the heat and stir in the orange juice until smooth. Cool, then store, refrigerated, in a tightly covered jar. Rewarm to serve.

Most caramel sauces are made by cooking sugar until it caramelizes, then adding copious amounts of heavy cream, and letting the sauce simmer until it is smooth and has reduced and thickened slightly. This sleek bronze gloss, on the other hand, is made without any cream, yet has all the intensity of a real caramel sauce, with citrus's sweet-tart edge.

This sauce keeps well in the refrigerator. Warm a little, in a saucepan or in the microwave, to serve over broiled pears, other fruits, plain cake, or any frozen dessert.

**Makes about
1 cup**

Lighter Custard Sauce

Unmatched for versatility, cool custard suits all sorts of fruit desserts and warm puddings. For an even simpler dessert, pass a pitcher of the custard sauce along with a bowl of cut-up fresh fruits and berries.

By using lowfat milk and whole eggs instead of yolks, you can cut back substantially on the amount of fat in this sort of sauce, while still retaining both flavor and body. Because this sauce contains egg whites, which curdle even sooner than yolks, it has to be watched even more closely than when you make a custard sauce with egg yolks. When it begins to thicken, you can feel it becoming slippery along the bottom

2½ cups lowfat (1%) milk
1 vanilla bean, split lengthwise but left attached at
 1 end, or 2 teaspoons pure vanilla extract
1 strip orange zest
2 large eggs
⅓ cup sugar

1. Rinse a heavy saucepan with cold water and shake dry, to help prevent sticking. Add milk, vanilla bean, if using, and orange zest to pan and bring the mixture nearly to a boil. Cover and set aside to steep for at least 30 minutes.

2. Return the milk to a simmer. Whisk the eggs and sugar in a mixing bowl until smooth but not fluffy. Gradually add a little of the hot milk to the eggs, then pour all of the egg mixture into the simmering milk.

3. Cook the custard over low heat, stirring constantly with a wooden spoon, until mixture thickens enough to coat the back of the spoon evenly, usually 7 or 8 minutes. Do not allow the sauce to boil.

4. Strain into a clean bowl. Discard the orange zest, scrape the seeds from the vanilla bean into the custard, and discard the pod. Add the vanilla extract, if using. Chill the sauce, covered, before serving.

This sauce can be flavored with herbs, nuts, coffee, or
liqueur, for example:

◆ With fresh mint leaves steeped in the milk in Step 1.

◆ With hazelnuts, roasted and chopped, infused in the milk
in Step 1.

◆ With 2 teaspoons instant coffee dissolved in 1 teaspoon
hot water added to the milk in Step 1.

◆ With bourbon, Grand Marnier, or fruit *eau-de-vie,* added at
the end, after straining.

*of the pot as you stir. The
sauce should thicken
enough to coat the back of
a spoon evenly, no more.*

**M a k e s   a b o u t
2 ³/₄   c u p s**

Cak

and other

bak

es

WE'RE NOT BIG BELIEVERS in concocting ersatz lowfat desserts. And this is even more true with baked goods. There is nothing like real butter for baking. And sugar and eggs not only add flavor but help baked goods to brown; and they keep them tender, too.

But certain types of cakes do lend themselves to adaptation, without sacrificing flavor, texture, or overall pleasure. The thing is to know which lowfat substitutions work and which aren't worth the trouble.

ed goods

Sour cream, for example, can be replaced, cup for cup, with lowfat or nonfat yogurt. We've done this for years in all sorts of cakes, muffins, and other baked goods, and the results are just as good. The yogurt adds a pleasant lightness, too. And just compare the figures:

1 cup	Calories	Fat g
Sour cream	493	48
Lowfat plain yogurt	140	4
Nonfat plain yogurt	110	0

Another easy way to lower fat and cholesterol is to replace whole eggs with a mixture of eggs and egg whites, eliminating some of the fat-rich yolks. In a cake that calls for three eggs, for example, using one whole egg and three whites will trim fat considerably, but the cake will still come out tender. (Too much egg white, without the yolk, can make a cake rubbery; the fat in the yolks helps keep cakes soft.)

COCOA FOR CHOCOLATE; OIL FOR BUTTER

Chocolate is composed of unsweetened cocoa, cocoa butter, and sometimes sugar. You can replace melted chocolate with cocoa powder in baked goods, and wind up with about one third of the fat. One ounce of chocolate has 140 to 145 calories and 15 fat grams; one ounce of cocoa has 90 to 120 calories and 3 to 4 fat grams. And you get all the deep flavor, which is found in the cocoa component of chocolate, anyway. Invest in a good brand of unsweetened cocoa powder; it makes all the difference in integrity of flavor. What you do lose is the luscious "mouthfeel" that fat adds; so you have to be sure, when baking with cocoa, to make up for it with enough moisture in the other ingredients.

Oil can be used instead of butter in cakes and pastry doughs, but remember that while many oils are largely unsaturated, *fat is still fat*. Substituting oil for butter will not make your cakes any healthier. But if you cut back slightly on the fat, oil can work well in cakes and pastries, and can also mean a major savings in cholesterol. A bland olive oil, traditional in baking throughout the Mediterranean, helps keep Orange-Chocolate Walnut Torte (page 398) moist.

Other baking substitutions that work include: light cream cheese for regular; part-skim ricotta cheese for whole-milk ricotta; and lowfat (1%) cottage cheese for ricotta. Generally, you can also cut back slightly on the sugar in just about any cake recipe. But remember that sugar melts in baking, adding moistness as it sweetens. You may need to compensate by adding a little more liquid when reducing sugar.

Also, rather than substituting, you can turn to baked goods that don't normally depend on fat to be good. Angel food cake is the classic example, made with just egg whites, sugar, and flour. No egg yolks, no fat at all. Sponge cakes derive their leavening, tenderness, and flavor from well-beaten eggs rather than creamed butter, and so are a healthier choice than butter-based cakes.

In our Lighter Brownies (page 404) and Pear and Dried Cranberry Upside-down Kuchen (page 388), we substitute applesauce for some of the fat. This is something of a recent trend in baked goods—replacing some of the fat in cakes, cookies, and muffins with such fruit purees as applesauce or prune puree, which keep them moist, while adding some flavor of their own.

We don't suggest lowfat substitutions for baked goods across the board; nothing will replace a home-baked pound cake, made with real butter. One can indulge in that—the real thing—only once in a while. But by relying on baked goods like angel food cake that are already naturally low in fat and finding substitutions that work without sacrificing quality, you can have your cake, and eat it, too.

Spicy Gingerbread with Warm Cider-Lemon Sauce

Gingerbread is another good candidate for reworking in a lowfat, low-cholesterol format, both because it's not that rich in butter or eggs and it's moist and spicy enough that the full flavor comes through. Serve it with a light warm sauce.

The cider-lemon sauce is based on a recipe from Beatrice Simmons, Marie's mother-in-law. When you thicken sauces with cornstarch, whisk the cornstarch with the sugar and other dry ingredients first. That way, you'll smooth out any lumps before stirring the starch into liquid.

Makes 12 servings

1	cup dark molasses
⅔	cup vegetable oil
½	cup firmly packed light brown sugar
1	large egg
2¼	cups all-purpose flour
1	tablespoon ground ginger
1½	teaspoons baking soda
½	teaspoon ground cloves
½	teaspoon salt
3	tablespoons minced candied ginger
1	cup boiling water
	Warm Cider-Lemon Sauce (recipe follows)

1. Heat the oven to 350°F. Lightly oil and flour, or spray with nonstick baking spray, a 9-inch bundt pan or tube pan, tapping out excess flour. Set aside.

2. Beat the molasses, oil, brown sugar, and egg in a large mixer bowl until well blended. Stir together the flour, ground ginger, baking soda, cloves, salt, and candied ginger in a separate bowl. Add gradually to the molasses mixture, beating after each addition. Add the boiling water all at once and stir to blend.

3. Pour the batter into the prepared pan and bake until the sides begin to pull away from the pan and the surface is just firm to the touch when pressed lightly, about 35 minutes. Cool for a few minutes, in the pan, on a rack. Carefully loosen the sides of the cake with the tip of a knife blade and invert onto the rack. Serve warm, with the cider-lemon sauce.

Warm Cider-Lemon Sauce

3 tablespoons sugar

2 tablespoons cornstarch

2 cups apple cider or unsweetened apple juice

½ cup fresh lemon juice

   Grated or finely shredded zest of 1 lemon

12 thin lemon slices

**Makes about
2 ½ cups**

1. Combine the sugar and cornstarch in a small saucepan until blended and lump-free. Gradually stir in the apple juice.

2. Bring to a boil over medium heat, stirring, until the mixture thickens slightly. Remove from the heat and add the lemon juice, lemon zest, and lemon slices. Serve warm, over slices of warm gingerbread.

Pear and Dried Cranberry Upside-down Kuchen

This cake is at its best served warm, topped with a spoonful of cool lemon yogurt. This lightly spiced cake batter contains only three tablespoons of sugar and a quarter of a cup of oil. Applesauce keeps the cake moist and tender.

This is a basic recipe. You can top the cake with sliced apples, peaches, or whole fresh cranberries tossed with a little extra sugar.

Makes 8

servings

Fruit Topping

4   small firm-ripe Bosc pears, quartered, cored, peeled, and thinly sliced (about 1½ pounds)

⅓   cup firmly packed light brown sugar

2   tablespoons fresh lemon juice

2   tablespoons dried cranberries, dried sour cherries, or muscat raisins

Cake Batter

1½   cups unbleached all-purpose flour

3   tablespoons granulated sugar

2   teaspoons baking powder

1   teaspoon baking soda

½   teaspoon ground cinnamon

¼   teaspoon salt

½   cup lowfat (1%) milk

½   cup unsweetened applesauce

¼   cup vegetable oil

1   large egg, beaten

1   teaspoon pure vanilla extract

Lemon lowfat yogurt, for serving

1. Heat the oven to 350°F.

2. Stir together the pears, brown sugar, and lemon juice in a bowl. Spoon the pears into a 9-inch round cake pan, spreading them in an even layer. Sprinkle the pears evenly with the cranberries. Set aside.

3. Stir together the flour, granulated sugar, baking powder, baking soda, cinnamon, and salt in a large bowl. Whisk the milk, applesauce, oil, egg, and vanilla together in a separate bowl until thoroughly blended. Add to the dry ingredients and stir just until blended, no longer. The mixture will be very thick.

4. Spread the batter evenly over the pear layer, without disturbing the fruit. Bake until cake is golden brown and the edges have pulled away from the sides of the pan, 30 to 35 minutes. Cool for 5 to 10 minutes in the pan, on a rack. Run a knife blade around the edges of the cake to loosen it, if necessary; then invert the cake onto a serving platter. Serve warm, topped with a spoonful of lemon yogurt.

Lemon Yogurt Cake with Fresh Berries

Made with yogurt, egg whites, skim milk, and a small amount of vegetable oil and sugar, this cake, based on a recipe from chef-author Jacques Pépin, is a good lowfat approximation of a basic white cake. Serve it with berries or other fresh fruits.

Makes 8 servings

3   tablespoons safflower or vegetable oil
½   cup sugar
    Grated zest of 1 lemon
1   teaspoon pure vanilla extract
¼   cup skim milk
¼   cup lowfat or nonfat yogurt
1   cup sifted cake flour (not self-rising)
½   teaspoon baking soda
2   large egg whites
    Salt
    Confectioners' sugar
    Ripe raspberries and blueberries, or other berries,
    tossed in superfine sugar, for serving

1. Heat the oven to 350°F. Spray an 8-inch round cake pan with nonstick cooking spray. Set aside.

2. Whisk together the oil, sugar, lemon zest, and vanilla in a mixing bowl. Add the milk and yogurt. Sift in the flour and baking soda and stir gently just until blended.

3. Beat the egg whites with a pinch of salt until nearly stiff. Gently fold into the batter. Transfer to the cake pan.

4. Bake until the cake is golden and springs back when pressed, about 30 minutes. Cool briefly, in the pan, on a rack, then invert onto the rack and cool completely. Sprinkle the cake with confectioners' sugar. Cut into wedges and serve, with berries alongside.

healthy substitutions for baking

TRADITIONAL INGREDIENT	HEALTHY SUBSTITUTE
◆ Butter	Canola and mild olive oil. Prune puree or applesauce to replace part of the butter
◆ 1 ounce chocolate	3 tablespoons cocoa
◆ 2 eggs	1 egg + 2 whites, or egg substitute
◆ Cream, whole milk (in batters, muffins, biscuit doughs)	Skim or lowfat (1%) milk
◆ Cream cheese (in cheesecake)	Lowfat ricotta + yogurt; light cream cheese
◆ Ricotta cheese, whole-milk	½ whole milk ricotta plus either part-skim ricotta or lowfat (1%) cottage cheese
◆ Sour cream	Plain yogurt
◆ Whipped cream, ice cream (to top cakes, pies, warm fruit desserts)	Frozen yogurt, lowfat yogurt
◆ 1 cup whipped cream (in mousse mixtures)	3 stiffly beaten egg whites or ¾ to 1 cup Yogurt Cheese (page 15)
◆ 1 cup whipping or heavy cream (for whipping)	1 cup evaporated skim milk

Angel Food Cake with Fresh Strawberries

We've cut back a bit on the amount of sugar usually found in angel food cake recipes and flavored the batter with a touch of grated lemon zest.

Makes one 10-inch cake

1   cup cake flour, not self-rising

1¼   cups granulated sugar

½   teaspoon salt

     Grated zest of 1 lemon

10   large egg whites (about 1¼ cups)

½   teaspoon cream of tartar

3   tablespoons fresh lemon juice

½   teaspoon pure almond extract

Honey-sweetened Strawberries

2   pints strawberries, rinsed, hulled, and sliced

2   tablespoons honey

1. Place the bottom oven rack at the lowest position and remove the middle rack. Heat the oven to 350°F. Have ready a 10-inch tube pan, preferably with legs around the rim, perfectly clean and free of any traces of grease.

2. Sift together the cake flour, ¼ cup of the sugar, and the salt onto a sheet of wax paper. Repeat, sifting the mixture again onto a second sheet of wax paper. This will help aerate the flour. Gently stir the lemon zest into the flour mixture. Set aside.

3. Using an electric mixer, beat the egg whites at low speed until foamy. Beat in the cream of tartar, lemon juice, and almond extract. Gradually increase the mixer speed and beat in the remaining 1 cup sugar, 1 tablespoon at a time, until the whites are glossy and form soft rounded peaks. Sift one-quarter of the flour mixture at a time over the whites, folding gently but thoroughly after each addition. Spoon the batter into the pan and gently smooth the surface.

4. Bake until the top of the cake is lightly browned and springs back when touched with a fingertip, about 50 minutes. Remove the cake from the oven and immediately invert, letting it stand until completely cooled. If your cake pan does not have legs, set the pan over the neck of a bottle (a wine bottle is good) or a funnel, so that the surface of the cake is at least 2 inches above the work surface.

5. While the cake is cooling, drizzle the strawberries with the honey and toss to blend. Let stand at room temperature until ready to serve.

6. When the cake is cool, loosen the sides with a long thin spatula and turn the cake out. Cut the cake into slices with a cake fork or a long serrated knife. Serve with lightly sweetened strawberries on the side.

Amazing New York–style Cheesecake

We honestly didn't think we were going to be able to come up with a cheese-cake that was low in fat yet also good enough to be worth the bother. We were both surprised and delighted by this one. Roughly based on the Lindy's New York origi-nal, it's light but rich and creamy. The flavor is mellow, with a lemony edge. And it bakes up perfectly—no cracks, with the palest gold edges.

Makes one 8¹⁄₂- or 9-inch cake

1 cup gingersnap crumbs (about 15 cookies)
1 tablespoon egg white (about ½ of 1 large) lightly beaten with a fork

Filling

1 pound (two 8-ounce packages) lowfat cream cheese (Neufchâtel), softened
1 cup Yogurt Cheese (page 15)
¾ cup sugar
Grated zest of 1 lemon
Grated zest of 1 small orange
1 pound lowfat (1%) cottage cheese, drained in a strainer for about 30 minutes
2 teaspoons pure vanilla extract
2 large eggs
4 large egg whites
¼ cup unbleached all-purpose flour
Fresh berries, for garnish (optional)

1. Heat the oven to 375°F. Separate the bottom and sides of an 8¹⁄₂- or 9-inch springform pan. Spray the bottom with non-stick cooking spray.

2. Combine the gingersnap crumbs with the beaten egg white in a bowl, moistening the crumbs. Press the mixture into the bottom of the pan. Bake the crust until golden, about 8 min-utes. Set aside on a wire rack to cool. Spray the sides of the pan and gently attach to the bottom. Set the pan aside. (If you don't trust the seal of the springform, wrap a sheet of foil tightly around the bottom and sides.)

3. Heat the oven to 550°F.

4. Combine the cream cheese, Yogurt Cheese, sugar, lemon zest, and orange zest in a large mixing bowl and beat with an electric mixer at medium speed until creamy. Meanwhile, process the cottage cheese in a food processor until smooth and creamy. Add to the mixer bowl and continue to beat until very smooth. Add the vanilla, eggs, and egg whites, one at a time, mixing until smooth after each addition. Add the flour and mix until well combined. Pour the filling into the pan. Bake for 12 minutes.

5. Reduce the heat to 200°F and bake 1 hour longer. The cheesecake should be set and lightly golden around the edges. Cool the cheesecake, in the pan, on a rack. While the cake is still warm, run a knife gently around the edge of the cake. When the cake has cooled to room temperature, cover the pan with plastic wrap, without letting the wrap touch the surface of the cake. Place it in the refrigerator for at least 6 hours, or overnight.

6. Remove the cake from the refrigerator about 20 minutes before serving. Carefully remove the sides of the pan and place the cake, on its base, on a serving plate. If you like, scatter fresh berries on the plate around the outside of the cake. Cut with a knife blade dipped in hot water between each slice.

Chocolate Bundt Cake

Prune puree stands in for some of the butter here. This is not as moist and luscious as bundt cakes made with lots of butter, melted chocolate, and sour cream, but it is a good cake with true cocoa flavor. This is best served on the day it is baked.

Makes one 9 ½-inch cake

Prune Puree

¾ cup moist pitted prunes

¾ cup water

Cake

1⅔ cups sifted unbleached all-purpose flour

1 teaspoon baking powder

½ teaspoon baking soda

¼ teaspoon salt

1 cup Dutch-process unsweetened cocoa powder

4 tablespoons (½ stick) unsalted butter, softened

1 cup sugar

1 teaspoon pure vanilla extract

2 large eggs

2 large egg whites

1 cup buttermilk (or a mixture of plain yogurt and water or lowfat milk)

Glossy Chocolate Glaze

2½ tablespoons Dutch-process unsweetened cocoa powder

2½ tablespoons lowfat (1%) milk, or as needed

1⅓ cups sifted confectioners' sugar, or as needed

1. Place the prunes and water in a saucepan and bring to a boil. Simmer, uncovered, for 10 minutes. Puree, with the liquid, in a food processor or blender. Set aside.

2. Heat the oven to 350°F.

3. Spray a 12-cup bundt pan, preferably nonstick, with nonstick cooking spray. Sprinkle the pan with flour to coat, shaking out the excess. Set aside.

4. Resift the flour with the baking powder, baking soda, salt, and cocoa onto a sheet of wax paper. Set aside. In an electric mixer at medium speed, beat the butter, then gradually add the sugar and vanilla, beating until as light as possible. Add the eggs, one at a time, then the egg whites. Add the prune puree and beat until combined. Add the dry ingredients alternately with the buttermilk, beginning and ending with the dry. Turn off the machine and finish mixing by hand with a large rubber spatula. Scrape the mixture into the prepared pan.

5. Bake until a toothpick inserted in the center of the cake comes out clean and the cake springs back when pressed with a fingertip, 40 to 42 minutes. Cool the cake, in the pan, on a rack for 15 minutes. Run the tip of a knife blade gently around the edges. Invert the cake onto the rack. Put a sheet of wax paper underneath the rack and cool the cake to room temperature.

6. Stir together the 2$^1\!/_2$ tablespoons of cocoa and the milk in a bowl until they form a smooth paste. Add the confectioners' sugar, stirring until the mixture is smooth. Adjust the consistency if necessary; it should be smooth, thick, and almost spreadable. Stir in a little more milk if too thick; sift in a little more confectioners' sugar if too thin. Spoon the glaze over the top of the cake, letting it drip down the sides, without covering them completely at the bottom. Let the glaze set for at least 15 minutes. Carefully transfer the cake to a serving plate and serve cut into wedges.

Orange-Chocolate-Walnut Torte

Olive oil is often used in baking in Greece, Italy, and throughout the Mediterranean. The oil keeps this cake moist. You have to use a mild-flavored oil, though, so that it doesn't intrude on the other flavors.

Processing the orange zest with the sugar is a good tip to remember; it helps release all of the orange's flavorful oils.

Makes 12 to 16 servings

1 cup walnuts
3 or 4 strips orange zest, coarsely chopped (about 1 tablespoon)
1 cup sugar
2 large whole eggs
2 large egg whites
¾ cup mild ("light") olive oil, canola oil, or other vegetable oil
¼ cup freshly squeezed orange juice
1 teaspoon pure vanilla extract
¾ cup unbleached all-purpose flour
½ cup Dutch-process unsweetened cocoa powder
1 teaspoon baking powder
Salt
2 tablespoons confectioners' sugar

1. Heat the oven to 350°F. Lightly oil and flour or spray with nonstick baking spray a 10-inch springform pan, tapping out excess flour. Set aside.

2. Place the walnuts, orange zest, and a few tablespoons of the sugar in a food processor and process until chopped fine. Set aside.

3. Combine the whole eggs and egg whites in a large mixer bowl and beat at medium-high speed until frothy. Gradually beat in the remaining sugar and beat until the mixture is very thick and pale in color, about 5 minutes. With the mixer on the lowest speed, beat in the olive oil in a slow steady stream. Add the orange juice and the vanilla.

4. Stir the flour, cocoa, baking powder, and pinch of salt together in a large bowl. Stir in the walnut and orange mixture. Fold in the egg yolk mixture until thoroughly blended. Pour into the prepared pan.

5. Bake until the edges begin to pull away from the sides of the pan and the center is firm to the touch when pressed lightly, about 35 minutes. Cool the cake, in the pan, on a rack.

6. Loosen the sides of the cake from the pan with a knife or small spatula. Remove the sides of the pan. Slide the cake onto a serving platter. Place the confectioners' sugar in a small strainer and sift evenly over the surface of the cake. Serve cut into wedges.

Deep, Dark Devil's Food Cake

This is roughly patterned after our friend and author Flo Braker's devil's food cake recipe in The Simple Art of Perfect Baking, upon which there is no improving. We've used oil instead of butter, cutting back slightly on the amounts of fat and sugar. Because devil's food cake traditionally doesn't contain many eggs, it comes out successfully in a low-fat version. The deep cocoa flavor still gives it that devil's food flavor, and it's so moist and chocolaty that it doesn't need icing. Cut this in thick squares directly from the pan, and enjoy it with a tall glass of cold skim milk.

¾ cup all-purpose flour, spooned lightly into measuring cup

¼ cup cornstarch

½ teaspoon baking soda

⅛ teaspoon salt

⅓ cup Dutch-process unsweetened cocoa powder

⅓ cup lukewarm water

¼ cup vegetable oil

1 teaspoon pure vanilla extract

½ cup firmly packed light or dark brown sugar

¼ cup granulated sugar

1 large egg, at room temperature (if very cold, briefly run the egg, in the shell, under hot water)

½ cup lowfat or nonfat yogurt

1. Heat the oven to 350°F, with a rack slightly lower than center level. Spray an 8-inch square or round baking pan with nonstick cooking spray. Lightly dust the pan with flour, tapping out excess. Set the pan aside.

2. Sift the flour, cornstarch, baking soda, and salt onto a sheet of wax paper; set aside.

3. Add the cocoa to the lukewarm water in a measuring cup; stir with a fork or whisk until a smooth paste forms; set aside.

4. Place the oil and vanilla in an electric mixer. Begin to mix at medium speed, gradually adding the brown and granulated sugars, and scraping the sides of the bowl once or twice. Add the egg and beat for about 1 minute, or until the mixture is smooth. Lower the mixer speed slightly. Add the flour mixture alternately with the yogurt, beginning and ending with the flour, and mixing only until the ingredients are partially blended. Turn off the machine and finish mixing with a large rubber spatula, just until there are no more visible traces of flour. Scrape the batter into the prepared pan.

5. Bake the cake for about 25 minutes, or until the top springs back when pressed gently with a fingertip, and a toothpick inserted in the center emerges clean. Cool the cake, in the pan, on a wire rack. Serve cut in pieces, directly from the pan.

Makes one 8-inch cake, about 9 servings

Dried Fruit Tart with Flaky Oil Pastry

While dried fruits are high in natural sugars, they really deliver when it comes to flavor and nutrients. This oil pastry bakes up flaky, with a crackerlike consistency. It can also be used for filled cookies and other small pastries.

Makes 8 servings

Dried Fruit Filling

1 cup diced (½ inch) dried apricots
1 cup diced (½ inch) dried figs
1 cup seedless raisins
2 cups unsweetened apple juice
1 cinnamon stick

Oil Pastry Crust

2 cups unbleached all-purpose flour
⅓ cup whole wheat flour
1 teaspoon ground cinnamon
½ teaspoon salt
½ cup vegetable oil
4 to 5 tablespoons skim or lowfat (1%) milk, as needed

Vanilla ice milk or frozen yogurt, for serving (optional)
Ground cinnamon (optional)

1. Combine the apricots, figs, and raisins in a medium saucepan. Add the apple juice and cinnamon stick and bring to a boil. Cover, reduce the heat, and cook over low heat until the fruits are tender and the liquid is almost absorbed, about 25 minutes. Uncover and continue to cook over low heat, gently stirring occasionally, until the liquid has evaporated, about 10 minutes longer. Cool the mixture thoroughly. Remove and discard the cinnamon stick. *(The filling can be made up to 2 days ahead.)*

2. Combine the flours, cinnamon, and salt in a large bowl. Gradually add the oil, tossing the mixture with a fork, until the mixture is crumbly. Stirring with a fork, add milk until the mixture comes together to form a ball. Shape into a disk. Cut off about a third of the disk, wrap the smaller piece in plastic, and refrigerate.

3. Roll out the remaining dough between 2 sheets of wax paper, or on a pastry cloth with the rolling pin protected by a rolling pin stocking, to a large circle about $1/8$ inch thick. Remove the top sheet of wax paper, if using, and invert the dough, without stretching it, into a 9- or $9^{1}/_{2}$-inch tart pan with a removable bottom. Carefully peel off the top sheet of wax paper. Fit the dough along the bottom and up the sides of the tart pan, trim the edges, and refrigerate until ready to bake.

4. Heat the oven to 400°F.

5. Spoon the dried fruit mixture into the prepared pastry and spread in an even layer. Roll out the remaining dough and cut with a pastry wheel or chef's knife into 8 strips about $1/2$ inch wide. Criss-cross the pastry strips over the filling, either weaving them together, or laying half the strips in 1 direction with the other half on top at a sharp angle. Press the ends of the pastry strips into the edges of the crust and trim off any excess at the edges. Bake the tart for 15 minutes.

6. Reduce the heat to 350°F. and bake until the pastry is lightly golden, about 25 minutes longer. Cool the tart on a rack. Loosen the crust from the sides of the pan and slip off the outer rim. Place the tart on a serving plate and serve, topped with vanilla ice milk or frozen yogurt, sprinkled with a little cinnamon, if you like.

Lighter Brownies

Brownies are among the good things in life that we feel shouldn't be tampered with. When you want a brownie, you want all that chocolate, butter, and nuts. That said, these lower-fat brownies, made with cocoa powder instead of melted chocolate, a little applesauce, and just enough walnuts for flavor, are moist and chocolaty enough to make them worthy of the brownie name.

Makes 12 brownies

½ cup sifted cake flour (not self-rising)

½ cup Dutch-process unsweetened cocoa powder

¼ teaspoon salt

1 large egg

3 tablespoons egg whites (about 1½ large)

¾ cup plus 2 tablespoons sugar

¼ cup plus 2 tablespoons applesauce, preferably unsweetened

2½ tablespoons vegetable oil

1½ teaspoons pure vanilla extract

1 tablespoon walnuts, toasted and chopped

1. Heat the oven to 350°F. Spray an 8-inch square pan with nonstick cooking spray. Set aside.

2. Stir together the flour, cocoa, and salt in a bowl. Whisk together the egg, egg whites, sugar, applesauce, oil, and vanilla in another bowl until smooth. Whisk in the flour mixture just until blended, no longer. Pour into the pan and sprinkle with walnuts.

3. Bake until a toothpick inserted in the center comes out with moist crumbs, 28 to 30 minutes. Cool, in the pan, on a wire rack. Cut into 12 squares.

Banana-Cinnamon Snacking Cake

1½ cups unbleached all-purpose flour

½ cup sugar

2 teaspoons baking powder

1 teaspoon baking soda

1 teaspoon ground cinnamon

½ teaspoon salt

1 cup nonfat or lowfat yogurt

¾ cup mashed ripe bananas (about 1½ bananas)

2 tablespoons vegetable oil

1 large egg

1 teaspoon pure vanilla extract

2 bananas, thinly sliced for topping (optional)

  Lemon juice (optional)

  Confectioners' sugar

1. Heat the oven to 400°F. Spray an 8- or 9-inch square baking pan with nonstick cooking spray. Set aside.

2. Stir together the flour, sugar, baking powder, baking soda, cinnamon, and salt in a large mixing bowl until very well blended. Whisk together the yogurt, bananas, vegetable oil, egg, and vanilla in a separate bowl, until thoroughly blended. Pour over the dry ingredients and gently stir just until blended. Do not overmix. Spread the batter in the pan.

3. Bake until the top of the cake has browned and the edges pull away from the sides of the pan, about 15 minutes. Cool the cake, in the pan, for a few minutes on a rack. Loosen the sides of the cake with a spatula and turn it out on a rack. Invert the cake right side up and cool thoroughly. If you like, top the cake with sliced bananas sprinkled with fresh lemon juice. Sprinkle confectioners' sugar lightly through a sieve over the cake before serving.

Cakes traditionally made with fruit purees in the batter, like banana bread and apple tea bread, are good candidates for reducing fat successfully. Here mashed banana adds texture and sweetness that would ordinarily be derived from butter, sugar, and eggs. Yogurt keeps the cake moist and light with much less fat than the sour cream often used in banana cakes.

Makes one 8- or 9-inch square cake

ACKNOWLEDGMENTS

First, we'd like to thank everyone at *Bon Appétit*. They came to us several years ago with the idea for our *"Cooking for Health"* column, and we've enjoyed working on it since. Thank you, Barbara Fairchild and Bill Garry, and all of our column editors: Laurie Buckle, Karen Kaplan, Scott Smith, James Badham, and Siobhan Burns. Pamela Cunha has also been a pleasure to work with.

Our cutting-edge nutrition experts, Marion Nestle and Eileen Stukane, are always there to help find the answers.

Without Judith Weber, our agent, and Harriet Bell, our patient, kind, and thorough editor, this never would have been a book. Kathleen Hackett is also a joy. Thanks, too, to Susan Lescher, Susan Derecskey, Skip Dye, and Don Morris.

Thank you also to Lisa Ekus and Merrilyn Siciak from whom we expect great things, as usual.

Index